Accessing Antiquity

Accessing Antiquity

The Computerization of Classical Studies

Jon Solomon, Editor

The University of Arizona Press

Tucson and London

The University of Arizona Press
Copyright © 1993
Arizona Board of Regents
All Rights Reserved

♾ This book is printed on acid-free, archival-quality paper.
Manufactured in the United States of America.

98 97 96 95 94 93   6 5 4 3 2 1

Library of Congress Cataloging-in-Publication Data

Accessing antiquity : the computerization of classical studies / Jon
    Solomon, editor.
        p.   cm.
    Includes bibliographical references (p.) and index.
    ISBN 0-8165-1390-2 (alk. paper)
        1. Classical philology—Data processing.   2. Civilization,
    Classical—Data processing.   I. Solomon, Jon, 1950–   .
    PA50.A23   1993   93-25963
    938′.00285—dc20   CIP

British Library Cataloguing in Publication Data
A catalogue record for this book is available from the British Library.

To Douglas C. C. Young
and
David W. Packard,

two men of different brilliances,
one goal

Contents

Contributors

Luci Berkowitz is Professor of Classics at the University of California at Irvine, California. She is Resident Scholar at the Thesaurus Linguae Graecae.

Jay David Bolter is Professor at the School of Literature, Communication, and Culture at the Georgia Institute of Technology.

Theodore F. Brunner is Professor of Classics at the University of California at Irvine, California. He is the director of the Thesaurus Linguae Graecae.

Dee Clayman is Professor of Classics at The Graduate School and University Center of the City University of New York and Principal Investigator for the Database for Classical Bibliography.

Gregory Crane is Editor-in-Chief of the Perseus Project at Harvard University in Cambridge, Massachusetts, and Assistant Professor of Classics at Tufts University in Medford, Massachusetts.

Carolyn G. Koehler is Professor of Ancient Studies at the University of Maryland, Baltimore County Campus, in Catonsville, Maryland. She is co-director of the AMPHORAS Project.

Philippa M. W. Matheson is co-director of the AMPHORAS Project Centre for Computing in the Humanities, University of Toronto.

Kenneth Morrell is Assistant Professor of Classics at St. Olaf College in Northfield, Minnesota.

Elli Mylonas is Managing Editor of the Perseus Project at Harvard University in Cambridge, Massachusetts.

John F. Oates is Professor of Ancient History at Duke University in Durham, North Carolina. He is co-director of the Duke Data Bank of Documentary Papyri and co-director of the Catalogue of the Duke Papyrological Collection projects.

Jocelyn Penny Small is Professor and director of the United States Center of the *Lexicon Iconographicum Mythologiae Classicae* at Rutgers, the State University of New Jersey, in New Brunswick, New Jersey.

D. Neel Smith is on the Executive Committee of the Perseus Project and Professor of Classics at Bowdoin College in Brunswick, Maine.

Accessing Antiquity

Introduction

Jon Solomon

The study of classical culture flourished for well over two thousand years before the advent of the computer age. Painters and poets consciously adapted the Homeric epics in the seventh century, and just two centuries later a rudimentary (even if entertaining) type of literary criticism was already fully developed in the Old Comedy of Aristophanes. Aristotle in the fourth century left as his greatest scholarly legacy the practice of formally organizing, cataloguing, and analyzing data both scientific and humanistic, and he is said to have collected the first scholarly library. He and his students intellectually inspired the great third-century Mouseion and Library at Alexandria, where the preservation and study of earlier Greek literature was carried out for several centuries. Chief among the scholarly tools they created were their literary catalogues (πίνακες), and the concept and frequent use of scholarly libraries continued among such learned Greeks of the Roman era as Plutarch, Strabo, and Athenaeus. Much of this scholarly tradition survived and even thrived in the medieval period, particularly in Byzantium, but even there not to the extent that it would become consistently dominant in the Renaissance. From that period, which was a "rebirth" of the *study* of Greco-Roman culture, to the present, classical studies have had phenomenal growth. In its initial growth phases, the study of "the Classics" also produced such scholarly progeny as the study of art history, archaeology, linguistics, epigraphy, and papyrology, and after the last century's expansion of universities, libraries, musea, and *Altertumswissenschaft,* the umbrella field of "Classical Studies" has now reached such an unwieldy size that specialization upon one historical period of one genre of one classical culture is the norm among contemporary scholars. The number of edited texts, literary commentaries, catalogued corpora of material remains, archaeological site reports, and secondary studies continues to mushroom. The most recent volume of *L'Année Philologique* bears witness to this

post-Renaissance proliferation in containing nearly 16,000 individual bibliographical entries in one year.

The means by which the classics have been preserved and the form in which
scholarly output has been issued has changed periodically over the centuries.
Homer, or at least his predecessors, had no physical means of recording their
writings. With the development of the Greek and Roman alphabets, papyrus
media, wax tablets, and ultimately the book roll, not to mention with intensive
scribal labor, classical literature was recorded, copied, preserved, and studied
in libraries by individual scholars of later antiquity. The development of the
codex increased library efficiency, and then the invention of the printing press
in the fifteenth century allowed for the mass dissemination of texts and the
proliferation of numerous private and institutional libraries. Such subsequent
scholarly tools and processes as the typewriter, photography, and xerography
increased not only the philologist's but also the art historian's and archaeologist's
ability to create study collections, teaching aids, and informed publications.

The past three decades have given to classical scholarship the most efficient
and productive tool yet developed, the electronic computer. By its very nature
it encourages new methods of cataloguing, analyzing, and processing data and
disseminating scholarship. Continuing a transformation already begun, the
computer will in the next decade have made most of the technological scholarly developments of the past two millennia immediately accessible. The computer records faster and more accurately than any means previously used, it
collects, stores, and searches data more compactly and with more precision
than ever before imagined, and with the flick of a fingertip it can send at the
speed of light one scholar's work to another scholar thousands of miles away.
Hidden behind these very words I am writing on my computer screen are
electronic storage disks that contain some 60 million words of Greek literature,
a Greek-English lexicon, maps of the Mediterranean basin, and photographs
of ancient works of art, and within a few years there will also be a nearly
complete bibliography of twentieth-century classical studies, catalogues of
most of the Greco-Roman vase paintings, sculptures, coins, papyri, frescos,
and inscriptions. All this data will share the ability to be accessed in seconds.

We are at a dynamic moment in classical studies. During this very decade
machines, processes, and tools are being created to revolutionize the way we
study and teach Greco-Roman antiquity, and the revolution is not over. To the
contrary, we are at merely an initial transition point. Within the last five years
the majority of classical scholars has "switched" from typewriter (or legal
pad!) to computer as a word processor, and within the next five years many
more will continue the adoption of the computer as a research tool. It is possible to speculate that in the near future a working session might involve calling
up a passage of ancient literature from the TLG CD-ROM with one's personal
computer, simultaneously calling up any bibliographical reference on the passage written within the last sixty years from the DCB, accessing the reference

from the local or some other U.S. library, and storing the material or one's own comments in a neat file easily found and brought up another day. Similarly, at some point in the near future (after appropriate copyright concepts have been established), a "publication" will leave the scholar's "desk" and see national dissemination in a matter of seconds, not months (or years).

While the preceding paragraphs serve as an encomium on the electronic computer as a research tool for the study of the ancient world, it should never be forgotten that computers do and know nothing by themselves. Even after the computers themselves, the hardware, are built, they must be programmed, told what to learn, how to organize it, how to store it, how to catalogue it, and how to format it. This is the task of classicists with expertise in computer hardware and software, and it is a vital task. A good database saves thousands of students and scholars hundreds and thousands of laborious hours. It makes data easily searchable and accessible, and it makes it practical to use. It will make a reality the modestly futuristic scenario just described.

On the other hand, a poor database will make the data difficult to access; any carelessness in entering, proofreading, formatting, or even selecting the hardware and software will perpetuate and disseminate errors. Perhaps it is fortunate that designing software and databases is so difficult, costly, and time-consuming, for all the scholars who have taken interest in carrying out the revolution have had to be very careful in their planning and execution. At the outset they have had to consider how large the particular corpus they would be working on might be, what the particular requirements and oddities of that corpus might be, what would be the most efficient and cost-effective method of entering, storing, and searching that corpus, how to check that the data entered was correct, and in what form to disseminate this data. Of course, funding had to be secured as well, and so did a team of knowledgeable, train-able assistants.

Each part of the planning was crucial. Underestimating the size of the cor-pus to be made into a database would cause a massive roadblock some months or years in the future. Choosing a program or format that would become obso-lete, obscure, or inefficient would defeat the purpose of the project. Entering incorrect data and not proofreading carefully would cause information to be lost; the computer is such a precise searching tool that what in printed format would have been a simple "typo" becomes an unrecognizable string of letters to the computer. And disseminating the information in a clumsy format or in one that scholars (or institutions) could not afford to purchase or in one that would become immediately obsolete would destroy the benefit of entering all the data so carefully. All the electronic databases described in the following chapters were created with all these potential pitfalls. What is remarkable is that some of these scholarly database creators, Theodore Brunner providing one superior example, foresaw all these caveats when they began their plan-ning over twenty years ago.

To see the future so clearly or, more accurately, to plan intelligently for what the future might provide and exclude is a gift innate in pioneers. The scholarly computer revolution is so dramatic and so far being carried out so successfully that it needs to be "celebrated" and recorded. The chief purpose of this volume is therefore to record the accomplishments of these dedicated pioneers who are changing the way classical scholars work and the means by which Greco-Roman culture is being studied. How valuable a document it would be if we had detailed statements from the persons who invented the alphabet and printing press, documents that explained whence the ideas for the inventions came, how they pursued and implemented their ideas, and what their hopes were for their inventions. We have that luxury in this case, for this volume contains essays written by creative, technically adventurous pioneers who are dedicating large portions of their professional lives to improving research methods for the rest of us and those yet to come.

The first essay, "Classics and the Computer: The History of a Relationship," introduces us to the very beginnings of the computerization of classical studies, and it is written by Theodore Brunner, the person most directly responsible for the *Thesaurus Linguae Graecae,* the entire 60-million-word corpus of ancient Greek literature already available on CD-ROM for several years now. Beginning with the meeting in 1949 between Father Roberto Busa and J. Thomas Watson, president of IBM at that time, Brunner traces the initial attempts at creating machine-readable versions of classical texts. His historical analysis, for which he drew from the earliest relevant records of the American Philological Association, traces an insightful and cooperative relationship between a traditionally conservative professional organization and the initial handful of scholars interested in computerization. Officially recorded discussions began as early as 1966, and by 1971 there were already computer-related papers included in the official program of the American Philological Association. In 1974, the association gave the *Thesaurus Linguae Graecae,* of which Brunner was now director, an administrative governing board, and together the TLG and APA created an exemplary atmosphere along the lines of which future large-scale electronic database projects could be conceived and nurtured. Considering the limited budget of the American Philological Association, the visionary diversity of its membership, and the potential political difficulties in administering, supporting, and continuing a pioneering project, we are left with the conclusion that the early days of exploring the desirability of computer-assisted scholarship were populated with sober scholars capable of envisioning a computerized world not yet apparent to many and steering a direct course which has led us there.

Luci Berkowitz's contribution, "Ancilla to the *Thesaurus Linguae Graecae:* The TLG Canon," complements the initial essay by exploring the conception, development, and deployment of the canon of Greek texts and authors which was fundamental to the creation of the *Thesaurus Linguae Graecae.* Before all the extant ancient Greek texts could be entered in the TLG, it was necessary to collect the corpus of ancient Greek literature and calculate its magnitude. Berkowitz traces the origins of the project to 1972 and describes the incomplete, inaccurate reference works from which the *Canon* had to be created, and she reminds us as well of the orthographic, bibliographic, biographical, chronological, and organizational difficulties, not to mention the difficulties inherent in examining fragments, duplications, incomplete texts, and questionable author attributions encountered while cataloguing over 1,000 years' worth of Greek literature. The resulting *TLG Canon*[3], which catalogues over 3,000 authors and nearly 10,000 works of ancient Greek literature, has become a scholarly reference work in its own right. Berkowitz completes her essay with an appropriate encomium of careful, painstaking, traditional scholarship. She reminds us that an electronic compilation of texts is valuable only if it consists of extremely accurate and complete data. Such a reminder helps makes those who have not made the "switch" to computerized scholarship aware that computers not only enhance searches and the efficiency of producing a printed/electronic product but also require absolute accuracy in the preparation of databases.

John Oates had a smaller database to develop and one which was quite technical in nature. He consequently begins his essay on the Duke Data Bank of Documentary Papyri (DDBDP) by discussing some of the problems inherent in entering editions of papyri, ostraca, and such media — how to report different hands, broken letters (sublinear dots were once a problem for their Ibycus System), symbols, abbreviations, variant spellings and readings, and the different formations of letters. But since the method of data entry and its attendant problems as well as the Ibycus hardware for the DDBDP were selected several years ago when the project began (1983), and since the data entry of published papyri is nearly completed, Oates chose a different emphasis for the remainder of his essay. He points out that the DDBDP, like the TLG, is not designed or expected to replace existing or new editions. Its value is rather in its ability to be searched, the ease with which scholars can use it to find linguistic parallels, analyze historical, economic, or sociological texts, and display various usages of technical terms. He demonstrates the ability to be searched by discussing the results of several searches he and colleagues have performed. His hope is that other scholars will make similar findings and develop new search methodologies when using the CD-ROM on which the DDBDP has been made generally available. However, he is well aware that in searching such a nonstandard database scholars will also come across, as has he, interesting findings they had not originally planned to discover. Ultimately, Oates concludes, the very specialized methodology appropriate to papyrological studies and the documentary texts of the DDBDP will by virtue of their computerization be made available to nonspecialists and become fully integrated into the broader areas of ancient studies.

"In the beginning there was no computer." So Jocelyn Penny Small with her characteristic wit begins her essay on the development of the Computer Index of the U.S. Center of the *Lexicon Iconographicum Mythologiae Classicae* (US-LIMC) and proceeds to narrate chronologically the computerization of her database, which incorporates all the ancient art objects that depict a mythological person, narrative, or character. She details how both "computer illiterati" and programming experts created order from the chaos of such a particularly complicated ("messy") database — a project that did not become practicable until the early 1980s. Unlike the exclusively text-based TLG and the DDBDP, the US-LIMC includes material objects as small as earrings and as large as architectural sculpture from all periods and all proveniences, and each of these objects, which might include one or several dozen figures, had to be described and defined — whether as a "statuette" or "figurine," whether of "clay" or "terracotta." Small discusses the multiple problems found in compiling a database of some 70,000 files and the solutions developed to address them, and then she turns appropriately to the future, when, it is hoped, all the databases described in this book can be searched along with hers by one scholar at one workstation. She appeals to you, the reader, to be honest in acquiring information from the database at cost from the US-LIMC, and she encourages you as well to let the US-LIMC know what needs to be done with the database. Her understated presence and the technical display throughout the essay heighten the direct appeal to classical scholars and computer enthusiasts to participate in the further development of the database.

Not all extant ancient objects can be categorized as art. The nearly 150,000 amphoras to be included by Carolyn Koehler and Philippa Matheson in their database have only historical and economic, but not aesthetic, importance. Their essay, "AMPHORAS: Computer-Assisted Study of Ancient Wine Jars," reveals many of the unique problems found in designing such a database and entering its data, problems which differ from those found by those working on the objets d'art of the US-LIMC. Here we have not objects containing depictions of mythological subjects but undecorated shipping containers of the type used all over the ancient world for several millennia. Their value lies not in their visual aesthetic but in their accessibility for comparative study through which we can trace their origins and destinations, the commodities they contained (usually wine, preserved fish, or oil), and their chronological development. Our authors describe to us how important these amphoras are for understanding ancient trade and economic history, with broad implications for investigating social and political history as well. They first vividly describe Virginia Grace's nearly 100 file drawers containing tens of thousands of handwritten file cards, and their essay then concentrates on the various methods they have devised for entering and sorting data in their first two phases, how they will scan in graphics in their third phase, how they are protecting their data until all of their files are entered, and, what is a concern for them even more than for the other projects represented here, how they will accomplish their goals and yet keep within their very limited budget. They conclude their essay with an assessment of the future, and their hope is that the exchange of such rudimentary, unartistic, but bountiful data as that derived from the amphoras database will help reduce the barriers that seem to keep scholars from regularly communicating with each other.

Of the first five databases represented in this volume, three contain written matter and two contain material objects. The database described in the sixth essay incorporates bibliography for all five of those databases and considerably more. Dee Lesser Clayman's essay on "The Database of Classical Bibliography" describes an ambitious project (some 500,000 citations) which will enter the entire international bibliography for classical studies, *L'Année Philologique* (*AP*), in electronic form and make it available to scholars and students on CD-ROM. The uniqueness of Clayman's essay derives from the preparatory state of the database, not at all a database which has been completed, corrected, tested, distributed, and updated, but one which is captured here in the design stage. Clayman discusses how the various bibliographic entries must be converted and tagged for effective searches, offers us a number of typical entries in their original *AP* format, demonstrates the conceptual and linguistic difficulties her database must simplify, and introduces us to the keyboarding codes and 71-field database template that she is using. To increase the efficiency of the Database of Classical Bibliography searches, Clayman has indexed all the fields in the database and provided for a master index of word/ subject searches. By looking at the nuts and bolts of her database, we see that it is to the advantage of all of us that she is building this bibliographical database after several other classical databases have already begun to be distributed. Clayman's ultimate hope, after all, is that in the near future scholars will be able to use her comprehensive bibliographical database with these other classical databases containing individual corpora.

Perseus is in some ways the most comprehensive collection of electronically accessible information available to classical scholars and students. While not itself a complete database of a particular corpus, Perseus contains a few dozen frequently used literary texts with side-by-side translations, an atlas of the Mediterranean, a historical survey, a bibliography, a classical encyclopedia, a Greek-English and an English-Greek lexicon, archaeological site plans, and hundreds of images of ancient Greek sculpture, architecture, coins, and pottery. The essay on Perseus, written (like Perseus itself) by a team consisting of Elli Mylonas, Gregory Crane, Kenneth Morrell, and D. Neel Smith, recalls the conception of Perseus and its timetable for completion. Because this is not an all-inclusive database, the authors inform us as well of their criteria for selecting material to include, criteria which range from the general usefulness of an author to the availability of legal copyright. We also learn of their methods and materials used for data entry, the different problems and solutions involved in preparing literary and archaeological material as well as a grammatical parser, and their rigorous evaluation procedures. In its comprehensiveness, this penultimate essay transfers us from the electronic versions of traditional databases to the broad range of materials the Perseus Project employs to complement them.

The final essay then takes us to a summary analysis of what the creation of the computer and the accessibility of multimedia, comprehensive classical databases means for contemporary and future classical scholarship. Jay Bolter in "Hypertext and the Classical Commentary" forces us to question some basic assumptions about the relationship between scholar and text. Contemporary writing spaces on which scholarship is both printed and studied are no longer entirely dependent on the printed page or bound volumes. The traditional classical scholar who had a printed text, a printed commentary, and a printed lexicon open during a work session is now the scholar who has electronic texts, commentaries, and lexica open in separate windows on the computer screen. No longer are these traditional reference volumes ordered from front to back. The contemporary scholar progresses instead in a nonlinear fashion and repeatedly makes various associative links between windows. Texts become networks of verbal references, and the reader by definition becomes the editor, selecting paths appropriate to his or her own work. The logical progression, then, is for scholars to consider the closure of the printed volume obsolete and become accustomed instead to the open-endedness of scholarship in electronic media.

When I contacted the contributors, I asked them in general to describe the history, the present state, and the future of their projects, but I gave them plenty of opportunity to write what interested them. Their responses are of course different for a variety of reasons. One of these reasons is that the projects are at different states of completion, with the *Thesaurus Linguae Graecae, TLG Canon,* and Duke Data Bank of Documentary Papyri nearly complete and already owned or leased by hundreds of scholars and institutions, with version 1.0 of Perseus just recently disseminated, and with the Database for Classical Bibliography only recently under way. Another is the nature of each project and the particular sets of problems encountered in each. The TLG had to enter some 60 million words and confront a profession that was not quite ready to accept computerization, the DDBDP has had to incorporate lacunae and uncertain readings which do not suit themselves well to electronic searches, the *Lexicon Iconographicum Mythologiae Graecae* must incorporate many different artistic genres, materials, and periods, and the DCB, which has a ready-made and uniformly printed database to work from, must nonetheless accommodate a number of languages, font types, and multiple markings.

The inspiration to invite these scholars to contribute to an edited volume of essays was in part the result of respect and admiration — respect for those who find computer programming and database architecture less difficult than nuclear fission and brain surgery, and admiration for men and women who foresaw these revolutionary means of improving modern scholarship and acquired the expertise and funding necessary to do so. But it was mostly the desire to record this revolution in accessing and working with the ancient corpora that inspired this volume. Unlike so many "computer books," therefore, this volume will hardly become obsolete even after the software and hardware its authors designed or employed have themselves become obsolete. It captures a period in history which has great interest for the technician and classical scholar of today as well as for the scholar of classical scholarship and the technological historian of tomorrow.

The resulting volume has a logical structure that ranges from the earliest attempts at creating machine-readable classical texts to the nearly completed CD-ROM containing the entire corpus of ancient Greek literature and from Egyptian-made papyri to dynamic, intangible hypertext. Its professional readers will find an inspiration to make these electronic reference tools available to themselves, their colleagues, and their students, and perhaps some of these will collect new databases or invent new search paths for the ones already developed. Perhaps this volume will even contribute to the creation of a scholarly climate in which printed publication and prioritized methodologies will give way to dynamically collaborative, open-ended work. The processing speed of the electronic computer is such that lexica, bibliographies, and large corpora of texts and images can be searched, sorted, and examined efficiently and rapidly. But the speed of electricity should also be applied to the swiftness with which scholarship is disseminated. As Jay Bolter concludes in the final essay of this volume, scholarship, which used to be the realm of carefully guarded individuals who produced printed publications over the course of months or years, has now the opportunity to become continual and immediate work in progress which we all share in the pursuit of knowledge.

1

Classics and the Computer
The History of a Relationship

Theodore F. Brunner

Meeting in New York City on October 17, 1987, the directors of the American Philological Association unanimously passed a resolution that compared the creation of machine-readable texts and other computer-related resources to "discoveries of such pioneers as Heinrich Schliemann and Michael Ventris" and that noted that the availability of these resources initiated "a revolution in Classics teaching and research far beyond the wildest dreams of previous generations."[1] In many respects, this action constituted a major milestone in the history of Classics: computers — and along with them scholarly notions and processes fundamentally different from those solely acceptable for centuries — were now fully legitimate. The road that led to this juncture deserves recording; a new generation of classicists, soon to move into the twenty-first century in which computer-aided scholarship will be a phenomenon so commonplace as not to warrant a second thought, should have a grasp of the events that shaped the research environment in which they will be functioning.[2]

It is already difficult to pinpoint precisely when Classics first made contact with the computer; if focus upon a text in one of the two classical languages qualifies for the honor, it occurred when Jesuit Father Roberto Busa met with J. Thomas Watson, then president of IBM, in 1949. Busa had begun his academic career in 1941, studying the concept of "presence" in the works of Saint Thomas Aquinas; the problem he encountered, however, was that the (manually prepared) word indices available to him did not carry words that were then considered to be "insignificant," e.g., articles, conjunctions, and prepositions. Prepositions, in particular, were of major importance to Busa: since the idea of "presence" is often expressed not by a noun but by means of a prepositional phrase in Latin, a *complete* index to Saint Thomas was crucial to his research. Creation of such a tool, Busa reasoned, might be facilitated via the use of computer technology, and he succeeded in persuading Watson to support the creation of a machine-readable version of the text of Aquinas. Data entry of the Aquinas corpus would not be completed until 1967, and another thirteen years would be consumed by text verification and data processing tasks leading, ultimately, to the production of a sixty-volume, 70,000-page concordance to the works of Saint Thomas.

Busa's work constituted the first major effort to create a large data bank in the humanities. Others would soon follow suit. In 1957, John Ellison converted the Bible into electronic form and published a biblical concordance. David W. Packard in the United States, Paul Tombeur and Louis Delatte in Belgium, Wilhelm Ott in Germany, R. A. Wisbey in England, Bernard Quemada in France, and Antonio Zampolli in Italy would spend much of the early 1960s creating or accumulating machine-readable versions of classical and other authors, and by the middle of that decade, Marvin Spevak in Münster, Germany, had begun work on his electronic Shakespeare texts.

It would be in the latter half of the 1960s and in the early 1970s, however, that the computer would make major and lasting inroads into the humanities. It is an era that is recorded, in some detail, in Joseph Raben's *Computer-Assisted Research in the Humanities: A Directory of Scholars Active,*[3] which lists no fewer than 923 computer-based projects in the humanities and the related social sciences in progress during the period from November 1966 to May 1972.[4]

Many of the projects listed in the *Directory* focused upon classical authors and texts. Computer-aided work being conducted then included the study of Homeric vocabulary and metrics (A. Q. Morton), a prosodical investigation of the Pindaric Odes (John C. Rouman), the linguistic and stylistic study of the fragments of Lucilius (Adriano Pennacini), grammatical analysis of Latin (Maurice Cunningham), stylometry in the works of Xenophon (Norman Duncanson Thompson), and the creation of a Plato concordance (Leonard Brandwood). Brandwood's concordance, in fact, was only one of scores of similar undertakings: of the 551 entries under the Language and Literature rubric in the Raben *Directory,* more than two thirds involve, in one way or another, index or keyword-in-context (KWIC) production.[5] The *Directory* also reveals that a sizeable majority of those using computers in the humanistic disciplines in the 1960s and early 1970s were Europeans.[6]

American classicists who did involve themselves with computers in this era were, for the most part, in the early stages of their careers,[7] and some of them paid a heavy personal price for their service as pioneers: many of their more senior (and conservative) colleagues, deeming preoccupation with machines frivolous and intellectually indefensible, expressed their disdain by responding negatively on those occasions when a young offender would be subject to departmental review for potential academic advancement. Quite a few computer-classicists, in fact, would leave the field entirely to pursue new careers in business or industry.[8]

The discipline's establishment, however, kept an open mind toward new concepts and methodologies. In fact, much credit is owed to the American Philological Association (APA) for its willingness to show not merely tolerance but also wisdom and foresight when confronted by phenomena which — several decades earlier — had effected fundamental changes in most of the nonhumanistic disciplines. Rather than to reject outright what could easily have been denounced as an unwarranted intrusion of technology into a field that had always prided itself in its humanistic purity, the APA's leadership took firm and deliberate steps to assure that Classics and the computer would not remain permanent strangers. The steady growth of the relationship is reflected in numerous documents issued by the Association and its constituent bodies.

One of the first references to computing in an APA publication is found in 1966 in volume 97 of the *Transactions and Proceedings of the American Philological Association (TAPA)*.[9] There, a "Report of the Delegates to the Fédération Internationale des Associations d'Études Classiques" (FIEC) mentions the admission of the International Organization for Computer Studies in the Ancient Languages to membership in FIEC; the same report also notes that the 1969 Fifth International Congress of Classical Studies in Bonn, Germany, will include a session "devoted to the uses of electronic machines." Another 1966 document, the APA's *Fall Newsletter and Announcement of the Ninety-Eighth Annual Meeting*, reports that the recently created National Endowment for the Humanities has earmarked a portion of its coffers for the production of "scholarly tools," an action soon to exert a major impact upon the growth of computer-based resources in the field.[10]

Nevertheless, the first computer-generated tool to be brought before the directors of the Association was to meet with a less than enthusiastic reception. The spring 1967 *APA Newsletter* carries the announcement that the journal *AGON*, "a new kind of venture in the field," has been founded by the University of California, Berkeley, Graduate Association of Classics, and that the first part of a "computer-sorted concordance to Lucretius" would appear as an appendix to its second issue. Still, the directors, meeting in New York City on October 28, 1967, voted "not, as a matter of policy, to give public endorsement" to this concordance, "but to refer [*AGON*] to other, appropriate agencies of the Association."[11]

However, the spring 1967 *Newsletter* also contains a computing-related item of far greater consequence. Referring to an "informal meeting of people interested in projects involving both computers and classics" at the 1966 APA Annual Meeting in Toledo as the impetus, it announces that *Calculi*, "a bimonthly newsletter intended primarily as a clearinghouse of information for classicists interested in or actively working in computer-oriented studies began publication in January," and that "a most informative March issue has subsequently appeared."[12] In retrospect, the "informal meeting" alluded to must be seen as a major milestone in the history of the APA: most of those who attended would play an instrumental role in the introduction of computing into the field.[13]

This group held its next informal meeting in Boston on December 29, 1967.[14] The meeting resulted in a formal request "that the Directors of the Association authorize appointment of a committee to investigate the implications and problems associated with the use of computers by classicists."[15] The directors' response was both prompt and positive. Meeting the next day, they voted:

> To authorize the President to appoint a special committee to report to the Board no later than December 27, 1968, on (1) the present applications of computer techniques in classical studies; (2) possible future applications; (3) specific problems already being encountered, e.g. the optimal method for providing output in Greek type, the feasibility of and conditions for instituting a central library of machine-readable texts and programs; the problem of publishing concordances already completed.[16]

At their next meeting (in New York City on October 26, 1968), the directors noted that Nathan A. Greenberg, David Packard,[17] Stephen Waite, William H. Willis, and Robert Dyer (chair) had been appointed by the Association's president to serve as a Special Committee for Computer Problems,[18] and they voted to "undertake expenses of [this committee] existing as of this date in sum not to exceed $550.00."[19] Not long thereafter, a formal Advisory Committee on Computer Activities (consisting of Lloyd W. Daly, James W. Halporn, David Packard, Alan E. Samuel, and chaired by Stephen V. F. Waite) was appointed to "advise [the directors] on current and future activities involving computers in classical studies."[20]

The Special Committee's recommendations (dated December 21, 1968) resulted, within slightly more than one week, in a major action by the directors. Meeting on December 30, 1968, in Toronto, they voted "to approve the establishment of a Summer Institute in Computer Applications to Classical Studies to be held at the University of Illinois in Urbana in 1969, and to authorize the Secretary-Treasurer to seek funds wherever he deems appropriate to support the Institute."[21]

Creation of such an institute had been urged emphatically by both the Special Committee and the Advisory Committee, and formal APA endorsement of the concept contributed much to its successful implementation. Supported by NEH with a $59,800 grant[22] and directed by Nathan Greenberg and John J. Bateman, the June-July Urbana Summer Institute[23] proved to be a spawning ground producing computing-related concepts and expertise with beneficial effects that would be felt by the field of Classics for years to come. Perhaps most important, however, the institute resulted in an effort to create what would become the first centrally located corpus of electronic Greek and Latin texts and other materials. According to its final report,[24] the institute had prepared (or acquired) the following texts upon its conclusion:

Homer, *Iliad* and *Odyssey*
Homeric Hymns
Isaeus, Oration III and selections from other orations
Sophocles, *Oedipus the King*
New Testament
Ammianus Marcellinus
Ausonius, *Mosella*
Appendix Vergiliana: Culex, Ciris, Moretum
Cato, complete works
Catullus 64
Cicero, *De Oratore,* Bk. I
Juvenal, complete poems
Livy, selections
Lucan, Books I and X
Lucretius, complete works
Ovid, *Metamorphoses,* Bks. I, II, V, XII
Rutilius Namatianus, *De Reditu Suo*
Persius, complete poems
Plautus, five plays
Tacitus, *Annales*
Vergil, *Eclogues* and *Aeneid,* Bks. I, IV, IX, XII
A dictionary of Latin
Corpus of Ugaritic texts

Today, this conglomerate of electronic materials seems paltry; in 1969, how-ever, it constituted a veritable gold mine for those beginning to apply com-puter-aided research methodologies to classical studies. Indeed, the Urbana Report leaves no doubt that the institute members were fully aware of the importance of these electronic resources:

> These materials comprise a valuable resource for future research. To prevent these texts from being dispersed and becoming difficult to obtain, Stephen V. F. Waite of Dartmouth College has been made temporary curator of the collection until final arrangements for its disposition can be made. The present understanding is that a library of tapes will be maintained at Dartmouth College. Copies of these tapes will be made available at cost to any researcher, although at present no responsibility is being taken by the Institute for guaranteeing the accuracy of these texts. It is hoped that these materials will be the nucleus of a growing collection of machine-readable texts in Greek and Latin which can become a repository of materials for future com-puterized research in classical studies.[25]

A copy of the Urbana Report was submitted to the APA directors, who took a flurry of computing-related actions at their meeting on November 1, 1969, in New York City.[26] They voted "to have Stephen V. F. Waite supervise until further notice the collection of Greek and Latin texts in machine-readable form acquired from the Summer Institute in Computer Applications to Classical Studies or from other sources." They authorized "the spending of up to $200.00 from the Monograph Fund to purchase magnetic tapes for recording machine-readable Greek and Latin texts for exchange purposes."[27] And Robert Dyer was "allotted a travel grant to deliver a paper at the Third International Congress on Computational Linguistics in Stockholm, Sweden, in September 1969 [*sic*]." Computer interests did not receive a carte blanche, however: the directors also voted to rescind a "previous approval of the preparation of a *Guide to the Use of Computers in Classical Studies* and the appointment of Donald W. Prakken as Editor," and refused to endorse "Professor Joseph Raben's proposal for a Summer Institute in Computer Application to the Study of Literature to be held at the University of Waterloo in 1970."

On balance, however, 1969 was a vintage year for computing in Classics. Nineteen seventy would prove to be a better year yet; in fact, *TAPA* 101 (1970) abounds in items attesting, in one way or another, to the fact that the computer was by now firmly established within the Association. To begin with, there is a lengthy "Report of the Advisory Committee on Computer Activities."[28] This report announces the availability of electronic materials resulting from the Urbana Summer Institute, but it also stresses the need for "a much more systematic library of computer material for classical research," noting that

> this would be a very large undertaking and one requiring substantial financial backing together with careful planning by a committee widely representative of the eventual users of such a resource. It is not likely to be achieved on the basis of chance contributions made by dozens of different researchers with different goals and standards of format and accuracy. In the end, it would probably be desirable to hire a full-time staff. Help could be offered to individuals willing to take responsibility for certain parts of the collection, but especially in the case of Greek a well trained full-time staff could prepare material at a much smaller cost than scholars are likely to find elsewhere. Any serious proposal in the future to found a comprehensive series of reliable texts should receive very serious consideration.[29]

Other portions of the report focus upon "Education in Computer Methods" (the committee accepted the fact that funds similar to that which supported the 1969 Urbana Institute could hardly be expected to become available annually, suggested that individual universities should be encouraged to offer computer courses as part of their regular summer sessions, and expressed the hope that an "authoritative guide to computer methods in classical studies" might still become a reality), "Bibliography" (alluding to *Biological Abstracts,* the committee noted that the Association should not overlook computer methods, were it to involve itself in the provision of bibliographical services),[30] and "Computers in Classical Publication" (the committee recommended that computer typesetting be viewed as a serious alternative to traditional means of publication, expressing the hope that "at least one book in the Association's Monograph series can be set in type by computer as a sample").

The committee report concludes with a section entitled "A Possible APA Computer Service Center." Here, the committee members acknowledge that their own affinity toward, and literacy in, computing may well "have blinded [them] to the legitimate claims of those who have neither inclination nor technical aptitude for computer programming, but whose research could clearly benefit from computer aid." A "central classics computing service center staffed with programmers conversant with classical problems" is mentioned as one possible solution; "if such a center possessed a comprehensive series of texts it . . . could ultimately become a resource like the *Thesaurus*."[31]

TAPA 101 also contains a report from Stephen Waite, now Supervisor of the American Philological Association Repository of Classical Texts in Machine-Readable Form, which notes that the Repository has already filled sixteen requests, and that "projects using texts from the Repository are now under way at such institutions as North Carolina and Minnesota on topics ranging from metrics to Latin phonology."[32] Waite also reports that "a proposal entitled 'American Philological Association Data Bank' has been submitted to the National Endowment for the Humanities."[33] This proposal received subsequent endorsement from the directors of the Association, meeting in New York on October 24, 1970.

Reports from the Supervisor of the APA Repository and from the Advisory Committee for Computer Activities again appear in *TAPA* 102 (1971).[34] Stephen Waite notes that the number of authors represented in the Repository has expanded from sixteen to thirty-three, and that between October 8, 1970, and October 15, 1971, fourteen requests for texts were filled for thirteen recipients in twelve institutions.

In addition, the Advisory Committee for Computer Activities[35] has, by now, agreed (though grudgingly) not to pursue production of *A Practical Guide to the Use of Computers by Classicists;* it had also decided that "despite the success of the Summer Institute held at the University of Illinois in 1969, [the] planning effort and the increasingly difficult scramble for funds necessary in order to hold [another] Institute would not be commensurate with expected results." With respect to the Repository, the committee notes that its curator "is acting for the Association," and that the committee "has the responsibility of determining policy with regard to the Repository."

The general tenor (if not tone) of the report would seem to suggest that policy-related disagreements had begun to arise between some committee members and Waite. Though being thanked for serving as both curator of the Repository and editor of *Calculi*, Waite is also "instructed to perform as curator no service beyond supplying machine-readable copies of materials in the Repository. He may choose to perform any other service, such as providing a concordance of a text, but only in his private professional capacity. The Committee feels that the Curator's task should be kept as simple as possible."[36]

Finally, the committee report notes that "for some years, an informal session for computer-oriented classicists has been held at the annual meetings of the Association," and that "the Committee has decided to attempt a more formal session for the meeting in December 1971 in Cincinnati." This session convened under the chairship of Nathan Greenberg in Parlor N of the Netherland Hilton Hotel in Cincinnati on Wednesday, October 29, 1971. Though only two papers were read,[37] the session constituted a major milestone: for the first time in the APA's history, a computer-related activity had warranted inclusion in the official program of the American Philological Association.[38]

Two days earlier, yet another milestone had passed virtually unnoticed. On December 27, 1971, this writer requested, and received, an audience with the directors of the Association. The request was motivated by a desire to apprise the Association of the fact that creation of a Thesaurus Linguae Graecae was being contemplated at the University of California, Irvine. The news was received by the directors politely, but it clearly failed to generate much excitement: the minutes of the meeting do not record the event.[39]

By the end of 1971, in fact, preliminary planning for a TLG had been in progress for the better part of a year, and a decision to proceed with the creation of a data bank of electronic Greek texts was virtually assured.[40] Notifying the directors was simply considered proper protocol, and there was little expectation on the part of those involved in TLG planning that the Association would involve itself to any degree in the new enterprise.[41] However, shortly after the Thesaurus Linguae Graecae began formal operations on July 1, 1972, its name and initials began to appear with ever increasing frequency in APA documents and publications. The next report of the Advisory Committee on Computer Activities,[42] though quite brief,[43] notes that "members of the Committee have maintained particularly close contact with the project currently being carried out by Professor Theodore F. Brunner of the University of California, Irvine. The long-range goal envisioned by Prof. Brunner is to complete a Thesaurus Linguae Graecae with the aid of the computer. The first, immediate step is to be the preparation of the extant texts of ancient Greek literature (up to a fixed cut-off date) in machine-readable form."

The 1972 "Report of the Supervisor of the Repository of Greek and Latin Texts in Machine-Readable Form"[44] also takes notice of the TLG; Stephen Waite reports that "some time also has been spent consulting with Theodore F. Brunner, who is directing the Thesaurus Linguae Graecae project at the University of California, Irvine. It appears to be a reasonable assumption that there will be extensive cooperation between the repository and the project in Irvine in the near future." Much space in the Supervisor's Report is devoted to a discussion of the problems inherent in assuring proper levels of uniformity and accuracy for the growing number of texts residing in the Repository. An Appendix reports on the status of *Calculi,* noting that 774 copies of the most recent issue of this publication (supported since July 1972 by a $300 APA subvention) were distributed outside Dartmouth College.[45]

A moment's pause is in order here. By the end of 1972, Classics had made vast progress in adapting to a new world defined by computers. A mere six years had passed since "electronic machines" were first mentioned in *TAPA* 97; yet, by now the Association was maintaining an active Advisory Committee on Computer Activities, a Repository of Greek and Latin Texts in Machine-Readable Form, and a journal devoted exclusively to computing matters. A highly successful Summer Institute in Computer Applications to Classical Studies had been organized, and the annual meetings of the Association now regularly scheduled sessions devoted to computing-related papers. Much of this progress was owed to deliberate actions by the directors of the Association meant to foster and facilitate computer-aided research by the APA membership. By late 1972, also, work on an electronic Thesaurus Linguae Graecae encompassing the entire extant corpus of Greek literature was well under way at the University of California, Irvine. For the next several years, much of the Association's energies would be devoted to the assertion of its interests in the TLG. Since (unlike the Repository) the TLG was not under the jurisdiction of the Association, occasional frictions would develop in the process.

The April 1973 *APA Newsletter*[46] reports that the directors voted "to establish an interim advisory committee on the Thesaurus Linguae Graecae at the University of California, Irvine, to assist with the furtherance of this project and to inform the Directors of its progress and status" (4).[47] Creation of this committee, in fact, was instigated by the Thesaurus Linguae Graecae: the TLG director felt that the responsibility for the selection of specific text editions for data entry should not lie solely within the project but should be shared by the Association. Initially, the committee was composed of Albert M. Henrichs, Bernard M. W. Knox, Miroslav Marcovich, Bruce M. Metzger, Lionel H. Pearson, John M. Rist, and Douglas C. C. Young (chair).

The 1973 Report of the Secretary, among several other computing-related items, again contains reports from the Committee on Computer Activities[48] and from the Supervisor of the Repository.[49] The computer committee notes that it "[has] kept in touch with Theodore Brunner and the TLG Project." In his capacity as Repository Supervisor, Stephen Waite reports that the APA collection of machine-readable texts has grown to over 180,000 lines. More important, however, he raises some issues which, in short order, will begin to exercise both the Association and the TLG. The pertinent portion of his statement reads as follows:

> During the past year, the Supervisor worked closely with the Thesaurus Linguae Graecae Project directed by Theodore F. Brunner at the University of California, Irvine, and spent two months in California as a Research Associate of the Thesaurus. The relationship of the Thesaurus, which is undertaking the preparation of large quantities of Greek text in computer-usable form, and the repository is by no means

clear. The Directors of the Association and the Association's Advisory Committees on these activities might wish to give particular attention to what form the connections between the two entities might optimally take. Even if the Thesaurus should wish to make its texts available through the Repository, it is far from certain that the Association is in a position to accept a sudden increase of the magnitude involved. On the one hand, there would be the advantage of having large quantities of texts readily available under the Association's auspices; on the other, the storing of 20,000,000 words of Greek text, the initial goal of the Thesaurus, would necessitate the purchase of at least $400.00 worth of magnetic tapes, assuming the maximum use of each tape. The Supervisor merely wishes to raise the question, the solution of which will greatly influence the nature of the Repository.

There is a hidden subtext. By mid-1973 (i.e., when this report was composed), the TLG data bank already contained considerably more electronic text than had been accumulated by the APA Repository over several years. The field, initially skeptical about the TLG's ability to implement its announced plans, was beginning to clamor for access to these rapidly growing resources. As a matter of policy, however, the TLG refused to disseminate "raw" (i.e., uncorrected) text material.[50] In consequence, some quarters within the field began to suggest that the Association undertake efforts to take over the TLG's product. The TLG, in turn, made it clear that such efforts would be futile. The directors, fully aware of these developments, chose to proceed cautiously. Meeting in New York City on October 14, 1973, they voted "to endorse the Thesaurus Linguae Graecae project as developed to date and to express their confidence in its present management," and "to extend the life of the [TLG] Advisory Committee to December 30, 1974, and to authorize the President to reappoint present members of the Committee and to add new members as circumstances may require."[51]

The year 1973, already full of significant computing-related developments in Classics, ended with a Colloquium on Computer Activities in Classics, again formally scheduled at the St. Louis Meeting of the American Philological Association, and chaired by James Helm. In addition to a report on the APA Repository by Stephen Waite, papers were delivered by A. P. MacGregor ("Computerized Taxonomy for Manuscripts of Seneca Tragicus"), Theodore Crane ("Machine-Detectable Figures of Speech in Lucan's *De Bello Civili*"), and David Packard ("Automated Morphological Analysis of Ancient Greek"). Furthermore, William Willis's Presidential Address contained the first public acknowledgment of the (now one and a half year old) Thesaurus Linguae Graecae by an officer of the American Philological Association. In his speech entitled "The Lost World," Willis referred to the TLG as "one of the most significant new developments . . . in the history of Greek studies since the onset of modern scholarship 150 years ago."[52]

Some problems were still simmering, however. As the field's attention continued to focus upon the TLG and its ever growing data bank of Greek texts, efforts continued to shift control over TLG policy and direction from the project to the Association. For the record, it should be noted that these efforts were not spearheaded by the Association or its officers; rather, the officers suddenly found themselves caught in a crossfire between voices within the field (advocating annexation of the TLG by the Association) and the Thesaurus Linguae Graecae (anything but willing to submit to such annexation). In any event, the directors of the Association passed, on May 13, 1974, the following resolution:

> That the President of the American Philological Association, in concert with such other members of the Association as he may designate, be authorized and directed to undertake conversation with the Chancellor of the University of California at Irvine, Professor Brunner, the officials of the donor and the recipient trust, and such other persons as he may deem appropriate, with a view toward framing a tentative agreement concerning the creation of a Governing Board of the *Thesaurus Linguae Graecae*, for the approval of the university, the trust concerned, and the Directors of the American Philological Association.

The issues involved were subsequently spelled out quite candidly and concisely by Harry L. Levy in a statement entitled "President's Corner" and published in the fall 1974 *Proceedings of the American Philological Association*.[53] In essence, Levy attempts here to effect a compromise that—while assuring continued TLG autonomy—would give the Association at least some opportunity to participate in TLG-related decision-making processes. Levy's statement, a masterpiece of diplomacy, deserves to be quoted here in detail:

> This Fall I shall avail myself of the hospitality of this corner to report to the members on the developing relations between our Association and the Thesaurus Linguae Graecae, now being created at the University of California, Irvine, under the directorship of Professor Theodore F. Brunner.
>
> Thus far, the official connection of APA with TLG has been limited to the valued services of our TLG Advisory Committee, advisory as much to the Directors of APA as to Professor Brunner. Opinion has been voiced in various quarters that, in the determination of policies and procedures for the budding Thesaurus, great benefit would be derived from the establishment of a more broadly based governing body than that provided by the UCI structure itself. In an attempt to meet this need, I proposed the creation of a new Governing Board. With the encouragement of the APA's Advisory Committee, with the unanimous approval of the Association's Directors, and with the warm cooperation of Professor Brunner himself, I placed my proposal before Chancellor Daniel G. Aldrich of UCI on a visit to his campus on 27 June 1974, accompanied by Professor Pearson, Chairman of the Advisory Committee, and by Professor Brunner. Chancellor Aldrich received the proposal with great interest, and promised to give it his close study and an early decision.
>
> If approved, the new arrangement will give the APA's representative one of the five seats on the Governing Board, with a degree of influence somewhat greater than the numerical ratio would suggest. For one thing, the APA representative's approval would be needed for the cooptation by the Board of a person 'eminently qualified to preside over' it to serve as Chairman; for another, the vote of either this Chairman

or of our APA representative would be required to validate any action or decision of the Board, which would control the policies and procedures of the Thesaurus.

One of the most important policy questions pending is that of access by scholars to the growing store of data which will in essence be the body of the Thesaurus. At my recommendation, the Directors of APA authorized and directed me to appoint a conference committee consisting of four members of the APA Committee on Computer Activities, four members of the APA Advisory Committee on the TLG, and the APA Secretary as Chairman, 'to discuss in detail the question of access to TLG material, and to reach such agreements as may be possible in the form of recommendations which might then be addressed to the appropriate body or bodies.' Besides Professor Carrubba, I have appointed the following members of APA, all of whom have kindly consented to serve: (Advisory Committee) Professors Bernard M. W. Knox, Miroslav Marcovich, Lionel Pearson, and William H. Willis; (Computer Activities) Professors Nathan A. Greenberg (who will replace Professor Helm on 27 December 1974 as a member of the Computer Activities Committee, and serve a full three-year term thereafter), Gregory Nagy, and [sic] John F. Oates, and Mrs. Cora A. Sowa.

On December 16, 1974, a set of Articles of Agreement for a Thesaurus Linguae Graecae Governing Board such as that suggested by Levy was ratified by all parties concerned; William Willis was appointed by the Association to serve as its representative.

Nevertheless, TLG-related issues continue to occupy a major portion of the 1975 Report of the Secretary. The APA's Advisory Committee to the Thesaurus Linguae Graecae is by now uncertain about its prerogatives and functions, and states in its Report that "future responsibilities of this Committee (or a new committee to take its place) will be dependent on decisions concerning TLG policy made by the Governing Committee of the TLG" (10). The Committee on Computer Activities notes that "the appointed members of the Committee also served on the Ad Hoc Committee on Access to the TLG project, out of which a statement was prepared to guide the Directors and the APA's member on the Governing Board of the Thesaurus Linguae Graecae," adding that "we are all hopeful that all questions of access can be settled by our December [1975] meeting" (11). The Supervisor of the APA Repository (which by now has grown to 314,204 lines of text) reports that "because of the thoroughly uncertain situation *vis-à-vis* the *Thesaurus Linguae Graecae,* [his effort to standardize texts] has been concentrated almost exclusively on Latin texts; to devote attention to Greek texts would be a waste of resources, since these texts could easily be superseded if the *Thesaurus* should decide to make its material available" (12). The Report of the Ad Hoc Committee on Access to the Data Bank of the Thesaurus Linguae Graecae deserves to be quoted at some length, since it comes close to an effort on the part of at least one APA entity to determine policy in behalf of a non-APA enterprise:

This committee met during the Annual Meeting of the APA in Chicago, on December 29, 1974. It recognizes that any policy regulating access to the material in the data bank must keep two goals in view. First, it must ensure that the integrity of the data bank is preserved. Second, in the interests of scholarship, it should permit and encourage access to the data bank to scholars on an international basis at lowest possible cost.

Ultimately access could take the following forms, with suitable organization to maintain proper control:

(1) The opportunity for individual scholars to obtain information from the data bank, either by submitting questions or obtaining duplicate tapes.

(2) The fullest possible availability, whether by publication or otherwise, of any products developed from the data by the staff of the *TLG*.

If the *TLG* is to be an ongoing organization, it will continue to expand and bring its data bank up to date and to develop and market new products, such as concordances and lexicographical or other statistical studies. As a center which uses computers for scholarly purposes, for the benefit of classical scholars, it will learn by experience exactly what form its organization should take. It can learn much from the experiences of existing models for the organization of scholarly banks (like the APA Repository).

The Committee notes that the matter of access presents certain immediate problems and wishes to make the following observations, to which it would draw the attention of the Governing Board of the *TLG,* the *TLG* staff, and all interested classicists.

(1) We agree that the *TLG* should continue to regard as its first priority the recording of Greek texts in computerized form, the expansion of its data bank.

(2) Since great progress has been made and the data bank is already a large one, with so many of the major Greek authors, up to 200 A.D., now on tape, the *TLG* could now begin to make certain services available to scholars, so long as the provision of such services does not impede the expansion of the data bank.

(3) It would be useful if the *TLG* could publish lists of services which it can perform and is willing to perform.

(4) The *TLG* should begin, if only in a modest way, to establish a basis on which charges would be made for such services. We would urge that the goal of the lowest possible cost be kept in mind.

(5) In order that the provision of services should not distract the *TLG* staff from its main task of data entry and in order to speed up the offering of a restricted set of services, it is suggested that the *TLG* explore the possibility of using the services of the APA Repository, of contracting out services without burdening their own staff.

(6) The Committee appreciates that the *TLG* is reluctant to release tapes or other material before their accuracy is fully checked. None the less, in the interest of making the material available to scholars with less delay, the *TLG* might consider releasing tapes before full verification, while warning the user in each case that verification has not been completed.

The APA through its Board of Directors and its various interested committees stands ready to continue its support of the *TLG* and to give scholarly advice in all matters pertaining to questions of access. (24–25)

Finally, the 1975 Secretary's Report contains a lengthy statement by the APA representative to the Governing Board of the Thesaurus Linguae Graecae. In it, Professor William Willis notes that the newly established TLG Governing Board (composed of one representative each from the University of California, Irvine, the UC Irvine Foundation, the TLG, and the APA, plus a coopted chair)[54] "has undertaken to establish policies governing the goals, priorities and conduct of the *Thesaurus*," describes the Board's newly established policies governing dissemination of TLG products,[55] requests "that the Association record and announce its unqualified endorsement and strong support of the *TLG* project," and recommends that the directors of the Association "authorize a subsidy to the *Thesaurus Linguae Graecae* equal to that provided to the *Thesaurus Linguae Latinae*."

Again, a moment's reflection is in order. While the period from 1966 to 1972 was marked by steady advances in Classics-related computing, these advances were also of an essentially small-scale nature. Even the APA Repository of Greek and Latin Texts in Machine-Readable Form, though steadily expanding, was primarily a reflection of individual efforts to create relatively small machine-readable texts. The appearance of the TLG in mid-1972 created virtual shock-waves in the field: here, suddenly, was a large project that — within a matter of a few months — was leaving no doubt in anyone's mind that it would succeed in creating vast electronic resources of major importance to research in Classics. The TLG, however, had adopted (what it considered to be legitimate) policies meant to assure that its product would be of the highest possible scholarly quality and integrity. In effect, the project refused to disseminate any of its texts until they were fully verified and corrected.

As Classics moved into the mid-1970s (and as is clear from the documentary evidence adduced here), computer-aided research was assuming ever-growing importance. Thus, it was inevitable that frictions would arise between the Thesaurus Linguae Graecae (the producer of electronic resources) and the field (i.e., the clientele for these resources). In essence, the rash of TLG policy-related issues filling the pages of *APA Newsletters, Proceedings,* and other similar publications and documents between 1973 and 1975 is simply a reflection of fundamental changes occurring within the field of Classics during that period. Clearly, Classics was not only ready but anxious to involve itself in computing; had this not been the case, TLG access and other similar policies would have failed to energize the field. Careful analysis of the actions of the directors of the Association leaves no doubt that the leadership of the APA was both fully sensitive to what was occurring within Classics and equipped to deal with a period of upheaval in a sensible and sensitive fashion.

After 1975, peace returned to the APA/TLG front; in fact, the reports from the Advisory Committee on the Thesaurus Linguae Graecae and from the representative to the Governing Board of the Thesaurus Linguae Graecae in subsequent *APA Newsletters* and other similar publications primarily note the steady growth of the TLG data bank. Activities of the Committee on Computer Activities became routine, and the committee members were now content "to stay in close touch with the *Thesaurus Linguae Graecae* Project."[56] By August 1977, the holdings of the APA Repository had grown to 397,416 lines.[57]

However, the computer was now making other (long-overdue) inroads into the Association. Meeting in Atlanta on December 27, 1977, the directors voted to affiliate the Association with Scholars Press.[58] As noted by the secretary, "two major aspects of the Association's system of doing business needed revision. The Secretary's office was inundated with the massive paperwork of billing, receiving, and recording dues, and maintaining the membership list — all done by hand. The rising costs of printing, plus difficulties in distribution, jeopardized the publication program."[59]

In essence, the directors' action provided computer assistance — long enjoyed by a wide segment of the field in the realm of research — to the Association's support structure: Scholars Press could offer computing resources sadly needed to facilitate the Association's administrative and publication functions. The ever-growing legitimacy of computing in Classics was, albeit subtly, affirmed by a small nuance in the summer 1978 *APA Newsletter* (8–9): here, for the first time, several candidates for office listed computing-related Association service in their résumés.

During 1979 and 1980, the Committee on Computer Activities continued "to stay in close touch with the *Thesaurus Linguae Graecae* Project," while the representative to the Governing Board of the TLG and the Advisory Committee to the Thesaurus Linguae Graecae attested to the rapid growth of the TLG data bank (which contained 32.5 million words of Greek text by 1979).[60] On December 27, 1979, the directors received a report from an Ad Hoc Committee on Basic Research Tools (created in 1976) and authorized its publication in book form;[61] the report's extensive and detailed focus upon computing-related issues further underlines the fact that Classics was by now fully at home in an electronic world. Included in the report are recommendations

> 1. That top priority be given to the continued development of data banks containing classical texts and bibliographical tools, and to providing direct access to them by computer terminal through whatever method proves to be most effective;
> 2. That mechanical compilations, whether by hand or by machine, be given low priority as involving in most cases a waste of resources in doing a poor job at what direct interactive computer use can do;
> 3. That a very high priority be given to the creation of the technical means . . . through which the computer's resources can be used effectively and economically for classical languages. (5)

The report also recommends that *L'Année Philologique,* along with several other specialized bibliographies, be converted into electronic form, and that further textual corpora like *CIL* and the papyri be added to existing machine-readable repositories as soon as possible (6–7).

As Classics moved into the 1980s, computing-related items in APA publications became routine. The spring 1981 *APA Newsletter* (11) announces the twentieth anniversary of the Laboratoire d'Analyse Statistique des Langues Anciennes and an International Congress on Automatic Data Processing organized in connection with this anniversary. It also invites information on research in computer applications to classical Greek and Latin in behalf of the British Association for Literary and Linguistic Computing (13). The summer 1981 issue (10) carries the first of a series of articles on computing-related issues written (or solicited) for the *Newsletter* by Roger Bagnall, now secretary of the Association.[62] The winter issue[63] (4) announces that a panel has been proposed for the 1982 APA meeting to discuss how computers are or can be used in support of instruction in the Classics. It also carries a report from the representative to the Governing Board of the Thesaurus Linguae Graecae noting that the TLG data bank contained nearly 41 million words of text as of June 30, 1981.

The pattern continues as time moves on. In fact, references to computers and computing become so commonplace that a few select references will have to suffice. The fall 1982 issue of the *Newsletter* (5) announces commencement of work on a data bank of documentary Greek papyri at Duke University under the direction of Professors William H. Willis and John F. Oates. The same issue (7) refers to an "Inventory of Machine-Readable Texts in the Humanities" being conducted at Rutgers University. The winter 1983 (9) issue contains items on Latin computer programs and on Verba, a computer-instructed course in medical terminology. It also lists several new computerized catalogues of ancient monuments (9–10). An article on "Reading Greek with the Kurzweil Data Entry Machine" by David Schaps (Bar Ilan University) is carried in the spring issue (14–15) of that year. The fall 1983 issue notes that "the staff [of the Association] is at work creating a database of information about classics programs and departments, to be computerized for ready access to a variety of information, ranging from statistics about faculty to address lists for departments" (4), and that "a large-scale project entitled 'Computer Assisted Tools for Septuagint Studies' is under way at the University of Pennsylvania under the direction of Robert A. Kraft of the Department of Religious Studies" (14). It also carries a report by the supervisor of the APA Repository noting that "since October 1, 1982, eleven requests for texts from as many institutions have been filled," and that "work has been concentrated on Latin texts due to the availability of Greek materials through the Thesaurus Linguae Graecae" (5–6).

However, not all appeared to be well now with the Repository. Although the Committee on Computer Activities reports in the fall 1983 issue of the *Newsletter* that "the APA Repository of texts in Machine Readable Form . . . is now functioning better," it also notes, in the same breath, that "the Repository remains a problem. At present it is dead storage, receiving no new texts and not handling other matters. . . . At our meeting in December the Committee will be seriously discussing the nature of the Repository and possible future roles and locations for it" (7).[64]

The winter 1984 *Newsletter* records the directors' approval of "an appropriation of $325.00 to launch a revived newsletter on computers and the classics, to be undertaken by Joseph Tebben of Ohio State University" (2); solicits (on behalf of the Committee on Computer Activities) information about machine-readable texts not in the APA Repository (7); and presents an article on "Text Processing on Computers" (12–13). An article on computer-generated Greek fonts by Roger Bagnall appears in the spring issue (8–9), while the summer issue contains a report on the availability of Gerald M. Culley's *Teaching the Classics with Computers,* the first of a series of APA Educational Papers (10). The fall issue announces a session for classicists "doing Greek-English word processing on the Apple Macintosh computer" at the Toronto APA meeting (3).

In its next report in the winter 1985 issue of the *APA Newsletter* (8–9), the Committee on Computer Activities appears far more sanguine about the APA Repository than it had been the previous year, noting that the Repository is "functioning well." The committee also reports that it "discussed the possibility of an APA-sponsored summer institute to introduce classicists to computing," but that "this project has not yet produced results, and may in fact have to be dropped." A report on the Repository of Texts in Machine-Readable [*sic*] Form, also carried in the winter 1985 issue (9), notes that ten requests for varying quantities of text were filled during the period from October 1, 1983, to September 30, 1984. The winter *Newsletter* also announces the forthcoming publication of *Word Processing and the Classicist* by Roger S. Bagnall, second in the series of APA Educational Papers.[65]

Scattered through the spring 1985 *Newsletter* are several items which, though seemingly insignificant, are indicators that computers are now a fact of life within the Association. To begin with, this newsletter (2–3) marks the first time that computing-related expenses are recorded in the report of the treasurer. For the calendar year ending December 31, 1984, the Association budgeted $1,200.00 for computer services; actual expenditures totalled $2,617.00. The report also mentions the acquisition of an IBM PC-XT depreciated over an estimated useful life of 3 and 2/3 years. The instructions for submissions to the Placement Book (6–8), formulaic for many years in the past in stressing the importance of using "a new black ribbon (and preferably a carbon ribbon) since typewritten copy that is too light does not reproduce well," suddenly also note that "copy from most dot matrix printers does not reproduce well." In the fall 1985 issue of the Newsletter (3–5), the Program Committee, too, frowns on computer-generated copy: "the awkwardness of handling computer print-outs and stationery of abnormal size led the Committee to recommend that all abstracts submitted for the 1986 meeting be typed on regular size sheets, namely 8 1/2 × 11 inches." Finally, the fall 1985 *Newsletter* (6) foreshadows the advent of what will soon become two major additions to the growing body of computer-based resources in Classics: the Committee on Computer Activities reports that "through the generosity of the Packard Foundation and the efforts of George Goold and Joseph Solodow a canon of Latin authors is being readied preparatory to the creation of a corpus of Latin authors in machine-readable form," and the Subcommittee on Epigraphical Bibliography notes that (again with financial support from the Packard Foundation) work has begun on a data bank of Greek inscriptions.[66]

In the meantime, the Thesaurus Linguae Graecae data bank continued to grow steadily, containing, by mid-1985, more than 56 million words of text. On July 1, 1985, the project announced plans to produce its first CD-ROM,[67] and the subsequent availability of massive amounts of Greek text in machine-readable form on an inexpensive CD-ROM medium can justifiably be credited with generating a quantum jump in computer use within the field. Continuous progress in technology also contributed to the rapid spread of computing in Classics. By the mid-1980s, microcomputers were readily within the financial reach of the average scholar; the steady growth of networks facilitated scholarly communication with the aid of the computer;[68] and processes such as optical character recognition were becoming sufficiently reliable (and economical) to warrant mention by the Association.[69] Computerized listings of various types of data and information were now commonplace: in the fall 1986 issue of the *APA Newsletter,* "the Women's Classical Caucus would like to make it known that it now has a computerized membership list" (17). Furthermore, the Association's Educational Papers Series published yet another computing-related title, *How to Choose a Database* by Jocelyn Penny Small.[70]

Yet more electronic resources were being built: at Rutgers University, work was in progress on the computer-based *Lexicon Iconographicum Mythologiae Classicae,*[71] and the directors of the Association were intimately involving themselves in the planning for the forthcoming "bibliographical database project undertaken by the Subcommittee on Classical Bibliography and the computer bulletin board project proposed by the Committee on Computer Activities."[72] In late 1987, "over thirty scholars from all over the world (that includes Japan, Sweden, England, and various European countries) attended a planning conference to establish international standards for encoding texts."[73] The creation of HumaNet, "an online newsletter of information about current activities in the field of classical studies," was announced by the Committee on Computer Activities in the spring 1988 *APA Newsletter* (21), and in the fall 1988 *Newsletter* the Subcommittee on Latin Lexicography reports that "the first Latin CD-ROM, promised by the Packard Humanities Institute for the APA meeting in New York, was duly delivered" (5). The fall 1988 *Newsletter* (12) also carries, for the first time, a directory of APA members' BITNET numbers. Eighteen names and numbers are listed; by the time a similar list is published in the

August 1989 issue of the *Newsletter,* this number will have grown to sixty-one.

These numbers are misleading, however. This author knows for a fact that scores of classicists *not* listed in these directories have access to, and frequently use, BITNET and other similar facilities. This is symptomatic of what is occurring in the field today. Computing in Classics has become so commonplace a phenomenon that documents and publications such as those periodically issued by the APA simply are no longer an accurate reflection of how the computer affects the Association and its membership. Today's classicist uses the computer as a matter of course, and concepts and procedures that seemed novel not too long ago no longer warrant even a second thought. A recent compilation of electronic resources available to the field[74] contains more than 600 pages of information about machine-readable texts, programs, and other electronic resources suited to support computer-based research and other similar processes, presenting an admirable picture of the progress that has been made by the field since the days depicted in the Raben *Directory.*

On reflection, this progress was made with astonishing speed. The history of Classics encompasses quite a few centuries; yet, there are few distinct periods within this history that can be said to have witnessed changes as rapid and fundamental as those brought about by the entry of the field into the electronic world. A mere two and a half decades after "electronic machines" first found mention in an APA publication, few (if any) members of the Association remain uninvolved in, and unaffected by, computing. The wide spread of TLG CD-ROMs throughout the world,[75] alone, is proof positive that research-oriented use of electronic texts is a commonplace phenomenon today. If *tempora mutantur,* then classicists can indeed claim to have demonstrated an ability to keep abreast with progress.

This paper has attempted to trace this progress as mirrored in documents and publications issued by the American Philological Association. There is clear evidence that the Association played a significant institutional part in the introduction of computing to the field, and that its officers, in particular, provided valuable and wise leadership as Classics set about to embrace computing. Today, one of the most traditional humanistic disciplines can pride itself in its ability to employ the most advanced aspects of modern technology to its best advantage. If the mid-1960s represent the era in which — after some preliminary flirtation — Classics and the computer first began to establish a serious relationship, then the onset of this, the last decade of this century, may properly be celebrated as the silver anniversary of a union that is solid and lasting.[76]

Notes

1. *APA Newsletter* (Winter 1988): 6. (*Editor's note:* The resolution was passed in connection with the presentation of Distinguished Service Medals to Theodore F. Brunner and David W. Packard for their accomplishments in Classics-related computing.)

2. This article is the nucleus of a subsequent (and far more extensive) study of the growing impact of computer technology upon classical studies.

3. Joseph Raben, *Computer-Assisted Research in the Humanities: A Directory of Scholars Active,* 3rd ed. (New York, 1977).

4. Some of the information scattered throughout the *Directory* makes fascinating reading. Computer technology in the late 1960s and early 1970s was not what it is today, and many of those who pioneered in the field did so in what is best described as highly primitive computing environments. Mainframes with as little as 8 kb core memory were the machines of the day, data entry was conducted on paper tape or punch cards, and disk drives (or "drums," as they were then called) were far beyond the financial reach of most users.

5. This says something about how many humanists viewed the computer two or three decades ago: for the most part, it was regarded primarily as a machine that could simplify and speed up the tedious processes involved in creating research tools. It was a tool to create yet *more* tools, and some time would pass before most humanists were able to accept the idea that the computer could provide *direct* access to literature, and that there was no longer any need to artificially and forcibly rearrange text in order to study and understand it.

6. Italy, Germany, and the United Kingdom are particularly well represented in the *Directory.*

7. Among the few notable exceptions was Cordelia Birch in Beaver Falls, Pennsylvania, who was busily creating machine-readable texts of authors such as Xenophon, Caesar, and Cicero for subsequent indexing and concording purposes.

8. One year ago, at a professional conference in Toronto, this writer made a similar statement, noting that the atmosphere of the late 1980s was entirely different, and that involvement in computing no longer carried a stigma in the field of Classics. To his surprise, several members of the audience disagreed, suggesting that — in some academic departments at least — computer-based research still ranks below "traditional" scholarly pursuits. This response is puzzling. The writer is sufficiently well connected with the field to know that even those alleged to be among the more reactionary in their attitudes toward computers have no qualms about calling upon their computer-literate colleagues when they need access to data and information difficult or impossible to obtain via traditional research methods.

9. Howard Comfort, "Report of the Delegates to the Fédération Internationale des Associations d'Études Classiques," *Transactions and Proceedings of the American Philological Association* 97 (1966): xlvi–xlvii.

10. The *Newsletter* notes that this allocation was "the result of strong pressure from the American Council of Learned Societies and its constituent societies, including the APA." The initial NEH allocation for tools purposes totaled $300,000. By comparison, NEH grant funds budgeted for tools purposes during fiscal year 1990 total $2,692,000. Between 1974 and the present, the TLG alone has received $3,403,839 from the Tools Division.

11. William M. Minton, "Report of Action by the Directors," *TAPA* 98 (1967): xxxviii. The record leaves it unclear whether this action was based upon disapproval of the concordance, or disapproval of *AGON.* In any event, the directors also voted at the same meeting "not to approve the request by *AGON* for financial assistance in preparing its annual catalogue of Ph.D. theses" (xxxix).

12. *Calculi* was founded by Stephen V. F. Waite (then at Dartmouth College) who, for many years, would provide invaluable yeomanship in the realm of computing for the APA and its membership.

13. The *Newsletter* does not list their names, but they included Lloyd W. Daly, James W. Halporn, David W. Packard, Alan E. Samuel, and Stephen Waite.

14. *APA Newsletter* (Spring 1968): 1. This issue also reports that Nathan A. Greenberg has been given a grants-in-aid award by the American Council of Learned Societies to conduct a computer analysis of Latin poetry.

15. The meeting also produced the formation of a group called "The Friends of Homer and the Computer."

16. "Report of the Special Committee for Computer Problems," *TAPA* 99 (1968): xli.

17. David Packard, *Concordance to Livy,* 4 vols. (Cambridge, Mass., 1968), was instrumental in alerting the field of Classics to what could be accomplished with the aid of the computer.

18. Willis, not yet as involved in computing as he would become in later years, was by far the senior member of the group. As Willis recalls it, his addition to the committee derived, to some extent, from a sense of uneasiness on the part of the directors over what they considered to be potentially precipitous entry into uncharted waters on the part of some relatively young classicists.

19. John Bateman, "Report of Action By the Directors," *TAPA* 99 (1968): xliii. Though small in present-day terms, the $550.00 allocation was sizeable in 1968. The subvention allocated by the APA to the *Thesaurus Linguae Latinae* for 1968–69 year totaled $500.00.

20. "Report of the Advisory Committee on Computer Activities," *TAPA* 100 (1969): liv. The Proceedings carried in this volume fail to provide the precise date on which the committee was appointed.

21. John Bateman, "Report of Action by the Directors," *TAPA* 100 (1969): lv. At the same meeting, the directors also voted to instruct "the Editor to investigate new technical processes in publishing as suggested by Recommendation IV of the Special Committee for Computer Problems, dated December 21, 1968."

22. Additional support was provided by the University of Illinois Digital Computer Laboratory, the Kiewit Computation Center at Dartmouth College, the National Science Foundation, the Ford Foundation, and the IBM Corporation.

23. The NEH-funded grant period actually ran from February 1 to September 30, 1969.

24. A complete description of the Institute, its members, and its activities can be found in the "Report to the National Endowment for the Humanities on the American Philological Association's Summer Institute in Computer Applications to Classical Studies at the University of Illinois at Urbana-Champaign, 1969: NEH Grant No. H69-0-150" (copy held by this author, and subsequently referred to as "Urbana Report").

25. Ibid. 19.

26. John Bateman, "Report of Action by the Directors," *TAPA* 100 (1969): lvi–lvii.

27. The Monograph Series did not suffer unduly: at the same meeting, the directors also voted "to transfer $10,000 from the Invested Fund to the Monograph Fund."

28. David W. Packard et al., "Report of the Advisory Committee on Computer Activities," *TAPA* 101 (1970): xliii–xlv. The committee was then composed of Lloyd Daly, James Helm, Alan Samuel, Richard Wevers, and David Packard (chair).

29. Some of these comments would prove to be prophetic. Although the collection of Greek texts in the APA's Repository would continue to grow modestly for a few more years, it would not be until the advent of the TLG that a truly comprehensive body of Greek text in electronic form would become a reality.

30. It is interesting to note that, according to the committee, "The existence of *L'Année Philologique* [made] automation in Classics less urgent." The late 1980s and early 1990s, of course, would witness strenuous efforts to convert *AP* into electronic form.

31. The reference here, of course, is to the Munich *Thesaurus Linguae Latinae;* in 1970, a comprehensive Greek thesaurus was still as inconceivable as it was when Diels declared it to be an impossibility in 1905 (cf. Preface to the 1925 LSJ edition, v).

32. Packard et al., "Report," xlv.

33. Stephen V. F. Waite, "Report of the Supervisor of the American Philological Association Repository of Classical Texts in Machine-Readable Form," *TAPA* 101 (1970): xlvi.

34. Nathan A. Greenberg et al., "Report of the Advisory Committee for Computer Activities," *TAPA* 102 (1971): xlv–l.

35. Then composed of Robert Dyer, James Helm, Cora Sowa, Stephen Waite, and Nathan Greenberg (chair).

36. In any event, and whatever the committee's views, Waite continued to command the confidence of the directors. Appointed as supervisor of the APA Repository in 1969, he still serves in this capacity in 1990 — perhaps the longest uninterrupted appointment ever granted by the APA to one of its members.

37. "Variety and Repetition in Hesiod and Aratus" by John Walsh, and "The APA Repository of Texts: Past, Present, and Future" by Stephen Waite.

38. Computer sessions at APA meetings would quickly become commonplace events; in fact, the attendance at such sessions today often exceeds that at many other sessions focusing on more "traditional" topics.

39. John Bateman, "Report of Action by the Directors," *TAPA* 102 (1971): lxii–lxv.

40. This article does not propose to cover, in detail, the history of the Thesaurus Linguae Graecae; much information on this subject has been published elsewhere, e.g., J. J. Hughes, "From Homer to Hesychius: The Thesaurus Linguae Graecae Project," *Bits and Bytes Review* 1.7 (1987): 1–6; also T. F. Brunner, "Data Banks for the Humanities: Learning from Thesaurus Linguae Graecae," *Scholarly Communication* 7 (1987): 1 and 6–9, and "Overcoming Verzettelung," *Humanities* 9.3 (1988): 4–7. For present purposes, a summary record of the interrelationship between the TLG and the APA will suffice.

41. It is also worth noting that those laying the groundwork for the TLG were totally unaware of what had transpired within the APA regarding computing, electronic resources, etc., during the preceding four or five years.

42. Cora Sowa, "Report of the Advisory Committee on Computer Activities," *TAPA* 103 (1972): xlviii. The committee was then chaired by Cora Sowa, who appears to have persuaded the directors to relent on the subject of a computer handbook: at their December 30, 1971, meeting in Cincinnati, they voted "to encourage the preparation of 'A Classicist's Guide to Computers' by Cora A. Sowa."

43. The report does, however, manage to note that "the other members of the Committee have made themselves available to give advice . . . to Dr. Waite (when it seemed necessary to have more than one opinion on an important matter)."

44. Stephen V. F. Waite, "Report of the Supervisor of the Repository of Greek and Latin Texts in Machine-Readable Form," *TAPA* 103 (1972): xlviii–lii.

45. Two hundred and two copies of this total were distributed outside of North America.

46. No *Transactions of the American Philological Association* volume was published in 1973, and subsequent volumes ceased to carry Proceedings. Between 1974 and 1977, the Association published its Proceedings separately; thereafter, *APA Newsletters* and periodic reports of the secretary constitute the only sources of information about actions by the directors and by APA committees.

47. According to the 1973 report of the secretary, the directors' action was somewhat different. Here, they voted (on December 30, 1972, in Philadelphia) "to authorize the President to appoint, in consultation with the Director of the Thesaurus Linguae Graecae at the University of California, Irvine, an interim advisory committee to assist the Director with the furtherance of this project" (32).

48. The Committee on Computer Activities was now elevated, by action of the directors at their December 30, 1972, meeting in Philadelphia, to the status of a standing committee of the Association.

49. Pp. 31 and 20–22, respectively.

50. The TLG continued to adhere to this policy, and rightly so: had TLG texts been allowed to circulate around the world in various stages of readiness, maintenance of TLG text uniformity and quality would have been totally impossible.

51. Report of the Secretary (1973), 36.

52. Text of Presidential Address provided by Professor Willis.

53. Harry L. Levy, "President's Corner," *Proceedings of the American Philological Association* 104.2 (1974): 71–72.

54. Dr. Robert S. Lumiansky, then President of the American Council of Learned Societies.

55. The Willis report carefully avoids any reference to the access issue with which other Association members were preoccupied. By late 1975, in fact, *verified* TLG texts had already been distributed to scores of users in the U.S. and abroad.

56. "Report of the Committee on Computer Activities," *APA Newsletter* (Spring 1978): 6.

57. "Report of the Supervisor," *APA Newsletter* (Spring 1978): 6.

58. *APA Newsletter* (Winter 1978): 4.

59. Ibid., 2.

60. *APA Newsletter* (Spring 1979): 8–9, 11, 12 and *APA Newsletter* (Spring 1980): 8. In its 1979 report, the Advisory Committee finds it necessary to note that "since 1973 the Committee has been asking that steps be taken to improve existing tapes (*sic*) by adding an apparatus criticus." The allusion is to a controversy of long standing that has no bearing upon the topic treated in this paper.

61. R. S. Bagnall, ed., *Research Tools for the Classics: The Report of the American Philological Association's Ad Hoc Committee on Basic Research Tools*, APA Pamphlets 6 (1980).

62. Bagnall, in fact, deserves much credit for having championed the cause of computing throughout his tenure as secretary.

63. This is volume 4, no. 4, of the *Newsletter*. Apparently as the result of a typographical error, volume 4, no. 1, is also entitled "Winter 1981."

64. In the same issue of the *Newsletter* (11), the committee invites inquiries from "institutions or individuals [that] might be interested in taking over responsibility for the corpus, and on what terms."

65. It is worth noting that the two titles thus far published under the auspices of the APA Educational Papers deal with computer-related topics.

66. Initially, this work was conducted only at the Princeton Institute for Advanced Studies; subsequently, data entry of inscriptions would also be also undertaken at Cornell University.

67. *TLG Newsletter,* no. 8 (July 1985).

68. In the summer 1986 issue of the *APA Newsletter,* "the APA invites members to send their BITNET identification numbers" and begins to consider "the feasibility of using BITNET for receiving advertisements for Positions for Classicists and announcements for the *Newsletter* (2)." As it turns out, some time will pass before the Association is ready to implement its electronic mail plans: in the summer 1988 issue of the *APA Newsletter,* Harry B. Evans (now secretary-treasurer of the Association) announces that "at long last we have a BITNET account and number for the APA office," conceding that "some things seem to take longer in the Bronx" (2).

69. Cf. "Optical Scanning," *APA Newsletter* (Spring 1986): 10.

70. *APA Newsletter* (Spring 1987): 22.

71. First mentioned in the *APA Newsletter* (Fall 1986): 15.

72. *APA Newsletter* (Fall 1987): 2. Before long, Dee Clayman will be actively engaged in converting *L'Année Philologique* into electronic form; cf. *APA Newsletter* (August 1989): 1.

73. *APA Newsletter* (Winter 1988): 14. The report notes that, "while Classics is one of the few disciplines where standards exist because of the *Thesaurus Linguae Graecae,* other fields have not been so fortunate."

74. John J. Hughes, *Bits, Bytes, and Biblical Studies: A Resource Guide for the Use of Computers in Biblical and Classical Studies* (Grand Rapids, 1987).

75. By July 1990, some 600 TLG CD-ROMs (which equals an aggregate of some 25 billion words of Greek text) were residing in thirty countries worldwide, and new CD-ROM orders were reaching the project each day. Since a large percentage of TLG CD-ROMs is licensed to institutions, the overall TLG user base can be assumed to be vast.

76. This paper was completed in mid-1990. Since then, computer use in the Classics has witnessed a phenomenal surge. By March 1993, the number of TLG CD-ROM licenses grew to almost 1,400, with TLG disks located in thirty-six countries, including Poland and Russia. Other phenomena include the Classics discussion group (CLASSICS@UWAVM), which has been active since August 1992; the TOC Project, which provides electronic tables of contents of journals of interest to classicists; the on-line availablility of the Bryn Mawr Classical Reviews; IBYCUS-L@USCVM, the Ibycus Computer users list server; and many other electronic resources and facilities now used by classicists as a matter of course.

2

Ancilla to the Thesaurus Linguae Graecae
The TLG Canon

Luci Berkowitz

In the administrative office of the Thesaurus Linguae Graecae at the University of California, Irvine, a large wall map dotted with colored pins illustrates the worldwide distribution of the TLG's CD-ROMS. The monthly tally for July 1990 confirmed that 595 compact disks, containing an aggregate 24.9 billion words of TLG machine-readable texts, were residing in some thirty countries on five continents. Not reflected on this map are the millions of words provided to individual scholars and academic institutions in the form of magnetic tape or paper printout. Clearly, the Thesaurus Linguae Graecae data bank has become a research tool that is widely utilized for scholarly enterprises; indeed, the growing number of publications that acknowledge use of TLG texts attests to the acceptance of the TLG as an indispensable resource for scholarly research. Yet, few of those who now consult the TLG daily are aware that the TLG data bank rests upon a literary-historical and bibliographic substructure linking the TLG's texts to the Greek authors who composed them. This substructure is designed to preserve a vast array of information about authors and works, including the chronological period (insofar as chronology is determinable) in which the texts were composed, the generic category to which each piece of writing can be assigned, the bibliographic details that identify the specific edition followed in creating each electronic text, and the citation system that enables scholars to find the precise locus of a word or word pattern. Known as the *Thesaurus Linguae Graecae Canon of Greek Authors and Works,* it exists in three forms: (a) as a comprehensive electronic information system that permits continuous updating and revision; (b) as a selective support system for texts on the TLG's CD-ROM;[1] and (c) as a printed volume published by Oxford University Press.[2]

Although the history of the TLG has been the subject of many papers, articles, panels, reports, and proceedings of scholarly associations,[3] discussions of the canon have generally been restricted to how it can be used, with only hints of how it developed, as a supporting instrument for those who consult TLG texts.[4] Yet, the canon, despite its principal function of providing guidance to scholars working their way through TLG texts, has developed a life of its own. Today, it not only supports computer-aided research in Greek literature but also contributes to the broader perspectives of Greek literary history. Like any eighteen-year-old, the canon has survived growing pains, setbacks, agonies, occasional indecisiveness, frequent challenges to reexamine and redefine its goals, and constant reminders of how much growth remains. Some of those reminders are still evident in the TLG's archives, many of them written by classicists as well as computer specialists in the form of memoranda, minutes of meetings, reports, and letters, dating from as early as 1972 when the TLG itself came to life. The record is incomplete because development of the canon was at first ancillary (and indeed incidental) to creation of the TLG data bank. Nevertheless, enough survives to reconstruct the birth and growth of the canon. Such a reconstruction is certainly worthwhile for its own sake; but more important, it demonstrates that the creation of electronic resources requires the application not only of modern computer technology but also of traditional methods of research. If technological progress is to have any meaningful purpose for Classics, technology and scholarship must work together; if they fail to cooperate, neither is served well.

The Background

When the Thesaurus Linguae Graecae was inaugurated in 1972, there was no comprehensive canon of Greek authors upon which to base an electronic data bank of the Greek literary corpus. To be sure, there were lists of authors that guided the compilers of the modern lexica,[5] but these lists were neither complete nor always up-to-date, although they would prove indispensable to the TLG in its formative stage. Recognizing that the incipient thesaurus would have to rely upon a carefully defined roster of authors, the members of the initial TLG Planning Conference that convened on the campus of the University of California, Irvine, in October 1972[6] urged the project to proceed gradatim; instead of trying to grapple with the entire mass of material that remained from classical antiquity until, say, the closing of the Academy in the sixth century, the Planning Committee proposed a number of project phases, fixing the scope of Phase I to encompass the period beginning with Homer and terminating with the arbitrary date of A.D. 200.[7] The committee's first directive to the TLG was to identify the surviving texts that could be dated within this period and to compile a list of the authors of those texts. Cost considerations made it imperative that the size of the literary remains in Phase I be accurately determined also.[8]

In 1972, the only available assessment of the extent of the Greek corpus was that Hermann Diels put forth in 1905, but it was not truly a word estimate fixed within a precise chronological framework.[9] In one and the same paragraph, for instance, Diels first posited a scope defined by Homer and Nonnus in the fourth or fifth century (presumably his own preference), then expanded the context to include Apostolius in the fifteenth century (Krumbacher's more ambitious prospectus).[10] Moreover, Diels's estimate of the Greek corpus now seems to have been more Pythagorean than precise. Declaring the Greek corpus to be "at least ten times as great [as that of Latin],"[11] Diels envisioned a final product of "(say) 120 volumes," if indeed the project were ever to see the light of day.

It is apparent that Diels was arguing against an effort that would yield a single unwieldy thesaurus and in favor of ten separate thesauri, each of which, by itself, would presumably rival the *Thesaurus Linguae Latinae* (*TLL*) in size.[12] Yet, no concrete figure had ever been put forth as a calculation of the size of the Greek corpus from Homer to Nonnus or, for that matter, to the early seventh century or to Apostolius in the fifteenth century. By 1972, however, the size of the Latin corpus under consideration by the *TLL* was known to us: 9 million words from the third century B.C. to the seventh century A.D. (i.e., from the beginnings of Latin literature to the death of Isidore of Seville)[13] had been collected on slips and had for nearly eight decades required the collaboration of scholars in Munich to establish meaning and usage.

With 9 million words of Latin as the only figure before us,[14] Diels's estimate for the Greek corpus began to assume a definitive (albeit misshapen) form: Greek literature, at ten times the size of Latin, must amount to 90 million words. Since we did not yet know the chronological framework that these projected 90 million words would encompass, we could only imagine a gargantuan body of literature that required definition and control. For the next eighteen years, it would be our task to determine how those 90 million words survived, that is, in what texts they were distributed. It would be our task also to identify the authors of those texts. We supposed that we would confront three- or four-hundred authors within Phase I and that their combined literary remains would amount to approximately 20 million words. These suppositions were derived from a conception of the bulk of Greek literature in the form of an inverted pyramid, with the point of the pyramid signifying the amount of the earliest surviving Greek texts and the widening base representing the size of extant later Greek literature. Our estimate of 20 million words between Homer and A.D. 200 was a guess that proved to be nearly correct, but the number of authors had been grossly underestimated and would have to be expanded to include more than 1,300 additional names.[15]

The Sources

With our crude estimates in hand, we began to explore the materials that form the core of collected information about Greek and Latin literature. Lexica, biographical and topical dictionaries, literary histories, and similar compendia provided the obvious starting points for locating authors and their contributions to Greek literature.

The lexica at our disposal generally carry disclaimers that help to specify their individual intentions of chronological scope and degree of completeness. Sir Henry Stuart Jones, in the preface to the ninth edition of *LSJ*, remarks that "Liddell and Scott, though they originally intended their work to be a Lexicon of classical Greek, admitted a number of words from Ecclesiastical and Byzantine writers, for many of which no reference was given except the symbols 'Eccl.' and 'Byz.' After due consideration it has been decided to exclude both Patristic and Byzantine literature from the purview of the present edition" (x). The editors of the *LSJ Supplement* also caution against expectations of exhaustiveness: "It should be emphasized that the list of Authors and Works is intended to be an indication not of best or most recent editions, but of the editions used in the lexicon" (v).

Exclusion of the patristic and Byzantine texts from *LSJ* and the Supplement is rectified, to some degree, in the *Patristic Greek Lexicon,* where Lampe's objective is "primarily to interpret the theological and ecclesiastical vocabulary of the Greek Christian authors from Clement of Rome to Theodore of Studium" (v), that is, from the first century to the ninth. Lampe's "somewhat arbitrary" limits, however, are not rigidly enforced, and the *Patristic Greek Lexicon* incorporates pre-Christian authors as well as later Greek writings of spurious attribution and uncertain date. E. A. Sophocles, on the other hand, adheres strictly to the first of his stated chronological limits, prefixing his list of authors for the *Greek Lexicon of the Roman and Byzantine Periods* with a terse reminder that the burden rests with the reader to recollect who wrote what before the demolition of Corinth in 146 B.C.: "The names of earlier authors are not given in this list, because Greek scholars are supposed to be familiar with them" (vii).

Several biographical and topical dictionaries helped us to form the skeleton of our list of authors and works, but limitations of chronology were pronounced in these sources as well. The editors of the first edition of *The Oxford Classical Dictionary* placed their emphasis upon the early part of classical antiquity: "The *terminus ad quem* is, generally speaking, the death of Constantine (337), and proportionately less space has been allotted to persons who lived later than the second century A.D."[16] Although Christian literature did not figure prominently within the pages of the first edition of *OCD*, the second edition gives due consideration to "leading Christian writers," as well as a number of important later Greek commentators, grammarians, scholars, and scholiasts.[17] For the early Christian authors, especially during the first few years of the project, we relied upon the second edition of the *Tusculum-Lexikon,*[18] *The Oxford Dictionary of the Christian Church,*[19] and the four volumes that comprise the *Dictionary of Christian Biography.*[20]

Unlike other more limited biographical dictionaries, the *Tusculum-Lexikon* encompasses the whole of Greek and Latin literature to the end of the fifteenth century. This broad perspective proved to be particularly useful as the TLG canon moved beyond its own initially prescribed terminus of A.D. 200.[21] The special value of the *Tusculum-Lexikon* lies in its compact articles with appended bibliographies for both Greek and Roman writers. A third revised and expanded edition was published in 1982,[22] thereby rendering this single volume a continuing source of useful biographical, historical, and bibliographic information.

If the biographical dictionaries presented us with disparity in coverage, they also revealed inconsistencies in their presentation of information, occasionally creating consternation as we developed the canon. The *Tusculum-Lexikon*, for instance, shows discrepancies in orthography, thereby separating otherwise similar names from one another. The editors claim that they are preserving the name in the form by which it would be recognized within the author's own cultural milieu.[23] Yet, orthographic distinctions such as *Constantinus Africanus* (176),[24] *Konstantin d[er] Gr[osse]* (447), and *Konstantinos VII. Porphyrogennetos* (448) emphasize only cultural differences and not true differences in name. Inconsistencies in the orthography of author names would later haunt us as we were trying to develop a *Namenregister* in the computer, an instrument that expects absolute consistency.

Less concerned with the merits of spelling variants, The *Oxford Dictionary of the Christian Church* resolves nearly every name, whether Greek or Latin, into an English orthographic pattern, although an admixture of Latin and English is not uncommon. Thus, the theologian and exegete Origenes is carried as *Origen* (991), whereas the author of the *Pratum spirituale* may be found under *Moschus, John* (928). In any event, *ODCC*, with its chronological scope extending into the second half of the twentieth century, proved to be a useful source of both biographic and bibliographic information.

The *Dictionary of Christian Biography* achieves greater consistency in orthography, opting generally for Latin spelling but settling also for English. The range of *DCB*, however, is less ambitious than that of either the *Tusculum-Lexikon* or *ODCC*, extending "from the time of the Apostles to the age of Charlemagne" (1:ix), and covering roughly the same period (although stated in remarkably different terms) represented by Lampe's *Patristic Greek Lexicon*. Despite exhaustive treatment of the Church Fathers, together with useful notations of the original sources that provide historical details and orthographic variants, *DCB* has grown outdated in many respects, not the least of which is the emergence of new scholarly findings and improved text editions. In 1973, this "Christian Cyclopaedia"[25] remained a useful mine of historical and biographical information; but with the announced publication of *Clavis Patrum Graecorum*, the bibliographic value of *DCB* began to decline.

Clavis Patrum Graecorum had been conceived by its editor, Maurice Geerard, as a three-volume bibliography identifying the current state of scholarship, including text editions, for the writings of the Greek fathers from Clement of Rome to John of Damascus (that is, spanning the first eight centuries of the Christian era). Writing to us on August 31, 1973, Geerard outlined the scope of his planned project: volume 1 would cover the literature up to the Council of Nicaea in 325; volume 2 would be devoted to authors of the fourth century, beginning with Athanasius and ending with John Chrysostom; volume 3 would conclude with authors from the fifth to eighth centuries, beginning with Cyril of Alexandria and ending with John of Damascus.[26] Eventually, a fourth volume focusing upon *concilia* and *catenae* and a fifth index volume would also be published.[27] But in 1973, the only part of this monumental work available for our consideration was the second volume that Geerard graciously shared with us in the form of his own proofsheets. We quickly came to regard the *Clavis Patrum Graecorum* as an indispensable work of reference, an *auxilium* of the highest calibre.

Another repertorial work that has assisted us since 1985 is the *Clavis Scriptorum Graecorum et Latinorum,* a three-volume conspectus of "authors from all periods, excluding modern Greek,"[28] alphabetized according to normative nomenclature and accompanied by chronological information, epithets, sources from which the data are derived, and abbreviated references to works that may be consulted further. Developed with computer assistance by a Canadian team under the direction of Father Rodrigue LaRue at the Université du Québec à Trois-Rivières, *CSGL* has provided numerous opportunities for cross-checking, verifying, and resolving discrepancies with the purpose of continually refining our own work on the TLG canon of authors. Unfortunately, *CSGL* was not yet available in 1972, when we began to concentrate our efforts upon the formidable task of identifying the precise remains of Greek literature before A.D. 200.

An important resource opened up for us soon after the TLG was inaugurated, and it became the basis for a long-standing international collaboration. The *Diccionario Griego-Espagnol (DGE)*, begun in the mid-1960s under the direction of Francisco Rodriguez Adrados, had already made considerable progress in identifying the corpus of material that would form the focus of a lexicon along the lines of *LSJ*, but with a plan for enlargement by some 20 percent. In a letter to us dated January 26, 1973, Adrados mentioned a list of approximately 2,500 authors to be cited in *DGE,* the first volume of which would be published in 1980. Covering the span between Homer and A.D. 600, this list of *Autores y Obras* included a date for each author, abbreviations (following those in *LSJ*) used to cite the author's works, and bibliographies both for the text editions cited for each work and for subsequent scholarly comment concerning individual works. Although it became apparent quickly that the

2,500 authors included many Latin writers,[29] this list proved to be an important instrument for checking and cross-checking information about authors in the developing TLG canon. In 1982, the collaborative effort between the TLG and *DGE* would culminate in the *Repertorium Litterarum Graecarum,* a conspectus of the authors cited in both the TLG data bank and the Greek-Spanish lexicon.[30] In 1972, however, the *RLG* was a decade away from realization.

Several standard literary histories gave us a firmer sense of chronology, alerted us to unresolved questions of identity, provided us with titles (and alternative titles) of works, and introduced us to problems of ascription and *genuinitas,* genre and individual literary character, and text tradition. Among the most valuable were the works of Schmid-Stählin,[31] Susemihl,[32] Lesky,[33] Rose,[34] and (later) the Cambridge histories of classical literature.[35] These were constantly supplemented, especially for questions of dating, by Pauly-Wissowa and *Der kleine Pauly.*[36]

For patristic literature we owed much to two standard works that require the attention of anyone who wishes to explore the full achievement of later Greek antiquity. Quasten's *Patrology*[37] provided us with a rich source of bibliographic information, details of chronology and ecclesiastical history, and learned discussions about literary works; Quasten's span, however, did not embrace events beyond the Council of Chalcedon in 451. Altaner's one-volume *Patrology*[38] completed much of the picture with details that ranged from the first century to the death of John of Damascus in 749.

With all of these materials at our elbows, the TLG's incipient canon of authors came into being as an alphabetized list of names that might have been found among standard graduate reading programs in American and European universities. Guided by the TLL's *Übersicht über das verzettelte und excerpierte Material nach Ordnungsnummern,*[39] we determined that each of our authors would be listed together with specific categories of information: (a) author's name with recognized Latin spelling; (b) literary epithet traditionally associated with the author and signifying the generic character of the author's major works; (c) geographic epithet when such a descriptor either has survived as part of the author's name or helps to distinguish between authors of the same name; (d) date by century (whenever available) in which the author lived or flourished. Later, the number of categories would be expanded in order to accommodate a wide variety of supplementary information.[40] Later too, when the Greek texts were to be converted to machine-readable form, we would add identifying numbers that would distinguish one author from another and one work from another.[41]

The Role of the APA

In its most rudimentary form, the TLG canon was nothing more than a list of Greek authors whose works would comprise the first shipment of texts to be sent overseas to the TLG's data-entry contractor.[42] It was this list that we submitted to the scrutiny of an advisory panel appointed by the American Philological Association.[43] On February 24, 1973, when this advisory committee met for the first time at the Center for Hellenic Studies in Washington, D.C., we presented the names of one thousand authors that we had compiled from a variety of sources. In addition to names, literary epithets, and geographical epithets (wherever informative), we supplied roughhewn estimates of the size of each author's works. Word estimates, we discovered, would enable us to assess the approximate size of each monthly data-entry shipment, but even more important, our calculations and computations would steer us toward a firmer grasp of the precise composition and extent of the Greek literary corpus.[44] By the conclusion of the Washington meeting on February 25, 1973, the APA Advisory Committee had sanctioned text editions for nearly ten million words of Greek. Not surprisingly, the first authors for whom text recommendations were secured included many familiar standards and favorites: Apollonius of Rhodes (author #0001), Athenaeus (#0008), Callimachus (#0533), Cassius Dio (#0385),[45] Demosthenes (#0014), Diogenes Laertius (#0004), Epicurus (#0537), Euripides (#0006), Galen (#0057) and Pseudo-Galen (#0530), Herodotus (#0016), Hesiod (#0020), Homer (#0012), Menander (#0541), Origen (#2042), Philo Judaeus (#0018), Pindar (#0033), Plutarch (#0007) and Pseudo-Plutarch (#0094), Pollux (#0542), Polybius (#0543), Sappho (#0009), Sophocles (#0011), Theocritus (#0005), Theognis (#0002), and Thucydides (#0003). Although several of these authors transcended the chronological boundary of A.D. 200,[46] the committee acknowledged that they were sufficiently important to warrant inclusion in our initial project phase. Several authors who lived even later, but preserved numerous quotations from earlier authors, were thought to have "a higher priority of interest for data capture";[47] without hesitation, the committee recommended text editions for Hesychius (fifth century), Himerius (fourth century), Nonnus (sixth century), Photius (ninth century), Stephanus of Byzantium (sixth century), Stobaeus (fifth century), and the *Suda* (tenth century). At the February 25th meeting, however, the committee deferred recommendations for Aeschylus, Aristotle, Hippocrates, Diodorus Siculus, Josephus, Lucian, Pausanias, Plato, Strabo, Theophrastus, and Xenophon, all of whom would provide stimuli for animated discussion before specific text editions would win majority acceptance.[48] Of the two Testaments, the New earned instant text approval,[49] while the Old (specifically the Septuagint) occasioned dissension, dispute, and disapproval that would continue almost unabated until the present day.[50]

The largest literary corpus represented on our maiden list belonged to the author with the worst text tradition, and the committee's recommendation did not resolve the problems we were to encounter: for Galen, who left us more than 2.6 million words, the committee recommended using "Teubner, ed. C. G. Kühn, except where more modern texts [are available], for which see OCD ed. 2 (L. Edelstein's list)."[51] Nevertheless, we would encounter vociferous opposition to the inclusion of any treatise edited by Kühn, whose credentials as a text editor have never won the wholehearted approval of scholars. Once again, we were faced with the recurring dilemma of either withholding from the data bank unreliable editions, thereby offering scholars only pieces of an author's collected works, or incorporating inferior editions in the hope that scholars would one day undertake the task of improving and therefore replacing those editions. The latter alternative has generally prevailed on the grounds that representation of some sort would be preferable to no representation at all; the Galenic corpus entered the TLG data bank via the *Corpus Medicorum Graecorum* and, where *CMG* was wanting, via Kühn.

By September 1973, the advisory committee had endorsed a program of data capture that focused upon entire literary genres, and the canon that was developing along generic lines had grown to include 1,800 authors.[52] Of particular interest was the corpus of the Greek medical writers that would become the focus of a special project funded by the National Endowment for the Humanities in 1974. Nearly 250 medical writers had already been identified, most of them *apud auctores alios,* and their fragments were being noted for inclusion in the canon.[53] For our work on the Greek medical corpus, we welcomed Helmut Leitner's timely bibliography,[54] but we were also mindful of the sense of dubiety that Erna Lesky had expressed in its preface: "Whoever makes a survey of the medico-historical literature of the last decades will meet with uncertainty and misquotations whenever ancient medical writers are cited. Unfortunately a correct quotation of ancient authors according to the latest standard of editions or translations is seldom given."[55] As we were to recognize over the years, these misgivings might well be directed to other generic literature, with only the words "medico-historical" and "medical" replaced by their generic correlatives.

Without question, generically related texts provide the richest veins of material for developing a canon of authors, but generic collections also present difficulties to both the task of data entry and the work of building a canon. Many generic collections present the fragments of a given author by recording the statements of later quoting authorities, but without distinguishing *ipsissima verba* from indirect quotation, paraphrase, or summary, and without separating quoted author from quoter. Poetic fragments, of course, are usually easier to detect because they present themselves in a metrical pattern, but prose fragments often invite question of where the quoted author begins and the quoting author ends. Yet, for several years, it was this decision that determined whether a given author merited inclusion in a canon of authors and works.

Editors of different generic collections also tend to tap the same source material for fragments, and one editor's *philosophus* may be another editor's *historicus.*[56] Thus, duplication of material is an ever-present risk when a data bank is in the making, and the risk of creating a cumbersome data bank escalates with the addition of each generic collection.

Generic collections also betray a high incidence of uncertain ascription of fragments, generated by a quoting source that may cite several names without isolating the author of the quotation or paraphrase. In the absence of other evidence that could settle the question of attribution, editors sometimes link the text indiscriminately to the entire group. In effect, this might argue for multiple listing in a canon of authors; in practice and in the interest of economy, only one of the named authors is retained for the canon, with the others acknowledged in an appropriate note.[57]

Also characteristic of generic collections is truncation of text that culminates in ellipsis or even, in lieu of text, cross references to altogether different editions.[58] Text foreshortened in an adopted edition is abbreviated in the data bank as well; the canon also reflects only what is there. The alternative would have been to excise the missing pieces from other editions, paste them onto the recommended text, capture them as appendages in the data bank, and record the resultant bibliographic nightmare in the canon. Editions that record cross references, but without benefit of text, may satisfy the curiosity of scholars who wish to know from what source certain fragments are derived, but the absence of text does not lend itself to data capture in a data bank of Greek text.[59] Nor does the absence of a work admit listing in a canon of authors and works.

All of these considerations — identification of fragments, duplication of text, unresolved attribution of fragments, incomplete text — were certain to affect the development of the data bank and the character of the canon. But there was no agreement among the members of the advisory committee regarding the advantages of depositing collections of fragments in the data bank in the first place.[60] Obviously, if the collections were to be disregarded, there would be no reason to carry in the TLG canon the (otherwise lost) authors represented in them. Although data capture of the later quoting authorities, especially scholiasts, commentators, and lexicographers, would constitute one way of resurrecting lost authors, the onerous task of rummaging through extensive quantities of connected prose would require years before all of the earlier authors *apud auctores alios* could be extracted and *then* assigned a place in the TLG canon. Furthermore, we were to be advised that "authors known only by name, of whom no word of their text was known, could be ignored by the TLG."[61] Eventually, we would realize that the importance of an author might rise or fall in accordance with individual scholarly interest, and there was no assurance that a lost author would remain lost. We would learn also that it is entirely possible to include lost authors in a canon of authors without destroying the equilibrium of literary history.[62]

In December 1973, the advisory committee could still concern itself with unquestionably extant authors, but the list of Greek authors requiring text recommendations was populated by names that, except for Aristotle, would not likely be found on a standard reading list in a university curriculum: Aelian the sophist, Aelian the tactician, Anaximenes of Lampsacus, Apollodorus the mythographer, Apollonius of Perga, Appian, Archimedes, Aelius Aristides, Arrian, Artemidorus of Dalda, Chariton, Clement of Alexandria, Epictetus, Euclid, Heron, Longinus, Longus, Marcus Aurelius, Maximus of Tyre, Rufus of Ephesus, and Soranus.[63]

More than a year after the advisory committee convened for the first time, the Septuagint "roused considerable discussion" for the last time,[64] when the Rahlfs edition was sanctioned as the text of choice for the TLG data bank. Also rousing considerable discussion, for the first but not the last time, were the vexatious and generally insoluble questions of chronology. Although accurate information about dates is seldom available, there was already a growing awareness that dates could be used to organize the material that was developing into a canon of authors and works. While some committee members argued strenuously (and convincingly) against "trying to establish firm dates for Greek authors between Homer and 200 A.D.," a compromise position was adopted "that some chronological identification (by periods or centuries) should be worked out, and that the matter should be given further consideration."[65]

No member of the TLG staff or, for that matter, of the APA advisory committee has ever presumed that it would be possible to establish a definitive chronology for Greek literature. Indeed, quite the opposite, a pronounced pessimism has prevailed to the present day, despite continuing efforts to assign dates by centuries wherever they can be assigned, sometimes with question marks, but often without confidence. Nevertheless, the advantages of affixing dates to authors became apparent as the TLG developed. When the committee met, on December 29, 1975, in Washington, D.C., the persistent fragment problem attached itself to chronological delimiters. Lionel Pearson, still wrestling with the recurring question of how to capture fragmentary texts, suggested that "the fragments of all Greek poetry up to 200 A.D. be recorded, a task which is practically more possible than that of recording all prose fragments, because the actual volume of words involved is comparatively small."[66] Adding that "to compete this task would be a notable achievement," Pearson did not see the irony in his suggestion: in order to record "the fragments of all Greek poetry up to 200 A.D.," all Greek poetry up to A.D. 200 would need to be dated. Pearson even betrayed his own predilection for prose fragments, linking them more precisely to dates as he proposed that "the fragments of authors earlier than 400 B.C. (or even 350 B.C.), for example, might be recorded, so that pre-Socratics and sophists could be included and early historians, as well as poets, and certainly the volume of text is far less for these early authors than for those of later centuries."[67] From this point on, the dating of authors by century became a fixed part of the information structure of the canon.

The canon now included also a system of abbreviations for identifying the several means that have preserved the Greek corpus: *Cod*(ex), *Pap*(yrus), *Epigr*(aph), *Q*(uotation). Toward the end of 1975, Pearson contributed one more abbreviation that would signify a legacy of titles, indirect quotations, paraphrases, references, summaries, and testimonia. *NQ,* meaning "no quotation," would be used to identify text material that might be carried under the name of a given author but could in no way be construed as *ipsissima verba.* By this time, Pearson had proposed a distinction between extant authors and lost authors. In retrospect, the distinction is interesting, for it is based upon two arbitrary criteria, an agreed quantity of surviving text and the method by which the text was transmitted; but in 1975, there were no other established guidelines. In effect, Pearson suggested, "the term 'extant' should mean an author of whose work a substantial quantity (five pages or more) survives in a codex or papyrus," whereas lost authors should be regarded as those "whose text is known only from papyrus scraps and quotations in later authors," with the tacit implication that the text occupies fewer than five pages.[68] Although a fixed quantity of surviving text has not prevailed for determining whether or not an author is extant, the abbreviation system has remained intact, and even today every work admitted to the electronic canon is marked according to the means of its transmission.

By the time the 1975 Washington meeting concluded, another expression had entered the TLG's working vocabulary. The "notable quoters," who belonged to the history of later Greek literature, would be identified for the canon, and their texts would be added to the data bank, thereby making "a large contribution to improving the record of earlier literature."[69] In 1976, the incipient roster of "notable quoters" included Photius, Stobaeus, the *Excerpta Constantini Porphyrogeniti,* the *Suda,* Harpocration, Hesychius, the *Etymologicum Magnum,* Stephanus of Byzantium, Aëtius, Eusebius, Pappus, Proclus, Plotinus, Eustathius, Tzetzes, and the scholia to Apollonius of Rhodes, Lycophron, Aristophanes, Pindar, Euripides, and Homer,[70] all of them now accessible in the TLG data bank.

In 1976 also, a growing concern with papyrus texts preoccupied the advisory committee in New York. Earlier, under the guidance of past APA president William Willis, who had been added to the membership in 1974, the committee had concurred "that literary papyri should be treated differently from documentary papyri, that they should be accepted as texts of ancient authors and handled together with other texts of Greek authors, and that the work of entering such texts into the data bank should be taken independently of any arrangements for documentary papyri."[71] Following this advice, the TLG added numerous Greek papyrus texts to the data bank, although only edited texts would be represented, with diplomatic texts ignored altogether. Though fewer literary texts have survived through inscriptions, we regarded epigraphical texts in the same manner, and these too have been deposited in the data bank.[72]

In order to avoid excessive duplication in the contents of the data bank, we would have to refine our thinking about papyrus texts: a distinction would have to be drawn between authors whose writings are preserved, either completely or in part, by codices, and authors whose known fragments derive entirely from papyrus and from quotations. Papyrus fragments of text supported by a manuscript tradition should be regarded as "alternative manuscripts,"[73] to be treated as all other manuscripts in an *apparatus criticus*. Inasmuch as solutions for successful data entry of an *apparatus criticus* had not yet been developed,[74] such papyrus texts were removed from the TLG's immediate consideration. But the numerous papyrus texts that had no separate manuscript tradition would have to be represented in the data bank, and "generally the text to be followed will not be that of the original publication in a papyrus collection, but a critical edition of the author's fragments."[75]

Although there was no thought of capturing *in toto* collections such as *The Oxyrhynchus Papyri*,[76] the problems generated by papyrus texts, especially in connection with their authors, were only beginning. It is a fact of classical life that scraps of papyri encourage debate about authorship, and different scholars are wont to assign papyrus texts to different authors on equally vigorous and meritorious grounds, although many papyrus texts, too scanty to warrant ascription on any grounds, continue as *adespota*. Moreover, many literary fragments still reside in the collection or journal in which they were originally published, and they have not been reedited, reprinted, reassigned, or reconsidered. While the TLG is cognizant of these puzzle pieces, much work needs to be done before every extant iota of Greek literature that owes its survival to the papyrus tradition is reflected in the canon.

The Computer Specialists

In mid-1976, the canon had outgrown its utility as an alphabetic register of authors, periodically presented to the world as an insert in the *TLG Newsletter*.[77] Already swollen by the names of hundreds of authors from generic collections and a growing number of later writers, especially the "notable quoters," the canon was in need of a new format that would facilitate consultation and permit frequent emendation. For four years, the TLG data bank had been housed in a computer; the time had come to make room in the computer for the TLG canon also.

Though fundamentally a computer project, the TLG had not immediately utilized the potential of computers for developing and preserving a canon of authors and works.[78] The earliest form of the canon was a file of 3″ × 5″ index cards (similar to the card catalogues found in libraries) organized alphabetically by Latinized names of the Greek authors. Each card included the author's standard literary epithet, a rough set of inclusive dates, shorthand notations of the author's extant works and editions of those works, and an indication of the sources from which the information had been elicited. For authors such as Galen and Plutarch, each of whose extant works number more than one hundred,[79] several index cards were required to record the essential details.

This pristine tracking system was in effect when the TLG, planning to submit sample texts to data-entry companies,[80] appointed an EDP systems analyst as a consultant. Brooke Tompkins Schroppel joined the TLG staff in April 1973, and although her stay would be limited to only six months, the impact of her expertise upon the data-entry program of the TLG and upon the canon would be felt for years to come. Under her guidance, the TLG research staff developed the techniques, still in use, for marking and preparing texts that would guide data-entry operators. Not a classicist, she nevertheless devised the set of codes that data-entry operators still use to convert Greek into computer-readable form. And though unaware of the full extent and nature of Greek literature, she designed a system for maintaining detailed records of the authors to be represented in the data bank, for cataloguing each work with complete bibliographic description, and for monitoring the status and progress of each text selected for inclusion in the data bank. Gradually, the sparse index cards were replaced by more detailed $8\frac{1}{2}'' \times 11''$ author and catalogue records. Author records contained provision for author names, epithets, word estimates in advance of data entry, word counts once the texts were deposited in the data bank, a listing of titles of the author's works, and a form of calendar identifying the precise data-entry shipment in which the texts were sent out for conversion to electronic form. Each author was assigned a four-digit identification number; each work attributed to a given author was assigned the same four-digit number and an additional three-digit number to distinguish it from the author's other works. Catalogue records compiled for each work included precise details of bibliography, citation system, and processing status, with provision for adding information about dialects and dates, as well as technical symbols and nonstandard editorial sigla encountered in a given text. For the next several years, this information system grew to occupy some thirty looseleaf notebooks, and although increasingly cumbersome to manipulate, it was used to provide supporting documentation for texts sent overseas for data entry, as well as to respond to scholars' requests for information about editions in the data bank.

With data capture of generic collections well under way in 1976, the number of authors that entered this paper-based information system was beginning to exceed manageable proportions. More than a hundred *philosophi,* some four hundred *historici,* and their thousand or so works had already been recorded.[81] The prospect of incorporating hundreds of additional authors into a system that could no longer accommodate them efficiently was greeted with exasperation by nearly everyone on the TLG staff. The paper canon, already bursting with more than a thousand author records and an additional several thousand catalogue records needed to maintain control over their individual works, would have to be replaced. In mid-1976, the project began the laborious task of transferring these paper records into computer files designed to preserve the information that had been compiled over a four-year period. The delicate work of keyboarding, proofreading, revising, and formatting required more than a year before the TLG could proclaim that its canon of Greek authors and works, like its data bank of Greek texts, resided in a computer and could therefore readily be accessed, consulted, updated, revised, and improved.

In late 1977, the combined results of this effort were published as the *Thesaurus Linguae Graecae Canon of Authors and Works from Homer to* A.D. *200*.[82] The advantage of this printed edition, that was quickly nicknamed "the green canon,"[83] was that it provided rapid reference to authors represented, or about to be represented, in the TLG data bank, as well as a bird's-eye view of the text editions selected for data entry. A set of numeric codes reflecting the status of each text informed the reader about the progress of data entry, and word estimates helped to define the magnitude of an author's combined works. Certainly an improvement over the sheaves of paper that for some years had to be gathered and sent out to inquiring scholars on an almost daily basis, "the green canon" was a source of great relief for the TLG staff. But more important, the availability of canon-based information in published form now gave scholars access to the literary-historical and bibliographic information that previously had been available only on the TLG premises.

Canon[1], however, had its shortcomings. Above all, it was impaired by its own chronological definition. At the time of publication, the TLG could proclaim the availability of a data bank that contained 1,688 authors and some 20 million words of Greek text, but since many of the authors in the data bank postdated A.D. 200, they were not represented in the volume. By this time, for instance, the Greek medical corpus had been added in its entirety to the data bank, but in *Canon*[1] there was no mention of Aëtius of Amida, Paul of Aegina, Nemesius of Emesa, Alexander of Tralles, or Oribasius, none of them earlier than the fourth century of the Christian era,[84] all of them major medical authors in their own right, and all of them important sources for the fragments of earlier *medici*. Furthermore, the bibliographies in *Canon*[1] generally comprehended an entire corpus without regard for individual works, omitted pagination except for fragments *apud auctores alios* or in generic collections, and disregarded work numbers even though they were already in use in the data bank.[85] Several bibliographies were also incomplete, lacking precise details of publication, and one author, Philodemus, was presented without any bibliographic information but with the promise that a bibliography was in the making. In essence, *Canon*[1] betrayed the shortcomings inherent in a printed document designed to reflect the essence of a data bank that continues to grow; a printed document is "frozen" at the moment of publication.

For the next several years, *Canon*[1] would be out of step with the rapid growth of the data bank. Between 1977 and 1981, with support from the National

Endowment for the Humanities and the Mellon Foundation, the TLG directed its efforts to later Greek literature, particularly but by no means exclusively the texts surviving from the years between 200 and 400. TLG Phase II was under way, and before it was over, some 41 million words would be included in the data bank, with an additional 825 authors assigned places in the canon. After several years of investigating texts for inclusion in the data bank, it was now apparent that the projected size of the Greek literary corpus between Homer and A.D. 600 could be revised downward from the putative 90 million words (based upon Diels's 1905 statement) to 65 million words.

In 1981, when the TLG's reconstituted advisory panel convened in Irvine[86] in order to consider the character and focus of data entry for the immediate future, the TLG itself was about to revise and restructure much of the methodology that had guided data entry, verification and correction, and development of the canon of authors and works. The impetus for this reorganization was the acquisition of an Ibycus hardware system. Donated by David Packard, this system was designed specifically to facilitate "manipulation and retrieval" of Greek texts in the TLG data bank.[87] In short order, the Ibycus system would alter radically the capabilities of the TLG, freeing it once and for all from its costly ties to UCI's Sigma-7, setting the vast holdings of its data bank at the disposal of scholars everywhere in the world, and accelerating the rate of verification and correction of TLG texts. It would also create a vehicle for the canon of authors and works that would facilitate revision, reflect the status of the data bank at all times, and result in a significantly improved work of reference. The expertise required to achieve these objectives was provided by William Johnson, a University of North Carolina classicist and computer programmer,[88] who, during the next three years, would direct his efforts toward the development of new software resources designed to sustain not only the data bank but also its canon substructure.

Thus, the arrival of the Ibycus opened new doors not only for the verification and correction staff, who had been in constant contact with computers since the early days of the project, but for the research staff as well. First, we were introduced to the techniques of interacting with the Ibycus, of applying Johnson's specially conceived programs that would transform the now unwieldy canon into an information system that promised consistency, flexibility, adaptability, rapid information retrieval, and unimpeded access to statistics. Then, we began the awesome task of transferring a decade's worth of accumulated data from UCI's Sigma-7 to the TLG's new Ibycus. This transfer required adjustment to a fundamentally different type of data structure: in the Sigma-7, canon information had been stored in linear form; in the Ibycus, the canon would be adapted to a data-base structure. Ultimately, we defined forty fields that could be planted with information regarding any author or work in the TLG data bank. Although an unlimited number of fields could potentially be used, the size of an average computer terminal screen argued for reasonable

limitation. In fact, forty fields have proven to be sufficient, with eleven reserved for information about the author and twenty-nine allotted for individual
works.[89] A few fields have never been used, and another few have changed
character over the years.[90]

We spent the next four years adapting the canon to the Ibycus format, refining and improving the quality of both information and structure, but also
incorporating new authors and works.[91] The new form of the electronic canon
proved to be easy to use, easy to consult, and for the first time, it was attuned
perfectly to the contents of the data bank that it had always been meant to
support. Furthermore, the canon had now matured into an efficient, independent, rapid retrieval system that could provide answers to a variety of questions
about Greek authors and their extant literary works. By 1984, both the data
bank and the electronic canon could also be consulted from offsite locations
by means of modem. To be sure, offsite access was limited, since in-house
operations consumed most of the system's ports. Nevertheless, between 1984
and 1986, several scholars in southern California and other localities availed
themselves of the opportunity to tap the TLG's electronic resources from the
comfort of their homes or individual offices.

In the dozen years since data entry had begun, the contents of the data bank
had grown to more than 50 million words, half of which had already been
corrected and could thus be distributed to scholars for their own research purposes. Yet, magnetic tape, long used as the medium for disseminating TLG
texts, had now outgrown its utility.[92] In 1985, it was apparent that a new
storage medium, the CD-ROM, would make dissemination and use of TLG
texts significantly more efficient.[93] With support from the Packard Foundation,
the TLG thus produced an experimental CD-ROM, "containing all currently
verified and corrected TLG texts, an electronic version of the TLG Canon, and
selected materials generated by other scholars."[94] Intended as a pilot project
that would stimulate the development of supporting software, the TLG's first
CD-ROM excited also a demand for wider distribution, improved compatibility with a variety of hardware systems, and an index to the words on the disk.[95]
In the meantime, the canon, about to be published in a revised second edition,
would constitute a bibliographic index to the authors and works on the CD-
ROM as well as to the complete contents of the TLG data bank.

*Canon*² offered a number of advantages over its predecessor. To begin with,
the record was fuller, representing 2,884 authors, 8,203 discrete works, and
56 million words in the data bank, a more accurate reflection of the TLG's
holdings. A new and more compact format removed the clutter of repetitious,
self-referential abbreviations.[96] Each author's literary corpus was resolved into
individual works, accompanied by detailed bibliographic information, precise
pagination for the specific text incorporated into the data bank, and reduction
of shorthand notations with only the most standard and most formulaic abbreviations retained. Author numbers and work numbers now assisted scholars in

identifying the material that yielded the results of their searches. Cross references helped to locate passages imbedded in quoting authors and also to link authors who might belong to a tradition of unresolved confusion. Most important, all authors represented in the TLG data bank were also listed in *Canon*[2], irrespective of chronological considerations; and the earlier promise of a bibliography to Philodemus was fulfilled.

The flexible, organic character of the new electronic canon lends itself quite readily to expansion, improvement, emendation, and innovation. Although intended, from the beginning, to serve as a handmaid to the TLG data bank, its utility continues to be appraised in terms of how well it manages to meet new challenges posed by scholars. In 1987, the contents of the data bank had grown so large (60,123,000 words)[97] that some TLG users were now seeking ways to isolate related texts that could then be examined and searched collectively as well as selectively, but independently of the entire data bank.[98] This effort provided the impetus for a new project that we began in the summer of 1987, classification of the works in the TLG data bank. Using broad generic descriptions, we scrutinized each work for the criteria that would define its appropriate category, then added tags to a classification field in the electronic canon, making it possible to organize all works affixed with a given tag into a circumscribed body of material. Although the software for manipulating this new feature is still being developed, the classification tags have been incorporated into the most recent edition of the *Canon*.[99] Henceforth, each work deposited into the data bank will be accompanied by classifying information as a standard prerequisite for listing.

In response also to scholars' needs, citation systems adopted for each work in the data bank are now routinely added to the electronic canon, and these also are represented in *Canon*[3]. For the most part, the TLG's citation systems reflect traditional conventions; a few are necessarily constructed because they were wanting, and some complex forms of citation are reduced to a more workable minimum.[100] More important, the information is accessible to scholars who consult TLG texts, and it will be found in all subsequent versions of the canon.

The Canon of the Future

As early as the initial TLG Planning Conference in 1972, the Thesaurus Linguae Graecae was conceived as a comprehensive collection of the surviving Greek texts, spanning the beginnings of Greek literature to some reasonable date of conclusion in the Christian era, based upon the best available editions, and preserved in electronic form for future scholars. But comprehensiveness did not then, and cannot now, imply an abstract concept of completeness. Even as the TLG approaches the end of its second decade, the size of the Greek corpus remains an estimate, and while there is continuing progress and the welcome assistance of many scholars, the identification of authors and works continues to be an ongoing process. The chronological terminus for the project's scope is still an elusive date, advancing as the literature of later antiquity is added to the data bank. The best available editions may not be the best editions, and indeed some texts stubbornly resist the data entry process.[101] Moreover, texts that were approved nearly twenty years ago may need to be replaced by improved editions that are only now available. All of these factors suggest that while "progressive completeness" remains a desideratum, "absolute completeness in the data bank is unattainable."[102] Nevertheless, as the TLG data bank grows, the TLG canon of authors and works will continue to provide the essential supportive substructure.

With 3,175 authors and 9,493 individual works now residing in the TLG data bank, the imperatives to organize, control, and monitor this mass of material are as compelling as ever. The techniques for meeting those imperatives are in place, and the electronic canon of authors and works is designed to facilitate expansion and refinement. The bulk of classical Greek literature has already been captured for the data bank and recorded in the canon. As the TLG turns its focus to Byzantine historiography and later Greek lexicography, new authors will be added to the canon.

The work of progressive completeness requires not only attention to new authors, but consideration of untapped categories of information for all authors. Updating, improvement, and refinement of the classification information (and indeed the entire taxonomic system imposed upon the contents of the data bank) will require the continuing collaboration of scholars who work with TLG texts, but the result will be greater facility in defining related texts. Systematic application of geographic epithets can help to present a fuller, if not a complete, picture of an author's movements and affiliations over a lifetime. The inclusion of *incipits* for all works that admit them, Greek titles where they survive, and relative dating where it is possible can only enhance the utility of the canon.

In the final analysis, the canon of the future is likely to be as different from *Canon*[3] as *Canon*[2] was from its predecessor, "the green canon." As organic as the data bank that it is meant to support, the TLG canon will always be expected to reflect advances in scholarship. As classicists gain increasing control over their subject matter, the canon, too, will grow to reflect our increased knowledge in areas such as literary history, bibliography, and taxonomy.

In a volume devoted to the marriage of computers and the classics, topics such as "notable quoters," spelling variants in the *Tusculum-Lexikon,* and the merits of Kühn would seem to have little to do with the gradual entry of classicists into an electronic world. Yet, scholarship and technology must work closely, hand in hand, if the electronic resources now being created are to serve useful purposes. Conversion of Greek text into machine-readable form is a simple task that can be performed without the slightest knowledge of Greek language and literature; this has been convincingly demonstrated by the TLG's commercial data entry contractors for eighteen years. However, creation of a data bank of Greek texts that is sound, capable of continuous growth, and suited to a variety of scholarly purposes must be predicated upon the existence of a solid scholarly foundation. In the absence of such a foundation, electronic texts are nothing more than strings of words flowing across a computer screen without literary and historical context, ill suited for anything but the most elementary research processes. The advent of the computer may have rendered the procurement of information easier and faster than it was a few years ago; by the same token, it also has increased the necessity for solid sources from which this information flows.

Over the years, the quality and integrity of the Thesaurus Linguae Graecae data bank have been recognized. Appropriately, this recognition has been directed to the high degree of accuracy that characterizes the TLG's machine-readable material. Indeed, the project takes pride in the awareness that a given text, upon leaving the premises, will be as error-free as human effort will allow. However, the project takes equal pride in its confidence that the text will be supported by a broad range of literary, historical, and bibliographic information designed to assist the user. It is this information that resides in the TLG canon and that guarantees the Thesaurus Linguae Graecae its integrity.

Notes

1. While an electronic version of the canon is included on TLG CD-ROM C, the software for utilizing it effectively has yet to be developed. Nevertheless, several enterprising computer-classicists have managed to tap its potential for their own use.

2. Until recently, scholars who subscribed to the TLG's CD-ROM received copies of Luci Berkowitz and Karl A. Squitier, *Thesaurus Linguae Graecae Canon of Greek Authors and Works,* 2d ed. (New York and Oxford, 1986). The more recent edition, idem, *Thesaurus Linguae Graecae Canon of Greek Authors and Works,* 3d ed. (New York and Oxford: Oxford University Press, 1990), is available from the publisher. Hereafter, the following abbreviations will also be used: *Canon*[1] = Luci Berkowitz, *Thesaurus Linguae Graecae Canon of Greek Authors and Works from Homer to* A.D. *200* (Costa Mesa, Cal., 1977); *Canon*[2] = the 1986 edition cited above; *Canon*[3] = the 1990 edition cited above. In lowercase Roman letters, "canon" should be regarded both as a general concept and as the developing record of TLG authors and works from 1972 on; "electronic canon" refers to the instrument that has resided in the TLG's computer system since 1981.

3. For instance, T. F. Brunner, "Data Banks for the Humanities: Learning from the Thesaurus Linguae Graecae," *Scholarly Communication* 7 (Winter 1987): 1 and 6–9, and "Overcoming Verzettelung," *Humanities* 9.3 (May/June 1988): 4–7; also numerous lectures delivered to scholarly societies, annual reports to the American Philological Association's Committee on the TLG, articles in both the domestic and the foreign

press, and a variety of invited papers presented to interested members of the world community. The TLG also publishes a semiannual newsletter that charts the project's progress.

4. For example, the preface to *Canon*[1] (i–xxix) and the introductions to *Canon*[2] (xi–xli) and *Canon*[3] (xi–lx); see also Squitier, "The *TLG Canon*: Genesis of an Electronic Data Base," *Favonius* 1 (1987): 15–20 (suppl.).

5. For example, H. G. Liddell, R. Scott, and H. S. Jones, *A Greek-English Lexicon*[9] (Oxford, 1940; repr. 1968), xvi–xxxviii, with E. A. Barber, P. Maas, M. Scheller, and M. L. West, *A Supplement* (Oxford, 1968), vii–x [hereafter, *LSJ*]; G. W. Lampe, *A Patristic Greek Lexicon* (Oxford, 1961; repr. 1978), ix–xliii; E. A. Sophocles, *Greek Lexicon of the Roman and Byzantine Periods from b.c. 146 to a.d. 1100*[3] (Cambridge, Mass., 1914; repr. Hildesheim, 1975), vii–xvi and 12–23.

6. Participants in the first TLG Planning Conference included Winfried Buehler, Peter Colaclides, Aubrey Diller, Wilhelm Ehlers, George Goold, G. M. A. Grube, Albert Henrichs, Charles Murgia, Brooks Otis, David Packard, Jaan Puhvel, Bruno Snell, and Stephen Waite.

7. Eventually, the TLG would divide its efforts into four separate phases: Phase I = Homer to a.d. 200; Phase II = 200–400; Phase III = 400–600; Phase IV = post–600.

8. Since the earliest days of the TLG, the number of words committed to the data bank in a given project period has been regulated necessarily by the funds available to support data entry.

9. *LSJ*, v, translated from *Neue Jahrbücher* (1905): 692. Acknowledging the enormous task of creating the *Thesaurus Linguae Latinae,* under way in Munich, Diels seriously doubted the feasibility of creating a Greek thesaurus.

10. One year earlier, Sir Richard Jebb had proposed a Greek thesaurus that would comprehend "the early part of the seventh century a.d.," but this option seems not to have survived the year in which it was suggested (ibid.).

11. Diels reiterated this estimate one paragraph later: "Since the proportion of Latin to Greek Literature is about 1 : 10 . . ." (ibid.).

12. The ten thesauri were proposed even earlier by F. A. Wolf, who wanted to represent the main branches of Greek literature as they were then conceived along mostly generic, but also ideological, lines, i.e., epic, lyric, tragic, comic, philosophical, historical, mathematical and technical, medical, grammatical, and Jewish-Christian (*LSJ,* vi). The generic concept would be resurrected by Bruno Snell when he sought to create a Greek thesaurus at the University of Hamburg in the 1950s.

13. Except for some of the *grammatici Latini,* a number of anonymously written poems, *passiones,* laws, and scholia, Isidore seems to be the latest author named in the TLL's *Index Librorum Scriptorum Inscriptionum ex Quibus Exempla Adferuntur* (Leipzig, 1904), 1–109.

14. The 9 million words did not, of course, embrace the entire extant Latin corpus up to the seventh century. Writing on the occasion of the seventy-fifth anniversary of the founding of the *Thesaurus Linguae Latinae,* H. Haffter (chairman of the International Thesaurus Commission) and H. Kratz (director of Teubner, Leipzig) recalled both the originally sought ideal and the contemporary attained reality: "In principle, the entire Latinity of antiquity was to be recorded, and for every occurrence of every Latin word a record was to be contained in the slip material, which was to be transposed into dictionary articles. It is more justified today than ever to acknowledge the judge-

ment and sense of realities of those planners, who did not allow themselves to be guided by a desire for encyclopedic completeness; instead, for the extensive literature of the later centuries, from about 200 to 600 A.D., they decided upon a procedure of selection that would record all essential linguistic and stylistic peculiarities, while facilitating processing the material." This reflection appeared in a Teubner announcement in 1975 that hailed the TLL's seventy-five years.

15. In December 1977, when the first edition of the *Canon* was published, we were able to confirm a figure of 21 million words representing 1,688 authors for Phase I.

16. N. G. L. Hammond and H. H. Scullard, eds., *The Oxford Classical Dictionary*² (Oxford, 1970), vii [hereafter *OCD*²].

17. See *OCD*², v. Among Christian authors added to the second edition are Athanasius, Gregory of Nazianzus, and Gregory of Nyssa. Later Greek commentators transferred from the first edition include Photius (ninth century), Eustathius (twelfth century), Thomas Magister (thirteenth–fourteenth century), and Demetrius Triclinius (fourteenth century), all of whom are now represented in the TLG data bank.

18. The full title of this volume is informative: W. Buchwald, A. Hohlweg, and O. Prinz, eds., *Tusculum-Lexikon griechischer und lateinischer Autoren des Altertums und des Mittelalters*² (Munich, 1963).

19. F. L. Cross, ed., *The Oxford Dictionary of the Christian Church* (London, 1957; repr. with corrections, 1958).

20. W. Smith and H. Wace, eds., *Dictionary of Christian Biography,* 4 vols. (London, 1877–87) [hereafter, *DCB*].

21. By the early 1980s, the TLG was well on its way toward capturing later Greek and patristic literature.

22. W. Buchwald, A. Hohlweg, and O. Prinz, eds., *Tusculum-Lexicon*³ (Munich, 1982).

23. Ibid., ix: "Die griechischen und lateinischen Autorennamen wurden in der Form genannt, die dem Kulturkreis des Autors entspricht."

24. Page numbers here refer to the third edition of the *Tusculum-Lexikon.*

25. *DCB*, 1:xii, n. 20.

26. John of Damascus is not in fact the last author listed, as volume 3 concludes with the bibliographies for three of his near contemporaries, i.e., John of Euboea, Cosmas Vestitor, and Andreas Cretensis, whom the Damascene outlived by nearly ten years.

27. The precise publication history of the *Clavis Patrum Graecorum,* published by Brepols in Turnhout, Belgium, is as follows: vol. 1 (1983); vol. 2 (1974); vol. 3 (1979); vol. 4 (1980); vol. 5 (1987).

28. Rodrique LaRue, *Clavis Sriptorum Graecarum et Latinorum,* vol. 1 (Trois Rivières, 1985), xiii. A fourth volume, containing an index, also appeared in 1985.

29. For example, Varro, Vergil, Valerius Flaccus, and Velius Longus.

30. Funded by a grant from the Spanish government, the *Repertorium Litterarum Graecorum* was published by the Instituto Antonio de Nebrija in Madrid.

31. W. Schmid and O. Stählin, *Geschichte der griechischen Literatur,* vols. 1.1–1.5 (Munich, 1929–48; repr. 1959–64); with W. von Christ in W. Schmid, ed., *Geschichte der griechischen Literatur*⁶, vols. 2.1–2.2 (1920–24; repr. 1959–61).

32. F. Susemihl, *Geschichte der griechischen Literatur in der Alexandrinerzeit,* 2 vols. (Leipzig, 1891–92; repr. Hildesheim, 1965).

33. A. Lesky, *A History of Greek Literature,* trans. J. Willis and C. de Heer (New York, 1966), and *Geschichte der griechischen Literatur*[3] (Bern, 1971).

34. H. J. Rose, *A Handbook of Greek Literature*[4] (New York, 1960).

35. P. E. Easterling and B. M. W. Knox, eds., *The Cambridge History of Classical Literature,* vol. 1: *Greek Literature* (Cambridge, 1985); and E. J. Kenney and W. V. Clausen, eds., *The Cambridge History of Classical Literature,* vol. 2: Latin Literature (Cambridge, 1982).

36. I.e., G. Wissowa, W. Kroll, K. Ziegler et al., eds., *Paulys Real-Encyclopädie der classischen Altertumswissenschaft* (Stuttgart and Munich, 1893–). Volumes 1.1– 24.1 were published between 1893 and 1963; a second overlapping series was published as vols. 1a–10a (1914–72); supplement volumes have been published since 1903. K. Ziegler, W. Sontheimer, and H. Gärtner, eds., *Der kleine Pauly,* 5 vols. (Stuttgart, 1964–75), although intended as an abridgment of "Der grosse Pauly," contains much new information and updated bibliographic details.

37. J. Quasten, *Patrology,* 3 vols. (Utrecht-Antwerp, 1950–60; repr. 1966). The subtitles of the volumes specify their chronological framework: vol. 1, *The Beginnings of Patristic Literature;* vol. 2, *The Ante-Nicene Literature after Irenaeus;* vol. 3, *The Golden Age of Patristic Literature from the Council of Nicaea to the Council of Chalcedon.*

38. B. Altaner, *Patrology,* trans. H. C. Graef (New York, 1961). Graef's translation is based upon the second edition of *Patrologie* (Freiburg, 1961).

39. The *Übersicht* was the basis for the TLL's *Index* (n. 13). Both the *Übersicht* and a *Canon Chronicus Scriptorum* had been presented to us by TLL Director Wilhelm Ehlers at the 1972 TLG Planning Conference.

40. See n. 89.

41. Since the TLL had fixed the order of its authors, the author numbers in the *Übersicht* could be used invariably to indicate the relative chronological position of authors in citing words and word forms within a specific lemma. For example, the numbers 3, 4, 5, and 6 respectively identify Ennius, Plautus, Terence, and Lucilius, but with emphasis upon their temporal sequence. The TLG has no fixed system of chronological order. Author numbers are simply computer substitutes for names without regard for chronological priority. Thus, Apollonius of Rhodes, who wrote during the third century B.C., is recognized by the computer as 0001, partly in order to distinguish him from the other twenty-eight authors named Apollonius, but partly also because he was the first author whose surviving literary work was consigned to the TLG data bank.

42. Since the beginning of its data-entry program, the TLG has used the services of overseas contractors for the conversion of Greek texts into machine-readable form.

43. At the December 1972 meeting of the APA in Philadelphia, the Board of Directors established the APA Advisory Committee on the TLG. The charter members of this committee (Albert Henrichs, Bernard Knox, Miroslav Marcovich, Bruce Metzger, Lionel Pearson, John Rist, and Douglas Young, chair) were appointed in order to provide the TLG with guidance in the selection of appropriate texts for its data bank.

44. Except for small fragments that were counted word by word, we arrived at word estimates for each work by random statistical analysis, which required our counting the number of words in ten randomly selected lines, multiplying the average by the average

number of lines determined from ten randomly selected pages, and then multiplying the result by the total number of pages involved.

45. Following *OCD*[2] (345), we carried this author as *Dio Cassius* until William Willis prevailed upon us to correct the name for the third edition of the *Canon*.

46. I.e., Athenaeus (probably), Cassius Dio, Diogenes Laertius, and Origen.

47. Minutes of the Washington, D.C., meeting of the APA Advisory Committee on the TLG (February 24–25, 1973).

48. Aeschylus, in particular, spurred considerable debate about the merits of replacing the standard Murray edition with Page's recently published text. Eventually, Murray's edition was adopted for the data bank.

49. I.e., K. Aland, M. Black, C. M. Martini, B. M. Metzger, and A. Wikgren, eds., *The Greek New Testament*[2] (Stuttgart, 1968).

50. Although the only complete edition available in 1972 was A. Rahlfs, *Septuaginta*[9], 2 vols. (Stuttgart, 1935; repr. 1971), the TLG met with criticism from a number of biblical scholars who felt strongly that the Göttingen and Cambridge editions were superior to the Rahlfs edition. While individual books of the Septuagint were being published, sporadically and out of order, in Göttingen and Cambridge, the state of the editions was then, and is now, in progress. The availability of the Rahlfs edition in the TLG data bank has given biblical scholars nearly two decades of research opportunities that they would otherwise still be anticipating.

51. Washington minutes (cf. note 47).

52. Minutes of the Irvine Meeting of the APA Committee on the TLG (September 21–22, 1973).

53. In July 1990, 417 *medici* were listed in the TLG canon.

54. H. Leitner, *Bibliography to the Ancient Medical Authors* (Bern, 1973).

55. Ibid., 5.

56. For example, Hecataeus of Abdera is represented in Felix Jacoby, ed., *Die Fragmente der griechischen Historiker*, 264, but also in Hermann Diels and Walter Kranz, eds., *Die Fragmente der Vorsokratiker*, 2:240–45.

57. In *D-K*, 1:443, Iamblichus's list of Phliasian philosophers (from *VP* 267), along with an addendum from Cicero's *De fin.* 5.29.87, yields five names. Since the emphasis in the testimonial statements seems to favor Echecrates (even though Diocles heads the list of five in *D-K*), the text is carried under his name, with a note acknowledging the others: *auctores alii nominantur Diocles, Polymnastus, Phanto et Arion.*

58. For instance in the *Grammatici Graeci*, there are numerous passages that trail off into ktl (καὶ τὰ λοιπά). See *Gramm. Graec.* 3.2, where there are three instances on page 35 alone, i.e., at lines 17, 32, and 35.

59. The remains of *paradoxographa*, for instance, are not so well served as other genres and are sometimes difficult to track down. The thirty-eight *paradoxa* ascribed to Sextus Julianus Africanus are noted in A. Giannini, ed., *Paradoxographorum Graecorum Reliquiae* (Milan, 1965), 372–73, without text, as cross references to the *Geoponica*.

60. In a letter addressed to the advisory committee following its first meeting (and dated March 30, 1973), Douglas Young notes that Lionel Pearson, in particular, considered it "a tremendous waste of time and money to feed all of [FGrH] or similar collections into the computer." In fairness, Pearson subsequently spent many hours on

the premises of the TLG, investigating the most effective means for data capture of the various collections. In the spring of 1973, however, his preferences lay with the later scholiasts and lexicographers. His letter of March 30 also states: "It is surely one of the principal objects of the data bank to provide information about the language used by important 'lost' authors like Ephorus; and it cannot do this without taking in the scholia and lexica, unless it wastes time and money by recording all of the fragment collections."

61. Minutes of the Chicago meeting of the APA Advisory Committee on the TLG (December 29, 1974).

62. Our neglect of lost authors during the early years of the project imposes a legacy upon our successors who will someday be faced with the task of recovering them from the heap of overlooked materials and restoring them to their rightful places in the canon. Some of this work has already begun, but it is far from complete.

63. List of approved texts from the St. Louis meeting of the APA Advisory Committee on the TLG (December 29, 1973). St. Louis also marks the site of the first committee meeting chaired by Lionel Pearson, following the death of the committee's first chair, Douglas Young, on October 24, 1973.

64. Minutes of the Irvine meeting of the APA Advisory Committee on the TLG (March 29–30, 1974).

65. Ibid.

66. Minutes of the Washington, D.C., meeting of the Advisory Committee on the TLG (December 29, 1975).

67. Ibid.

68. Ibid. Pearson did not address specifically epigraphical texts in this distinction, but in subsequent deliberations he clearly regarded them as he did papyrus texts.

69. Ibid.

70. These are named as examples of desiderata in a statement by Pearson entitled "Fragments of Greek Authors in the Word Bank" (4–5), distributed to members of the advisory committee.

71. See note 64.

72. Subsequently, the Duke Data Bank of Documentary Papyri was established, with support from the David and Lucile Packard Foundation and the Packard Humanities Institute. DDBDP would create an electronic data bank of documentary texts on papyri. Similar projects devoted to data capture of inscriptions would soon be under way (also with Packard support) at Princeton and Cornell Universities.

73. Pearson, "Fragments," 1 (cf. note 70). Actually, this proposal had been put forth as early as March 1974 in discussions with Willis at Duke University.

74. The advisory committee had begun to discuss the data-entry problems posed by an *apparatus criticus* as early as its meetings in Urbana on October 11–12, 1973. These discussions are still in progress.

75. Pearson, "Fragments," 2 (cf. note 70).

76. B. P. Grenfell, A. S. Hunt et al., eds., *The Oxyrhynchus papyri* (London, 1898–).

77. Published sporadically before 1984, the *TLG Newsletter* now appears twice yearly.

78. Until 1981, when David Packard dedicated an Ibycus system to the TLG, the project's computer needs had to be met by the Xerox Sigma-7 computer at the University of California, Irvine. The high monthly cost of disk storage prohibited use of the Sigma-7 for purposes other than text verification and correction.

79. In *Canon*[3], 109 works are listed under Galenus, 25 under Pseudo-Galenus, 147 under Plutarchus, and 4 under Pseudo-Plutarchus.

80. Prior to undertaking full-scale data entry, the project conducted a series of pilot studies in order to assess the financial implications in converting large amounts of Greek text into electronic form.

81. By July 1990, the TLG canon would list 358 *philosophi,* 700 *historici,* 983 discrete philosophical works, and 1,138 remnants of historical works.

82. See note 4. Laurence Shick, the TLG's programmer, designed the format for Diablo printer output of *Canon*[1].

83. Though nicknamed for the color of its cover, *Canon*[1] could also be considered green because the canon then was in an early stage of development.

84. Nemesius and Oribasius belong to the fourth century A.D., Aëtius and Alexander to the sixth, and Paul to the seventh.

85. In a few exceptional cases, work numbers were provided to facilitate consultation of a lengthy bibliography, for example, the Anonymi Historici in FGrH, the Anonymi Medici, and the Aristotelian corpus (*Canon*[1], 24–26 and 59–60).

86. The APA Advisory Committee on the TLG, now appointed by the APA's standing Committee on Research Materials, had been renamed APA Subcommittee on the TLG. Guided by an interim chair, Glen Bowersock, the subcommittee began to express new interests in accordance with the wishes of the APA directors. Its new mission, as set forth in the minutes of the Irvine Meeting of the APA Subcommittee on the TLG (September 12–13, 1981), was "to provide advice and support on matters of scholarship and policy with a view to helping the TLG both internally and in dealing with outside bodies."

87. *TLG Newsletter* 5 (June 1982): 3; also *APA Newsletter* 4.4 (Winter 1981): 9.

88. Johnson joined the TLG staff as programmer in July 1981 and left the project in June 1984 in order to collaborate with David Packard in the development of a new scholarly computer. This Ibycus SC is now widely used by scholars in the humanistic disciplines.

89. The current list of fields permits the following kinds of information about authors: author name (or where lacking, work name); sorting information (denoting alphabetical placement of complex names as well as order of listing for identical names); synonyms or alternative names by which the author may be recognized; author epithet traditionally used to characterize the author's major work; generic epithet applied to a work name that stands in lieu of an author name; other descriptive labels such as an author's nickname, patronymic, affiliations, and official titles; geographic epithet designating place of birth or principal site of literary activity; date by century in which the author wrote; expanded frame of time within which the author wrote (i.e., Phase I = Homer to A.D. 200; II = 200–400; III = 400–600; IV = post-600), especially useful when dates cannot be determined, but assigned to all authors; bibliographic sources providing information about the author; cross references to other authors if appropriate. Information about discrete works is found in the following fields: bibliographic source providing information about the work or text edition; type of bibliographic format in which the approved text edition is to be cited (e.g., book, book in series, or article); conventional title of the work (with preference for Latin, but permitting Greek or even both); computer-verified word count for works deposited in the data bank; word estimate for works planned for data entry; *incipit* (especially of prose works with identical

titles); means by which the work has been transmitted (e.g., codex, papyrus, inscription); classification of the work according to genre, category, or form; dialect(s) represented in the work; overseas shipment in which the approved text edition for the work was sent out for data entry; date (used especially of a specific codex or papyrus containing the work); status of the text in the correction process; form of citation system adopted for the preferred edition (e.g., chapter, section, line; page, line); reference locating a work imbedded in another work and cross-referenced to another text; editor of the adopted edition; title of the edition; name of series or journal (when required to complete information about a book in a series or an article); place of publication; publisher; year of publication; place of reprinting; reprinting publisher; year of reprinting; pages included in the data bank; breakdown (where warranted) into titles of treatises, chapter headings, fragments, or papyrus information; cross references to other appropriate works or other authors; new editions that may be used to replace currently adopted texts; comments, questions, and problems related to the work or text edition; an injunction suppressing the entry when printing, together with the rationale for suppressing (e.g., *verba Latina solum; inedita; nullus textus*).

90. While all of the fields are useful for constructing new entries and building the electronic canon, only the most cogent are introduced into printed editions of the *Canon*. It is unlikely, for instance, that scholars would be interested in knowing in what shipment a text was sent out for data entry. Information about dialects, although surely of interest, is not yet available, and *incipits* are still only sporadically used.

91. The focus of data entry between 1981 and 1985 was upon authors who dominated patristic literature. The most voluminous author added to the data bank during this period is also the most voluminous extant Greek author, John Chrysostom, who left us more than 4 million words.

92. By now, more than a dozen 1600-foot reels were required to provide a user with copies of the verified and corrected portions of the TLG data bank.

93. In late 1986, the TLG discontinued modem access to its resources; by then, the CD-ROM had established itself as the principal medium for dissemination of TLG data.

94. *TLG Newsletter* 9 (December 1985): 1.

95. *TLG Newsletter* 10 (July 1986): 1–2, 3.

96. For example, in *Canon*[1], word estimates were introduced by *WE,* means of transmission by *Trans,* and status of the text vis-à-vis data entry by *St.*

97. *TLG Newsletter* 12 (December 1987): 1. Of this total, more than 44 million words had been corrected.

98. It makes little sense, for instance, to require a user to consider all of Greek literature when searching for a passage that is clearly within the realm of epic poetry.

99. *Canon*[3], esp. xxxi–xlix ("Classification of Works in the TLG Data Bank").

100. In the absence of a convenient form of citation, the TLG sometimes found it necessary to incorporate titles into the citation system for the *comici.* See, for instance, the fragments of Cratinus in A. Meineke, ed., *Fragmenta comicorum Graecorum,* vol. 2.1 (Berlin, 1839; repr. De Gruyter, 1970), 15–232, where the citation system adopted is according to play, fragment, and line. Where there are competing citation systems, only one is retained for the electronic text. For example, K. Jacoby's system of book, chapter, section, and line is retained for the *Antiquitates Romanae* of Dionysius of Halicarnassus, whereas the pagination of Reiske's 1774–75 edition (printed in the inner margin of Jacoby's text) is necessarily ignored.

101. For example, F. Field's two-volume edition of Origen's *Hexapla* (Oxford, 1875; repr. Hildesheim, 1964) presents genuine problems for text preparation but no clues for salvaging the Greek text, discarding the interlocked Latin and Hebrew, or satisfactorily representing the three *interpretes veteris testamenti,* Aquila, Symmachus, and Theodotion.

102. Irvine minutes (cf. note 86).

3

The Duke Data Bank of Documentary Papyri

John F. Oates

My purpose in this chapter is twofold.[1] I will first present a description of the Duke Data Bank of Documentary Papyri detailing its development, the history of the project, and the methodologies used in the process of creating this research tool. Secondly I will consider some of the future effects of the data bank on papyrology and ancient historical studies.

The Duke Data Bank of Documentary Papyri project began in January 1983 at Duke University under the direction of myself and my colleague, Prof. William H. Willis,[2] and will be substantially complete in two to four more years. We are aiming to construct a machine-readable data bank comprising all published Greek and Latin documentary papyri. By "papyri" we mean all papyri, ostraca, parchment, and tablets inscribed with Greek and Latin documents from the third century B.C. to the eighth century of our era. ("Papyrology" is a discipline difficult to define; generally speaking we practitioners know what it is, and no one will be surprised that we exclude Latin charters of the early Middle Ages from the scope of our project.) Although we are independent of the Thesaurus Linguae Graecae, we have collaborated closely with them and in some ways we are a complement to their vast data bank. We currently work on a contract basis with the Packard Humanities Institute, which in January 1989 issued its CD-ROM 2, containing the 2.5 million words of papyrological Greek and Latin which we had entered up to September 8, 1988. In June of 1991 PHI issued its CD-ROM 6, which contains the more than 3.6 million words entered by the DDBDP through April 5, 1991. Funding for the project has come from the Packard Foundation and the Packard Humanities Institute, with one small equipment grant from the National Endowment of the Humanities. Duke University has provided generous space and other support, including the original purchase of the Ibycus minicomputer system.

The purpose of the Duke Data Bank is to make instantly accessible through search programs the total corpus of published Greek and Latin papyri. It is not intended to substitute for printed editions but rather to serve as a means of searching such volumes and of making concordances.

From the beginnings of modern papyrology, the key research tool has been the index. From this beginning individual volumes containing documentary texts have been systematically provided with indices of words and names, at least, and frequently of royal and imperial titles, measures, etc. In 1922 Friedrich Preisigke brought out the *Namenbuch,* and from 1926 to 1931 there appeared the three volumes of his *Wörterbuch der griechischen Papyrusurkunden,* which is still a major research tool for papyrologists. It will indeed remain so because of its lexical analysis in a lemma for each word occurring in documentary texts to that point. Emil Kiessling subsequently produced four fascicules of volume 4; the last, reaching the middle of epsilon, was published in 1971. Volume 4 was intended to include everything published from 1924 to January 1, 1940. In 1969 Kiessling brought out as a Supplement the *Wörterlist,* a listing of all words occurring in papyri published between 1940 and 1966 with no attempt at lexical analysis. In 1966 there appeared the useful *Spoglio lessicale papirologico* prepared by Sergio Daris and basically an index of the indices of individual volumes. In 1969 Daniele Foraboschi's *Onomasticum alterum papyrologicum* was published. In effect, then, our latest lexical aids cover most of the papyri published to 1966. The extensive publications since that time had to be accessed through the indices of the individual volumes until January 1989, when the first Duke Data Bank CD-ROM became available.

When we began in 1983, we had already made the decision to enter text beginning with the most recent publications. Our Phase One includes all texts published since 1966 and is kept up to date as each new volume of documentary texts takes priority for data entry. There are currently 172 volumes entered in Phase One. Phase Two extends from 1966 back to 1924, the closing date for material contained in Preisigke's *Wörterbuch.* All 161 volumes in Phase Two have been entered. (These figures are those of April 5, 1991.) Phase Three will contain the rest of papyrological material, that published before 1924. Forty-two of the 88 volumes in this phase have been entered. Three hundred seventy-five of these volumes, representing more than 80 percent of all published material, are available on the Packard Humanities Institute CD-ROM 6.

For the most part, data entry has been done at Duke University by project staff and by graduate students. The Project Coordinator is Dr. Louise P. Smith and the Assistant Coordinator is Ms. Catherine Rine.[3] The Oxyrhynchus texts were entered by our British colleagues. Of 38 volumes in that series containing documents, 22 were entered at Oxford under the direction of Peter Parsons, and 16 by Dr. Traianos Gagos at the University of Durham; the two latest have been entered by us at Duke. Once we have entered text volumes, printouts are sent to the University of Michigan where they are proofread under the direction of Professor Ludwig Koenen and his assistants. At this time 284 volumes have been proofread, verified, and corrected.[4]

Our main equipment is the Ibycus minicomputer system as developed by Dr. David W. Packard. It is a self-standing mainframe system with central processing unit, twelve terminals, a tape drive, a 404 megabyte memory disk, and a laser and a dot matrix printer. Most of the equipment is manufactured by Hewlett Packard. This set of machinery is the basic equipment for the data-entry part of the DDBDP. We have in addition two Ibycus Scholarly Computers and a Macintosh IIsi with ink-jet printer and laser disc reader. The Ibycus mini system is antiquated, but no easy replacement which would offer sufficient work stations and the requisite storage is currently available. As I write this, we are hopeful that Hewlett Packard will continue to support this equipment until initially planned data entry is competed. At that time we will have to shift to an arrangement whereby we can enter new volumes as they appear and manage the data bank as created.

In matters of data entry, we have attempted to avoid any editorial work and any matters of interpretation. We have endeavored to enter the text provided by the editor, even where probably wrong, in order not to destroy the bibliographic record. Often, however, editors have been ambiguous in their texts and we have had to reach some resolutions. Furthermore, we have not attempted to reproduce precisely the appearance of the papyrus on the printed page any more than the printed text represents the appearance of the writing on the papyrus original. Thus primarily we are trying to create a data bank that is a guide to editions of papyri. The computer medium, however, differs from that of print, and a certain number of escapes and conventions have been used. When more extensive graphic capabilities are readily available, it may be that many can be resolved. Currently they are arranged in logical fashion in different categories, but such may not be readily discernible. Lists of symbols, escapes and conventions are provided in the instructions included on the laser disk.

We enter texts by typing the Greek (or Latin) directly into the machine. The Greek is converted to Beta Code, the ASCII character set system developed by David Packard and used also by the TLG. The display in the search program is also in Greek (or Latin). The relatively small volume of our material did not allow for contracting out data entry as was done by the TLG. Furthermore, the nature of papyrological data entry is infinitely more complicated than data entry from the standard printed volume of literary texts. Finally, the almost endless varieties of typeface used in presenting papyrological volumes, ranging from the different hands of the early *BGU* volumes to more recent typewritten and photographed editions, precluded the use of any kind of scanner.

Data entry posed problems of a magnitude much greater than we had expected. The early years of the project entailed lengthy staff meetings once or twice weekly to resolve problems never before imagined. There were all the symbols, abbreviations, signs, numbers and fractions, etc. that had to be dealt with. There were problems of reprinted texts and especially partially reprinted texts, duplicate texts which the editor had combined into one, and duplicate texts where the editor reported only significant variations, etc. One great problem was what to do with broken letters, marked in printed editions with sublinear dots — a significant matter for the edition of papyri. In the older Ibycus system, when we began, a sublinear dot was not possible. We solved this using the dim reverse function to indicate a dotted letter.

Perhaps the biggest question facing us was that of the apparatus criticus, particularly the matter of how to deal with very common variant spellings used by various scribes. If the scribe's spelling is not standard, we enter the standard spelling, koine or classical, and follow the word with the scribe's spelling enclosed in braces with the exponent ^{4}, thus πόλεως{^{4}πώλαιος}^{4}. Similarly, {^{5} }^{5} encloses a form altered by the scribe, {^{7} }^{7} an editorial error, {^{9} }^{9} an alternative reading found in a duplicated copy of the text. There are exceptions: Egyptian proper names including month names are entered as they are written on the papyrus; also γείνομαι (and its inflection) and πρόκιται are not normalized. The user must, therefore, search both γείνομαι and γίνομαι, πρόκιται and πρόκειται. In fact, all words in which ι and ει are possible variations should be searched in both spellings.

As I have indicated, the first CD-ROM disk, PHI 2, which contained what had been entered up to September 8, 1988, into the Duke Data Bank, was issued on January 5, 1989. This disk was made generally available at the annual meeting of the American Philological Association in Baltimore, Maryland. The second disk of the DDBDP material was issued in May 1991 and can now be ordered from the Packard Humanities Institute in Los Altos, California.[5] It is specifically designed to be used with an Ibycus Scholarly Computer, with which the user has the advantage of speed in searching. For a word which occurs 316 times in the 3.6 million words, the full search takes a few seconds more than four minutes. (#ovov#) was the pattern I used.) The default citation gives three lines of context; this context may be expanded, and in the browse mode a whole volume of texts can be read. While this last feature was not our primary intent, it can be valuable to scholars without an extensive papyrological collection at hand. The CD-ROM can also be used with the Macintosh and IBM systems for which a number of programs have been developed.[6]

Each match is accompanied by a citation of the text; the volume number, papyrus number, and line are given along with column or fragment number and indication of recto and verso where relevant. Also the letters *rp* are used if the text as entered also exists in another edition. This information is included in the first protected 'header' line which precedes each entered text (the ~ line). A second protected 'header' line provides information on provenience and date, the earlier edition if *rp* is indicated, and on the material if other than papyrus. The header lines are invisible in a word search, but their information is displayed with every match. The information contained in these headers should be susceptible of manipulation, but database management programs have not yet been written. We have ourselves manually created pointer files which allow us to search volumes which contain, e.g., Ptolemaic papyri, all papyri whose provenience is Oxyrhynchus, and all ostraca. The possibilities are endless but very time consuming in manual construction. Database management programs should provide the answer.

The first and foremost value of the data bank is to the editor of papyrological texts both quantitatively and qualitatively. The speed of searching for parallels is the most obvious advantage, and such searches can much more quickly locate the context of any given papyrus. I can illustrate from my own work with a Duke papyrus, the sale of a donkey from the year 382.[7] Having found the word ὄνον in the text, by word search I could locate other such sales including the lists provided by Sophie Lith in her edition of *CPR* VI.2 (along with her discussion of donkeys in general) as well as the update by Jaako Frösén in his edition of *CPR* VII.36. In addition I could quickly locate all such sales published since 1979. Of course these would have been found eventually, but the discovery was very much quicker. The seller is identified with his mother's name; only the first three letters ταψ- were clear. Searching showed that Ταψοῖτος was the most likely reading, and the ink traces then seemed quite clear. Even if it had been impossible to interpret the ink at the end of the word, there is a 90-percent certainty that Ταψοῖτος was the correct reading. Again, eventually this might have been resolved, but the statistical certainty would not have emerged. Furthermore, the buyer and seller are from the same village τοῦ Μοθίτου, that is, from Dakleh Oasis of the Great Oasis in the southwestern desert. When I was first working on the text, Guy Wagner's magnificent *Les Oasis*[8] had not been published, and the computer led me to all Oasis texts in swift and efficient fashion. Thus the computer and the data bank make editing texts faster, and they also make for better texts.

Success depends on words and lexical searches. (I am leaving aside for the moment the great value of being able to search a string of readable letters which do not immediately suggest a word.) The first difficulty is that Greek is an inflected language. In ideal cases a search of the stem will produce all forms of the word. Clearly, searching for ον would result in chaos. Since the search program on the Ibycus allows word boundary markers, one might think of #ον# but this would create an equally chaotic overload of information. My strategy, since I was interested in texts where the form occurs, was to search #ονον#. This proved to be satisfactory and even eliminated many of the intrusive custom house receipts from the matches. This case, however, is simple. Suppose, for example, that one wanted to find all the occurrences of παῖς in all cases singular and plural. My search patterns would look like this: #παι# ̌ #παις ̌ #παιδος ̌ #παιδι# ̌ παιδα#. Since I did not put a word boundary after παις I will also capture παισί in this search. I would then construct another string to capture the other plural forms.

The value for editing texts justifies the creation of the data bank, but it also opens doors for historical, economic, and sociological studies as well as linguistic and stylistic analyses. Just what will be done remains to be seen as more and more scholars and graduate students have access to the data bank, but I would like to do some speculating. First of all, the data bank does away with the need for a new Preisigke. Studies of individual words, however, will be greatly facilitated. Other tasks will be facilitated as well. The late Sir Moses Finley[9] excluded Egypt from his study of the ancient economy ostensibly because of the peculiarity of Egypt but really, I suppose, because of the intractability of the evidence. All sorts of new economic studies are now possible. I think first of the tax system, where the only guide is woefully out of date. Another area that will be a fertile ground for examination will be the family, another hitherto neglected area. Agriculture calls for in-depth study. In both these areas and in the area of taxation, much more complex sets of data can be put together than was previously possible. Individual sites will be more susceptible to in-depth analysis.

I have never run an extensive search without noticing something not germane to my inquiry but which looked interesting in itself. One of my graduate students last term, examining monetary terminology centering on the fourth century, turned up very interesting patterns in the Ptolemaic period, including radical changes in the terminology in the early second century B.C., which apparently coincide with the debasement of Ptolemaic silver coinage. There are other intriguing findings in this study, but I have not yet tried to see what they mean.

In a recent examination of the word μηχανή (which is interesting in itself), three side issues presented themselves. First there is the spelling of the word for "fuller." Κναφεύς and γναφεύς appear in about equal frequency, about 50 times each. Egyptian scribes apparently found it difficult to distinguish the gamma from the kappa sound at the beginning of the word. Second, although fullers and fulling activities are referred to more than 200 times in the data bank, they have never been studied as an occupational group. Third, μηχαναί frequently are fitted with ἀργαλεῖοι or is it ἐργαλεῖοι?

At the end of his article, "The Camel, the Wagon and the Donkey," in *BASP* 22 (1985): 1–6, Roger Bagnall says, "A detailed history of patterns of usage remains to be written; it would be worth the trouble." I have not yet done such a study, but I can report that on the CD-ROM of the Duke Data Bank there are 1,509 occurrences of ὄνος in all cases singular and plural and that there are 454 occurrences of κάμηλος in all cases singular and plural. Clearly the data bank is the starting point for Bagnall's desideratum.

Of course, as always, the computer data bank will give smart answers to smart questions, and once questions have been formulated search strategies will be devised. But I do believe that as more and more papyrologists, historians, linguists, and jurists make use of the data bank, solutions will emerge to problems whose very formulation was impossible before this technological development took place. Recently James Keenan pointed out that papyrologists are good at making lists,[10] but not necessarily are they equally good at synthesizing the papyrological evidence. In their surveys of Ptolemaic and Roman Egypt published in 1983, Keenan and Bagnall pointed out the lack of historical work on the papyri since the great work of Rostovtzeff, *The Social and Economic History of the Hellenistic World,* published in 1941.[11]

What then does the future hold as the Duke Data Bank nears completion? The major entry project will be finished in two to three years. Proofreading and verification must continue, and corrections to the data bank will be an unending task. Papyrological publication will continue; we know there is as much more material awaiting publication as currently exists in printed editions. These new editions will have to be entered as they appear. There will also be the necessity of caring for the existing material in whatever form it is stored. These are basically housekeeping tasks and do not pose major problems. The essential and major undertaking, that of data entry of approximately five million words, has been, or shortly will be, accomplished.

Additional refinements can continue to be added. As noted, the header lines currently contain information on date, provenience, and other editions if any. Other information can be added: current location and inventory number and the existence of photographs, etc. Also at some point the corrections or suggestions indicated in the *Berichtigungsliste*[12] can be included. The list can be extended for any useful information desired in the future.

A larger question can be posed concerning the use of the data bank: What use will be made of it and what effect will it have on the study of Graeco-Roman antiquity? First, as noted above, it will expedite the editing of texts and the understanding of them. It will replace the lexicons and word lists currently available. Thus it will speed up and make more accurate the kind of work that currently and traditionally has gone on in papyrological work. But second and beyond, one hopes that the existence of the Duke Data Bank will lead to more sophisticated and profound studies of the material on a broad basis, that it will allow papyrological evidence to be more readily integrated in the broader areas of ancient studies.

Such new approaches will first of all depend on the insight, knowledge, and skill of the individuals using the material, an asset that the computer will never replace. Nonetheless, with the data bank in existence and begging for use, techniques will have to be developed to manipulate the material. Currently the tool that comes to mind is the database management system and particularly the kind of manipulation available through the various "hypercard" systems and the like. I certainly do not know what the advances in computer technology will be or how easily these can be adapted to ancient materials. The market is not large, and commercial companies are not likely to develop products for it. Remember that Greek fonts were not available for any computers until recently. The model may well be in bibliographical database systems developed for larger fields but which can be easily adapted for the use of classicists and other students of antiquity. We would also hope that, along with the advances in technology, the computer would become increasingly user-friendly.

I would add here my own experience, although at the moment it is only work in progress. I am working on the Ptolemaic bureaucracy and have specifically selected the *Basilikos grammateus,* a key official, who has not been studied since the early part of the century. I have been using a card-file system on a Macintosh which allows me to retrieve and correlate information through any of the categories I have provided for and entered. To be sure, this is a refinement of the manual card-file system, but it is faster and more flexible. I have retrieved all the Greek material through use of the Duke Data Bank.[13] This has been a manual process. In the future I would hope that the card file could be created programmatically from the data bank. In any case the hope is that studies of the papyrological material can go beyond list-making and that the evidence of the papyri can be used to add significantly to our understanding of Greek and Roman antiquity.

Appendix I: The Origin of the Duke Data Bank of Documentary Papyri

The precise beginnings of the DDBDP were somewhat adventitious, as is probably true of a great many large research projects. The TLG itself is a case in point. In the winter of 1982, Kent Rigsby, an associate professor at Duke and then senior editor of *Greek, Roman and Byzantine Studies,* was seeking an expeditious mode of producing our journal. On leave at the Institute for Advanced Study at Princeton, he made use of the Ibycus minicomputer and the composition machinery of Steve Waite to set up an issue of the journal. Finding this process satisfactory, he began to inquire into the possibility of acquiring one of the Ibycus systems for Duke University. When David W. Packard, the creator of the Ibycus and then residing in Princeton, heard of this interest, he contacted Bill Willis and asked if Bill and I were interested, if Duke acquired an Ibycus, in undertaking to create a data bank of documentary papyri.

Bill and I did not hesitate a minute. This desideratum had long been on our minds and on the minds of papyrologists generally. We also had wanted to acquire an Ibycus system for the department of classical studies and the university. David Packard had created the first Ibycus system at the University of North Carolina at Chapel Hill, and we had envied its possession by our near neighbor for some time. Both of us saw enormous possibilities for use of the computer in papyrological studies and classical studies in general, and we had both been active in promoting such work. Willis had been one of the first supporters of the TLG and brought the support of the American Philological Association to its efforts. He served on its governing board for a lengthy period from its infancy to its maturity. In 1973 he devoted his presidential address to the American Philological Association to the possibilities of the TLG data bank of all Greek literature for classical scholarship. I had as early as 1965 discussed the possibilities of a computer data bank of the papyri with Eric Turner and others in London and subsequently with IBM and others in North America. The technology was not feasible at any reasonable cost at that point. I subsequently in 1974 and 1975 served as chair of the American Philological Association's Committee on Computer Activities and as a site visitor to the TLG for the National Endowment for the Humanities.

In addition to Bill's and my great interest, the Duke University Library possessed the necessary resources to undertake such a project. Bill and I had assembled in a dedicated room of the library all the necessary bibliographical material, all of the printed editions of documentary papyri, and the requisite reference tools. We also had a supply of graduate students in the department who would be available for data-entry purposes.

The decision to go forward was easy, especially because David Packard promised to help us with acquiring and setting up the Ibycus system materials and indicated that the David and Lucile Packard Foundation would be interested in funding its operation. The rest was not easy and involved hectic activity on a variety of fronts over the period from mid-March 1982 until the middle of July of the same year. Bill Willis and Francis Newton, then chairman of the department of classical studies, which was giving the proposed purchase and the project its unqualified support, were tireless in pursuing the goal. The first and most important step was convincing the university to purchase the equipment, an expenditure projected at $40,000. The Dean of the Faculty, Ernestine Friedl, was a key person and entirely supportive, but even this relatively small figure, previously unbudgeted and in a time of tight budgets, represented a difficulty. Many had to be persuaded of the project and the equipment. Many helped; Ted Brunner and Luci Berkowitz from the TLG came to Duke and met with the concerned persons in the administration. David Packard spent a good deal of time with them and with us. Finally in May after continuous and concerted effort by Bill Willis, Francis Newton, and me, the university agreed to go ahead.

Then came another round of feverish activity in acquiring the equipment, arranging space for it, installing the requisite wiring, etc., and finally plugging it in. Once again Bill Willis was tireless in attending to an incredible number of details. Finally in mid-July David Packard came and did the final hookup. We were almost in business. The Packard Foundation provided us with a small planning grant to cover the period from July 1982 until the first of January

1983 and then a full grant to begin on the latter date when we officially began work on the Duke Data Bank of Documentary Papyri.

Appendix II: The Checklist of Greek and Latin Papyri

The creation of the *Checklist,* which is an essential tool for the data bank, was also rather accidental. The circumstances are set out in the preface to the first edition (most conveniently found in the third edition, *Bulletin of the American Society of Papyrologists* Supplement 4 [1985]: xi–xiii.) The *Checklist* was created before and independently of the Duke Data Bank. Upon coming to Duke in 1967 I began to assemble the materials to teach papyrology to our graduate students. I discovered that the library possessed many more papyrological editions than were evident and that these were hidden in various series. Perforce I began to make lists of bibliographical data to bring these all together. To acquire other editions, either in original editions or in reprints, I also had to compile full bibliographic information for the library staff to complete orders.

By 1971 I had rather full bibliographic material on papyrus editions and made this known at the International Congress of Papyrology in Marburg that year. At the urging of a number of scholars, I began to ready it for publication and to arrange it by a preferred set of abbreviations. This last was not my choice of task, but it has been done. In 1974 the first version was published and the third edition in 1985. The *Checklist* has now become the standard reference for papyrological citation. If it had not existed in 1983 when we began the Duke Data Bank, we would have had to create it, as Luci Berkowitz had to create the invaluable tool, *Canon of Greek Authors,* to serve the TLG.

After the Marburg Congress, when I proceeded to prepare the *Checklist,* my colleague, Bill Willis, and then Roger Bagnall aided in the effort. Bagnall took charge of the second edition with the collaboration of Willis and me and with help from Klaas Worp. I again took on the third edition with the help of the same three collaborators. On this occasion I put the text into the computer and it has so remained. The most recent version can be found on PHI CD-ROM 6 current to April 5, 1991. We now keep a current version on line, updating it as necessary in connection with the DDBDP. Bill Willis has been largely responsible for the latest additions to the *Checklist.* Presumably, another print edition will be issued within the next few years, but the computer version can be provided to users on disk.

Notes

1. An earlier and shorter version of this chapter was delivered to a conference, "Sciences de Passé et Nouvelles Technologies d'Information," held at the University of

Lille, March 16, 1989, and subsequently published as "The Duke Data Bank of Documentary Papyri," in S. Cacaly and Losfeld, eds., *Sciences historiques, sciences du passe et nouvelles technologies d'information* (Lille, 1990), 253–60.

2. See Appendix I.

3. The original project coordinator was Dr. Elbert Wall. Other research associates have been Dr. Peter Witt, Dr. Stalo Monti-Puagré, and Dr. Robert Babcock. Numbers of graduate students in the departments of classical studies, history, and philosophy at Duke University have worked on data entry.

4. Currently proofreading and verification is under the charge of Dr. Peter van Minnen. His predecessors at Ann Arbor have been Dr. Randolph Stewart, Dr. Gregory Schwender, and Dr. Traianos Gagos.

5. Packard Humanities Institute, 300 Second Street, Suite 201, Los Altos, CA 94022.

6. For the Macintosh computers, the Pandora program is available from the Perseus Project, Department of Classics, 319 Boylston Hall, Harvard University, Cambridge MA 02138. For IBM computers, there is a program available from the Humanities Computing Center at the University of California in Santa Barbara. Further information may be obtained from the Thesaurus Linguae Graecae at the University of California, Irvine.

7. "Sale of a Donkey," *Bulletin of the American Society of Papyrologists* 25 (1988): 129–35.

8. G. Wagner, *Les Oasis d'Égypte à l'époque grecque, romaine, et byzantines, d'après les documents grecs,* Institut Français d'Archéologie Orientale du Caire, Bibliothèque d'Étude, no. 100 (Cairo, 1987).

9. M. I. Finley, The Ancient Economy (Berkeley, 1973).

10. Cf. James G. Keenan's survey of recent work on Roman Egypt, "Papyrology and Roman History, 1956-1980," *Classical World* 76 (1982): 23–31, esp. 23 (introductory remarks). For an overall view and some tentative approaches, see the double number of the *Bulletin of the American Society of Papyrologists* 26, nos. 3–4 (1989), printing the papers read at a symposium, "Comparative Approaches to the Social History of Roman Egypt," held at the annual meetings of the American Philological Association in Boston in December 1989.

11. See the additional survey of work in Roger S. Bagnall, "Papyrology and Ptolemaic History, 1956–1980," *Classical World* 76 (1982): 13–21.

12. Currently published in Leiden under the direction of P. W. Pestman and H. A. Rupprecht. Volume 8 is promised shortly, and there is an index to vols. 1–7.

13. I am also dealing with the demotic material which is essential for a study of the *Basilikos grammateus* or "scribe of Pharaoh." The Demotic Dictionary Project at the Oriental Institute of the University of Chicago, also computer related, will help with this aspect, but I have not yet taken advantage of its resources.

4

The Computer Index of the U.S. Center of the *Lexicon Iconographicum Mythologiae Classicae*

Jocelyn Penny Small

In the beginning there was no computer.[1] The *Lexicon Iconographicum Mythologiae Classicae* (*LIMC*) was organized by Prof. Lilly Kahil in the early 1970s as an international project to produce a pictorial dictionary of classical mythology (ca. 800 B.C.–A.D. 400). It follows its predecessor, Roscher's *Mythologische Lexikon* (1884–1937), in being organized alphabetically by the name of hero or divinity but differs in its emphasis on the visual representations, which are published in a separate companion volume to each volume of text. The U.S. Center (*US-LIMC*) was established in 1973 at Rutgers University. Its immediate aim was to provide the scholars writing entries with photographic and descriptive documentation of the classical antiquities in American collections.[2] Everything was done manually. By "everything" I mean absolutely everything from ordering photographs to recording the information about objects to anything involving words.

Early Efforts at Computerization

The first attempts at computerization were fairly typical of the period, with the two poles of scholarly opinion on the subject represented by the executive director and various members of the Executive and Advisory Committees. Computers were wonderful and needed only occasional attention or were not worthy of more than that amount of attention. No matter which view was espoused, only casual advice was considered necessary. The mainframe IBM program Text-Pac was used for about six years to record approximately two thousand objects on keypunch cards.

I became director in 1976 and had nothing to do with the work being done on the computer until the fall of 1978, when the executive director was on sabbatical. It was then that I first really looked at the computer printouts and realized that they suffered from basic misunderstandings of our material. A series of meetings with the staff of the university's computer center were not terribly fruitful, in part because university computer centers are woefully undermanned; and even today one is lucky if there is a single person responsible for all humanities. The following fall (1979) we hired a New World archaeologist in my department with extensive computer experience. After the first week of discussions he told me that our needs were by no means simple. I responded that I was glad we had provided a challenge. The following week he informed me we had "messy data." I told him that the whole point was to preserve the mess. In a number of day-long sessions, three of the computer illiterati (classical archaeologists) worked with him on developing a stripped-down grammar (syntactic parser) to encode the figured representations. Remember this was the era of the mainframe and the minicomputer. It slowly became clear that computerizing a manual catalogue system is not a simple task that can be done in one's spare time. It is not only a full-time job, but also, as I now know, a continuing full-time job. The other lesson I learned then was that I was right to be wary of those offering quick fixes. The anthropologist was the first person I had met who did not begin with a purported solution, but wanted to know first what the nature of our material was and then what we expected to retrieve from a computerized system. There are no shortcuts. As a result, for the next four years we abandoned computers and concentrated on completing the survey of American collections for the *LIMC,* which was the Center's original and primary purpose.[3]

Revelation

By 1984–85 the world of computers had changed drastically. No longer were mini- and mainframe computers the only possibilities. No longer did we need to develop a syntactic parser, as discussed in 1979–80. We could use an off-the-shelf database program. Since the other national centers of the project and the *US-LIMC* agreed to use IBM PCs, we chose a database program for that machine called, perhaps appropriately, *Revelation.*[4] After my previous experience, my first question in seeking a database program was, "What do I have to do to get all of my data out of your program and into another, when I realize I have made a mistake?" After that, three capabilities were and continue to be paramount. First, the *US-LIMC* material ranges from a simple statue or gem with a single figure to many-figured objects like Roman sarcophagi and South Italian vases. Thus I had to have variable length storage. Second, scenes with numerous participants, as well as other types of information like the material an object is made of, work best in a system with repeating or multi-valued fields. That is, rather than storing the information as a string ("Priamos, Hekabe, Achilleus, Hektor, etc."), each item within that string is treated as a separate entity that can be separately retrieved and sorted into appropriate alphabetical order (fig. 4.4).[5] Moreover, any given entity can be linked to modifying information. Thus Achilleus' shield with a triskeles as its device is never confused with the undecorated Boeotian shield of Automedon. Third, the program had to have a *full* programming language so that someone — not me — could write a way out of the program's limitations. Revelation stores its data in ASCII, has up to 64kb per record (a luxurious size I have not exceeded), allows for linked multi-valued fields, and comes with a highly praised version of BASIC. The program proved far more capable than anticipated and was sufficiently, but just sufficiently, user friendly to allow me to do most of the work of designing and setting up the database.[6] I attended a three-day training course in the program — a novel experience — and hired its teacher for certain customizations. I still hire him for various programming tasks that are beyond my capabilities.

I spent a year experimenting with various designs, and I cannot stress enough the importance of allowing enough time at this stage (figs. 4.1–4). A database is an artificial construct that has less connection to the original catalogue card

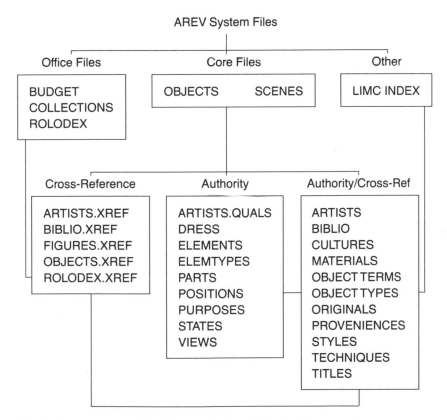

4.1. Database structure of the Computer Index of Classical Iconography.

```
US NUMBER:              13

CITY:                   Boston
COLLECTION:             Museum of Fine Arts
INVENTORY NUMBER:       63.473
EX COLLECTION:

DISCOVERY DATE:
PROVENIENCE:
FINDSPOT:

OBJECT:                 Vase
TYPE:                   Hydria
  SUB-TYPE:
PURPOSE:

CONDITION:              Intact
DIMENSIONS:             H — 0.496
MATERIAL:               Clay              TYPE:

CULTURE:                Greek
REGION:                 Attica
SITE:
TECHNIQUE:              Black-Figure
STYLE:                  Attic
ARTIST:                 Leagros Group     BASIS:   Beazley

ORIGINAL:

DATE:                   520 BC–510 BC     BASIS:

INSCRIPTIONS:           Body:   GK: EKTRWR PATROKLW :GK

DECORATION:

REMARKS:

BIBLIOGRAPHY:           Para              164 No. 31 bis
                        CVA USA 19        24–25; pl. 82
                        Addenda           47
                        LIMC 1            139 Achilleus 586
                        BosTrojWar        No. 26
                        Vermeule 1965a    35–52, fig. 1, 13
DATE ISSUED:            09-22-89
```

4.2. Objects record.

than a word-processed document to a typewritten manuscript. Converting continuous text into machine-readable form, as the Thesaurus Linguae Graecae has done, presents not just different but in some ways simpler intellectual issues. A text exists. One may not like a particular reading, but that reading exists as a printed interpretation or version. A person or committee can decide on which edition to use and then has that fixed entity to follow slavishly. The *US-LIMC* material has to be constantly interpreted, because cataloging visual images means describing them in verbal terms anew every time. It quickly became apparent that no standard descriptions exist for the variety of objects that range from earrings to textiles to vases to censers to architectural sculpture, that date from 800 B.C. to A.D. 400, and that come from any part of the classical world in any material with a varying number of scenes.

Take a simple example. What is the difference between a statuette and a figurine? When I was asked this by a colleague faced with similar problems at the Getty Photo Archive, I quipped, "A figurine is something advertised in the *New Yorker*?" Quips may be good for informal conversations, but I needed something more concrete. Dictionaries define figurine and statuette in terms of each other. Finding no help there, I then examined scholarly usage in classical art. Note the emphasis on "classical," because art historians of the post Antique often use the same terms differently or even different terms. I managed to find a colleague who had used both words in a publication. We discussed the matter and came to the conclusion that my quip was right: figurine is used pejoratively by classical archaeologists to refer to statuettes of less than stellar quality. In a situation where one has to make all too many judgments, I had decided that we should avoid as many qualitative ones as possible. All our figurines are statuettes with, and this is very important, a record in a linked file where "figurine" is entered as a synonym. Multiply this one example by all the information we have to record and you will get some idea of the magnitude of what we faced and continue to face.

If I can allow for synonyms, why go through all this trouble for all those terms? Someone has to determine first which terms are indeed synonyms and under what conditions. For example, "clay" and "terracotta" are not truly synonymous. "Terracotta" is fired clay, which means that any object made of terracotta is obviously made of clay, but not the reverse. Yet scholarly usage is maddening. Scholars tend to refer to vases of fired clay as clay, not terracotta, while statuettes of the same fired clay are made of terracotta and even sometimes called "terracottas." Never is a vase called a "clay." Do keep in mind that I have discussed only English and that the *US-LIMC* is part of an international project with entries in French, German, and Italian. I pass over problems like the occasional misapplication of ancient names by modern scholars to objects.[7] Another nice twist to the vocabulary screw is culture. If a vase is called a phiale in Greek and a patera in Latin, should phiale be used for Greek objects

US NUMBER:	13
SCENE NUMBER:	13-B1
CITY:	Boston
COLLECTION:	Museum of Fine Arts
INVENTORY NUMBER:	63.473
PHOTOGRAPH(S):	MusPh
VIEW:	Front
PART:	Body
POSITION:	
TITLE:	Achilleus Dragging Hektor
DESCRIPTION:	At far left, standing to face right, underneath an architrave supported by a Doric column, are Priamos (white hair and beard, himation) with a staff in his left hand, his right hand outstretched, and — in the background by his side — Hekabe, tearing her hair in mourning. Ahead of them Achilleus (short chiton, greaves, Corinthian helmet, two spears, shield-device, in white, triskeles) mounts his chariot to right, with a backward glance. Below, bound by the heels to the chariot-box, is the body of Hektor (nude, bearded, identifying inscription). Standing in the box and facing right, the reins in his hands, is Achilleus' charioteer, Automedon (short chiton, corslet, greaves, Corinthian helmet, sword, spear, Boeotian shield-device in white, wreath). Running up to him from right is Iris (chiton, himation, necklace), her hands raised in excitement. In the background at far right, partly concealed by the horses, is the white tomb which carries the inscription, Patroklos. Flying forth from it is a winged eidolon of Patroklos (short chiton, animal skin, greaves, Corinthian helmet, spear, shield-device, in white, six balls). Coiled at the base of the tomb is a bearded snake, looking left. Vine above tomb.
OTHER TITLES:	
REMARKS:	
DATE ISSUED:	09-22-89

4.3. Scenes record

and patera for Roman ones? What do you then do with Etruscan examples of precisely the same shape, but for which we do not know the Etruscan term?[8]

Sometimes the object itself presents a problem. If you have a fragment of an object (e.g., an amphora), do you catalogue it as a fragment (lid) or as the object (amphora) with a notation under condition that it is fragmentary? The solution to this question is not easy. What happens when you have a leg which could be from a table or a *kline*? Furthermore, no matter how hard one tries, words and terms will be omitted. When I made up my original lists for just the terms for the objects themselves, I left out "incense shovel." In fact, every controlled field needs an entry for "Problem," which can then be explained in a "Remarks" field.

SCENE NO. 13-B1: Achilleus Dragging Hektor

SCENES	NO.	ELEMENTS	TYPE	DRESS/ATTRIBUTE
13-B1	1	Porch	Doric	
	2	Priamos	Clad	Beard; Himation; Staff
	3	Hekabe	Clad	
	4	Achilleus	Warrior	Chiton, Short; Greaves; Helmet, Corinthian; Spears; Shield, Triskeles
	5	Hektor	Nude	Beard; Inscription
	6	Automedon	Warrior	Beard; Chiton, Short; Cuirass; Greaves; Helmet, Corinthian; Sword; Shield, Boeotian, Beads; Goad; Reins
	7	Chariot	Quadriga	
	8	Iris	Clad	Chiton; Himation; Necklace; Wingless
	9	Eidolon/ Patroklos	Warrior	Chiton, Short; Skin; Helmet, Corinthian; Shield, Balls; Spear
	10	Tomb	Omphalos	Inscription, Patroklos
	11	Snake		Beard
	12	Vine		

4.4. Scenes record: The "grid."

Second, the advantage of databases over free text is precisely their use of controlled vocabulary. If someone "normalizes" usage, it is much easier to get full sets of data in answer to queries. Clearly the "normalizer" has to know what he/she is doing so that information is not lost or problems smoothed over. Hardly an object can be entered without some judgment call being made at some point in the cataloging process. Moreover, the scruffier the piece, the harder it is to decide whether a round object in a scene is a ball, a piece of fruit, or, that wonderful archaeological invention, a "foodstuff." At this point one of the most important lessons of designing a database should be apparent: there is no such thing as an objective database. Everything is subjective, although some databases can be more objective than others. The conversion of *L'Année Philologique* into machine-readable form has far fewer problems of this nature than my project because it is working from words that have a fixed version in printed volumes.

If controlling the vocabulary does not seem sufficiently nightmarish, then consider the actual design or structure of the database. To be useful, it must reflect the way archaeologists think about and organize their information. The degree of detail needed and the way it is arranged differ for the classical historian, the literary scholar, and the art historian, to name just three possibly interested parties. For instance, the classical art historian is very much interested in representations of the Trojan Cycle — a category often too broad for the classicist. Furthermore, certain common usages, which work as individual units, imply categories (fields) that must be specified. For example, "Attic red-figure" requires four fields: Culture (Greek), Style (Attic), Technique (Red-Figure), and Material (Clay).

At the same time a balance has to be struck between what is reasonable to record and what can be omitted. While everything is indubitably of potential interest to someone somewhere sometime, budgetary and even intellectual constraints place real limits on the amount of detail included. The *US-LIMC* does not do pose, which I believe will be best captured in machine form through pattern analysis of digitized pictures. It does, however, do a more detailed analysis of the components of a scene than any other project I know. Instead of recording just the title of a scene, all of its elements (figures, structures, objects, flora, fauna, etc.) are listed with their "attributes" (figs. 4.3 and 4.4). As a result the *US-LIMC* can tell you what vases Dionysos holds in what scenes on which objects.[9]

The other unusual and notable component in the *US-LIMC* database is the use of classification files. Originally these files began as fairly ordinary authority files to control vocabulary (use "Clay" not "Terracotta"), but they have evolved into a very powerful search tool. Unlike most authority files, the *US-LIMC* ones record information that is "informational." For example, the fact that "Achilleus Dragging Hektor" occurs in the *Iliad,* which, in turn, is part of the Trojan Cycle, is hierarchical, but that it takes place at Troy is not.

Similarly, that Myron is Greek and a Sculptor is informational. It tells one about Myron, but the bits of information do not necessarily imply each other. The use of these classification files enables us to answer questions like "all objects from Umbria" or "all titles of scenes with women in Greek art between 600 B.C.–400 B.C."

Because the entire system is modular, each classification file can be produced separately without touching the data in the Objects and Scenes files, provided that the most specific information has always been recorded. That is, if an object is found in Gela, Gela, not Sicily, is entered in the Objects record. Later in the Proveniences file a record can be added to note that Gela is in Sicily which is in Italy. In fact, these files can be added to existing data from other sources to improve dramatically their retrieval of data. In a test of *L'Année Philologique* material all references to the Trojan Cycle could be found, although the "Trojan Cycle" appeared nowhere in the L'Année Philologique record.[10]

Advanced Revelation

I do not make up these names. *Advanced Revelation,* a major upgrade to old, run-of-the-mill *Revelation,* appeared in 1987. While I would not dream of going back to the old version, the period of acclimation was longer and far more arduous than it should have been. They changed many of the commands and all the keyboard assignments with the result that during the period of transition, which took several months, I was often in a state of near paralysis. Delights such as these were and are constant. The end result, however, is a system that enables one to follow one's train of thought through a succession of screens or windows. For example, you can get all objects by the Providence Painter, note that one of them comes from Capua, find out where Capua is, see what other objects we have from there, find a particular one by Brygos, and then look at its scenes.

In addition, pop-ups with choices, definitions, and the like make everyone's life easier. For instance, each file has a field for bibliographical references (and a separate field for the precise citation) with the abbreviation spell-checked by the Bibliographical file. If you cannot remember how a particular work by Beazley or a book or article with Etruscan somewhere in the title is abbreviated, press F2 for a pop-up. You curse (the verb for using the cursor?) to the appropriate field (Last Name, etc.), type in the information you want, press F9, and instantaneously the possible choices appear. Choose the one you want by pressing 'Enter' when on it and that is all. In fact, it takes longer to describe than to do. The only problem was that it took me a year to realize that you could use the indexes of any file within any other file as many times and in as many ways as you like. Nothing in the documentation said you couldn't. Nothing in the documentation, however, said you could.

ENTRY NO.	13323 VOLUME 1 LIMC NAME Aias I NO. 49
PHOTOGRAPH	
PH. SOURCE	
CITY	Athens
COLLECTION	Agora Museum
MUSEUM NO.	AP1044
CULTURE	Greek
OBJECT	Vase
OBJECT-TYPE	Krater Cal
MAT/TYPE	ABF
PROVENIENCE	Athens, Agora
DATE	530 BC–520 BC
ARTIST	Exekias
REMARKS	

4.5. Index to *LIMC*.

Today

In 1988 we completed the task of converting the typed catalogue cards into machine-readable form. Now all new cataloging is done directly on the machine to save time and reduce errors. We are again making study trips to collections, which in the United States have been extremely active. In addition, we have indexed the first three volumes of the printed *LIMC,* although not in the same kind of detail as for the *US-LIMC* material (fig. 4.5).[11] That file will eventually be fully integrated into the *US-LIMC* system so that even its simple index can be enhanced to give all objects, e.g., "from Etruria" or "with women."[12] We have, including indexing files, somewhere between 65,000 and 80,000 records systemwide.[13]

   With the system up and running for four years, what do I, its creator, do now? Too much. I never anticipated that the amount of time I would spend just on system problems would remain a constant. Either some new software or upgrade appears and has to be installed and coordinated with all the other programs, or the hardware needs to be upgraded. I pass over the time spent deciding which type of machine, part, or software is necessary, then determining which specific brand and where to buy it. At the same time both the assistant director and I have not lost our rosy-eyed view of computers, which means that we expect them to produce what we want the way we want it. That takes time, because our demands seem to be increasing. One of this year's accomplishments enables us to list our bibliographical references with multiple authors, no authors, articles, etc., by merely entering "List Biblio."

Another task that never ceases is minding one's words. As more data accumulates, it frequently becomes clear that whole classes of information need to be reconsidered and their vocabulary cleaned up. More classification files are added and have to be added to. The data itself are always in flux. New objects are entered; new interpretations are recorded.

We now have enough data to answer queries. That almost everyone so far wants our information in hard copy offers not just a sad commentary on the state of computerization among archaeologists, but, I believe, a reflection of the conceptual problems that databases present to the average scholar. At first we used to give just a selection of the fields we record, but we found that we spent more time trying to squeeze information into an 8 1/2″ wide format than if we just gave the full record. This method also works better for the inquirer, since frequently they are unsure of what we record or do not really know what they want until they see it. We can also produce machine-readable records in ASCII for those who want to use their word processor. While the program has an easy conversion into *dBase* and *Lotus 1-2-3,* the results are less satisfactory, because *Advanced Revelation* has two capabilities that cannot be transferred into either program: variable length storage and repeating fields. We are currently experimenting with making the full set of data available at a few test sites, but the problems of easy use are not simple to solve (see the next section). At the moment, since the queries we currently receive are one-time questions for specific projects with narrow definitions, it is simpler and cheaper for the scholars to have us perform the searches. Our information is available at cost, and we very much welcome queries.[14]

Because computerized information can be easily changed, our data can always be kept up-to-date. This malleability, however, comes with a negative side. What can be altered simply by us can be altered simply by anybody. The *US-LIMC*'s policy is that only data received directly from the *US-LIMC* has any guarantee. If you get a copy of our information from someone else, it is at your own risk.[15] We hope that by pricing our information reasonably enough that it will be more worthwhile to buy the most-up-to-date version from us. While someone out there is bound to be less than scrupulous, I think that the ability to manipulate information is far more important than trying to copy protect our data or to give only printouts, which can, in any case, be either scanned or even, good grief, retyped into a database. In fact, I assume that as scholars become more database literate, more will want to be able to work with our data directly or even to use it as a base for adding their own information. As long as the *US-LIMC* data are treated like any other copyrighted information, we foresee no problems.

The Future

The *US-LIMC* database is just one small part of what should be available in the Completely Computerized Scholarly Emporium. Everything, absolutely everything, should be available on-line and work together with one search engine for both text and structured data, as well as for all disparate projects. Although the computer companies, both hard and soft, seem to be doing their best to prevent any such coordination, a number of us in charge of various classical projects are doing our best to get around such problems. To give an idea of the magnitude of producing such a system, both myself and everyone I have discussed the matter with sees it as a three-year project to make a friendly interface for just my database. But it will all come.

As an example, if you get a reference from *L'Année Philologique,* you should be able to call up the full text immediately, and, in turn, to find the objects and texts it discusses in the *US-LIMC* database or the TLG respectively. Photographs should be digitized so that they can be manipulated and themselves searched for patterns.[16] Plans of sites should also be available, not just with findspots and buildings noted but also with links to databases so that you can get an idea of the change in sites over the centuries. These plans should change dynamically, as different dates are requested. Complete assemblages of sites should be possible no matter what the modern dispersal of the objects may be. Moreover, the idea of classification files that the *US-LIMC* has developed needs to be vastly expanded and coordinated across all aspects of classical studies. For example, the same mythological module could retrieve all Greek objects with scenes from the Trojan Cycle, as well the references from the TLG and *L'Année Philologique.*

Having control of such vast amounts of information will inevitably affect scholarship, because different kinds of questions will be capable of being reasonably answered. I do not think that I can in any way anticipate all the possibilities. I can only try to insure that the system I build now is made as flexible as possible so that it will form a good base for the future.

Conclusion?

The question mark is intentional. There is no conclusion. Databases are like Heraclitus' stream. You never step twice into the same system. Either the design has changed or data are added. I do, however, have some more general observations.

It should be clear that no stage is without its unexpected problems. I have tried to show that, unlike Zeus giving birth to Athena, I did not immediately produce a perfect system. It still needs and will continue to need adjustments. Computerization is a full-time job — a fact that is only slowly being realized. Computerization is a full-time job not just to set up the system and add the bulk of the data, but to maintain that system. Maintenance consists not just of adding new information but of keeping both the hardware and software up-to-date. You cannot fall too far behind current developments, because you may then be stuck with a wonderful trove of data that cannot be used on any system. It is also easier to upgrade in smaller rather than larger increments. At the same time magnetic media die. Tapes and disks have to be "refreshed" by being transferred to fresh media.[17] I am most concerned that universities, libraries, and funding organizations realize what such maintenance involves. Computerized information is not like a book that needs only storage space and no "manipulation" other than dusting over the centuries.

Finally, a plea to you. Use these new tools. The more users, the more likely we are to continue. Tell us what is wrong, so we can make corrections not just of data, but of design. Just as important, tell us what we are doing right. The more you tell the designers, the better the tools will become and the more you will benefit. Face the issues, be it of costs, data corruption and misuse, or new modes of working. No matter what, be patient. Remember Rome was not built in a day.[18]

Notes

1. The early history of the computerization of the project is described more fully in "The NEH and Research Data Bases: A Classical Experiment," in T. F. Moberg, ed., *Databases in the Humanities and Social Sciences 1985* 3 (1987): 467–69, which in some parts is reproduced verbatim here for the very good reason that the past history of the project has not changed since I wrote that article. See Bibliography for my publications on the computerization.

2. The *US-LIMC* is especially grateful to the National Endowment for the Humanities, Research Tools, and Rutgers University for their extremely generous, continuing support. In addition it is a pleasure to acknowledge the assistance, in chronological order, of the Andrew W. Mellon Foundation, the Getty Trust, the Lucile and David Packard Foundation, and the Kress Foundation, as well as a number of private donors.

3. When I first came to the project in 1976, I thought we could record everything within a reasonable amount of time. As time passed, I realized not only the extent geographically and numerically of the major American collections, but also that there was hardly a college without a museum without a donation of some Greek pot or Roman lamp.

4. The program was originally produced by Cosmos, Inc., which was bought and renamed Revelation Technologies, Inc. All of the programs I considered belonged to the category called "relational," which has both restricted and loose definitions that depend on the user and context. The narrow definition refers to the way the fields can be mathematically "related," that is, work together in retrieving information. The looser definition indicates a database that contains more than one file or table that work together. The basic idea is to streamline entry, storage, and retrieval by not repeating information. If Chiusi is in Etruria, enter it once and not in every record for every object found in Chiusi. Then, if modern Tuscany secedes from Italy, only one record

need be changed. For issues of designing a database, see, among others, *How to Choose a Database* in the Bibliography.

5. The *US-LIMC* uses the orthography of the publication for the names of its figures — the only ready-made standard we have.

6. I have a love-hate relationship with the program. The hate primarily arises from the abysmal quality of the documentation. E.g., in the main index to the six volumes of opaque verbiage accompanying the ten 360kb diskettes there is no reference to "back up." When I asked why, I was told that "back up" was not one of their terms and so obviously need not be indexed. The love comes from the incredibly consistent design of the program that uses the same format not just for the files you create, but for their system files, and also from a number of features simply not available or as easy to use in other database programs.

7. For example, *askos* means "wineskin" in Greek, but is used today for "flat round flasks with oblique round-mouthed spouts and an arched handle." J. Boardman, *Classical Review* n.s. 29 (1975): 119. For fuller discussion, see J. Boardman, *Athenian Black Figure Vases* (London 1974), 191–92.

8. Our solution for all problems of this type is to use the Greek term in conjunction with the field "Culture" to control who produced the object. Obviously, when a Greek term does not exist, we use a Latin, Etruscan, or modern term, depending on the situation. This solution has three advantages: simplicity of entry; consistency; and the ability to search more easily for all of anything, while still not losing the culture. For example, all representations of Athena can be found with one question on one field (Figure in the Scenes file), but if one wants only Etruscan examples then one also searches for "Culture equal 'Etruscan'" in the Objects file. This kind of two-file search is easily accomplished in *Advanced Revelation*.

9. It may be of interest that a very large number of ancient representations do not lend themselves to easy titling, which has implications for the way classical artists conceived of their representations — a research project on which I am now working.

10. The two projects are naturally cooperating. See Bibliography for a list of articles where I discuss this aspect in more detail.

11. The primary reason for the more limited recording rests in the nature of the catalogue entries themselves, which focus, as to be expected in a dictionary about figures, on just the segments with the figures. To do a full analytical cataloging requires either the object itself or a full set of photographs.

12. Integration consists of tasks like taking the current usage of "ABF," similar to "Attic red-figure" discussed in the text, and entering it by its component parts rather than as a single term.

13. In *Advanced Revelation* the number of records is limited only by the storage system. Last year the biggest application they knew of was Helsinki Hair Tonic with, I believe, 1.5 million records.

14. As a guideline, current prices, subject to change, are: $12.00 for doing the search, postage and handling; $5.00 for a diskette; and $0.10 a page no matter what is on the page (list, catalogue entry, or xerox of a photograph).

15. There is probably more of a problem of someone making minor changes, forgetting that he/she did so, and inadvertently passing that version onto a colleague as the "real" *US-LIMC data*. Caveat emptor. One, perhaps, unexpected benefit of direct purchase is that it is a way of directly registering your support of the *US-LIMC,* which is

crucial for continued funding. Remember that your costs can be covered by a research grant, or, failing that, are tax deductible.

16. This is a major topic in itself. Manipulation of photographs, like that of data, also lends itself to gross abuse, but can produce wonderful results. Visual pattern matching, I believe, will be a solution to many problems like pose or migration of motifs over time and across cultures.

17. While those who purvey CDs as records claim a lifetime of listening pleasure, those who sell CD-ROMs say that they will probably last about fifteen years. As a result, with regard to my record collection, I have often wondered whether this means I have fifteen years to live, although I am trying to hedge that one by continuously buying CDs.

18. Addendum, February 1993: *The US-LIMC* is currently working on a user-friendly version of the U.S. Database for formal release in 1994. It is no small matter to design a simple interface that masks the complexity of the arrangement of the data and, indeed, of the subject matter. The most important rule to keep in mind is that users want information, not functions. You buy a hammer not for its beauty, but to pound nails. You use a computer database not for its arcane design, but for its data. While the initial-release version will run on IBM clones, we are currently considering porting to the Macintosh and running as an independent database on the Internet. None of these possibilities is mutually exclusive. Stay tuned.

5

AMPHORAS
Computer-Assisted Study of Ancient Wine Jars

Carolyn G. Koehler and Philippa M. W. Matheson

Capturing significant facts about the trade and economic history of the ancient Greeks cannot be done from literary sources alone; "the economy" was not a concept that Greeks articulated when discussing the elements central to the functioning of their society, and intellectuals such as Thucydides, Plato, and Aristotle generally ignored most issues connected with commerce as being beneath their consideration. Although a certain amount of evidence can be pried out of writers like Demosthenes and Xenophon, they fail to define the scope of the numerous transactions conducted over centuries by Greek city-states from Massalia on the Rhône to Naukratis in Egypt to Sinope on the Black Sea. Laws and decrees inscribed on stone and records preserved on papyri add details here and there, but our best source of information is archaeological, and of a very specific sort: finds of the large clay jars used throughout the Mediterranean for shipping in bulk an array of goods, including wine and oil, processed fish, nuts, honey, pigments, and pitch. These transport amphoras, as they are known to archaeologists, are large, undecorated, two-handled vessels with a neck sufficiently narrow for stoppering and a pointed lower body designed for convenient stowing on shipboard and for maneuverability on land. While their capacity ranged from 4 to over 40 liters, most commonly they held 25 to 30 liters.[1]

Jars of this sort, which first appeared in Canaan and Egypt before 1900 B.C., proved so efficient that they remained the primary shipping container in the ancient world for three millennia.[2] A number of Greek city-states each manufactured amphoras in a variant of this general shape, by which the point of origin (and often, by extension, the contents) would have been recognized. Scholars can now identify the place of manufacture for amphoras that transported, for instance, wine from Rhodes, Knidos, Thasos, Kos, and Chios; oil from Samos; and dried fish from the Atlantic coast of North Africa (fig. 5.1).

5.1. Study collection of transport amphoras from the Agora Excavations of the American School of Classical Studies at Athens, in the basement of the Stoa of Attalos. Jars are arranged by classes in chronological order (*top row,* jars from Lesbos; *center,* from Mende; *bottom,* from Thasos). Photograph by Craig Mauzy.

Hundreds of thousands of such jars belonged to cargoes moving in and out of every port, and they are ubiquitous at excavation sites both on land and under water throughout the Mediterranean and the Near East.

Most obviously, the remains of these transport amphoras serve as an index of ancient trade. Before they can be so used, however, they must be dated, and in turn their initial aid to the excavator lies in the dating of archaeological contexts. For many series of jars, the handles were stamped before firing with

a   *b*

5.2. (*a*) The stamp on a Rhodian amphora handle found in the excavations of the Athenian Agor (SS2148), dated by name of the magistrate (Αριστογιδαω) to ca. 222 B.C. and showing the same rose symbol as appears on (*b*), a coin of Rhodes (private collection).

pictorial devices and/or the names of the potter and an official of the state (figs. 5.2*a* and *b*). Such stamps reflect a degree of control over the production of the jars (perhaps guaranteeing a certain capacity, within tolerances) and, to at least some extent, the interest of the state in export commodities. They also enable specialists, of whom Virginia R. Grace of the American School of Classical Studies at Athens is preeminent, to work out chronological lists of magistrates from groups of amphora stamps excavated in contexts that have been independently dated. Over several decades at the Agora Excavations of the American School of Classical Studies, Dr. Grace has amassed an archive on Greek amphoras and their stamps that is recognized as the most complete in the world. In establishing dated sequences for the officials of Rhodes, Knidos, and other states, Dr. Grace has turned these ancient containers into a vital dating tool. Her chronology for the eponymous priests of Halios on Rhodes, whose annual terms formed the basis for official record-keeping, and whose names appear on amphoras manufactured in Rhodes during the third through first centuries B.C., dates the terms of office of the majority of these officials to within five years, many to the exact year — a precision not even numismatic evidence can yield.[3]

Hellenistic contexts dated in this fashion by amphora stamps have made possible the analysis of many kinds of archaeological finds, such as the mouldmade bowls with relief decoration found in the Athenian Agora.[4] Because this tableware is common at so many sites, and the workshops in which it was made can be identified through the style and even the moulds linking individual examples, dating the evolution of this popular pottery by means of stamped handles has expanded our knowledge of another aspect of the manufacture and export of ceramics in the Hellenistic period.

Even when amphoras are not stamped, they provide help in dating other material because of gradual changes in the shape of jars within a series. George

Bass, excavator of the eleventh-century A.D. shipwreck at Serçe Limani, Turkey, got his first indication of the date of its now famous cargo from the amphoras on board, which Dr. Grace was able to match with similar pieces from Byzantine contexts at the Athenian Agora.[5]

The study of amphoras has broad implications for social and political history. For instance, amphora stamps provide us with the names and dates of the Rhodian priests of Halios during the time Rhodes was one of the wealthiest and most powerful cities in the Mediterranean. Elsewhere, the 885 Rhodian and the 382 Knidian plus the six Sinopean handles in the construction filling of the Middle Stoa in the Athenian Agora together posit a date of ca. 183 B.C. for that building which flanks the south side of the marketplace. This date led Virginia Grace to suggest that the Stoa was a royal donation made by Pharnakes of Pontus, who ruled a kingdom on the Black Sea that controlled important centers of the grain trade and was thanked in an Athenian inscription for benefactions to the city, and who may have intended the Stoa as a municipal granary.[6] In another case, Knidian amphoras help throw light on the problem of the occupation of ancient Corinth in the "period of abandonment" between its destruction at the hands of the Roman general Mummius in 146 B.C. and its re-founding as a Roman colony under Julius Caesar in 44 B.C. At Corinth enough Knidian handles from that century have been discovered to suggest an unexpected level of occupation before the site's official renewal. A thorough analysis of their dates is under way.[7]

Amphoras have long been recognized as the sine qua non for studying the history of ancient commerce and trade since they supply qualitative and quantitative information about the movement of commodities such as oil, wine, and preserved fish throughout the ancient world. An outline of exports and imports can be drawn for individual sites, as is now being done, for example, for ancient Corinth, one of the great emporia of Greece from the eighth century B.C. until the Roman sack. Jars made at Corinth itself and at its colony of Corcyra constitute the greatest percentage of amphora finds there before the middle of the third century (and showed a healthy export to the west). After that, according to the stamped handles, Knidian and Rhodian imports of wine, in roughly equal proportion, took over the market but faced strong competition from Italian shippers of the Roman republic. At Athens, by contrast, where the Roman army did not strike until 86 B.C., the stamped handles are 62 percent Knidian and 23 percent Rhodian; deposits like the Middle Stoa Building Fill reveal that, although Rhodian wine was chiefly imported in the third and early second centuries, Knidian vintages were increasingly consumed thereafter. By the second half of the second century B.C., wine shipments from Rhodes to Athens were few and far between.[8]

Rhodian amphoras traveled widely and in huge quantity; such exports, correlated geographically and chronologically, are beginning to show patterns of trade between many cities in ancient Greece and their neighbors. Large collec-

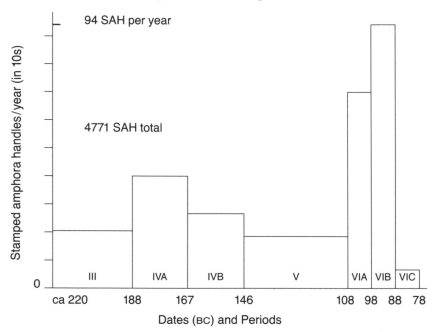

Knidian Imports into the Agora at Athens

5.3. Classification of stamped amphora handles from Knidian jars found at the Agora Excavations in Athens. The Roman numerals show the periods for Knidian amphoras assigned by V. P. Grace (see note 3). Only "datable" stamps are included; the figures therefore represent only relative imports and cannot be reliably converted into actual trade totals; however, the relatively low rate of import in Period V (146–108 B.C.) as opposed to earlier and later periods gives an indication of Athens' depressed economic condition, particularly when these figures are compared with the total *exports* of datable Knidian jars in this period, which shows a much higher volume of production in Period V than in Period III, and much more similar quantities of jars made in Periods IVA, IVB, and V.

tions, such as that in the Musée Gréco-Romain in Alexandria, which stores over 100,000 stamped handles, provide solid information about trade (once the work of recording and identifying has been completed, no mean task). However, the proportions of amphoras from the various different manufacturers found at any site, even quite small ones, can tell us much about the site's commercial connections, as, for instance, at the City of David in Jerusalem, where the preponderance of Rhodian amphoras was striking;[9] at larger sites the chronological breakdown of the import pattern of a given type of container can also give important evidence about economic factors affecting the site, as in the case of the Knidian wine import at Athens (fig. 5.3).

None of these studies, nor many others recently carried out by a variety of scholars pursuing questions of ancient history, sociology, economics, and trade, could have succeeded without the evidence from amphoras and their stamps. Amphoras can be related to a wide range of subjects, and the information they give has a ripple effect upon scholarship. By fixing chronological points of reference for a single excavation or type of jar, they document a significant segment of the imports and exports of a particular city or region. These studies can then provide the framework for examination of trade in larger scope, and help synthesize patterns of economic supply and demand and of socio-political structures promoting the growth of enterprise. With the creation of her unique archive, Virginia Grace has established the chronology for many series of amphoras and published a number of such studies since 1934, most in the last 35 years. At the same time, she has continually responded to the questions about Greek amphoras and related problems that have come from scholars all over the world, and scholarship has gained a double value in the exchange of information with a central office. New material keeps adding to the general pool, sometimes bringing more stratigraphical contexts, and expanding the data on which quantitative studies are based. By now, however, the workload in the Stamped Amphora Handle Department at the Agora has become overwhelming, as amphora finds continue to increase year by year; and as economic questions become a focus of intense interest for students of the ancient world, the number and complexity of inquiries are correspondingly greater. To incorporate new examples, and to deal effectively with the influx of requests for information, computerization became essential.[10]

By putting the information in Dr. Grace's files on computer, we expect in the long term to continue all facets of her work: adding new material from excavations and publications, analyzing and publishing significant series and groups of amphoras, and providing individual scholars with information tailored to their particular needs and questions. Retrieval of information from the computerized database will be faster and more efficient than it is using the original card file and can be accomplished without travel to Athens. It will also be possible to ask questions of the computer database which cannot at present be asked in the same form of the card file (fig. 5.4 demonstrates one possibility).

The Original Card File System

Information about any given object is entered in several different places (usually four, often more) in the original card-file system. Since the different files in which the object has been entered are set up for different purposes, different types of information are given in each place, and the complete information about the object is distributed among the files. Cross-referencing is extensive and laborious: a change in detail or identification of any given object made

INVNO	STUDY	CXT	PHT + PUBL + NB
C-1937-0645	KT 0259	Forum NE. c-e: 23-25, Strosis 2. NB169 p411 10.v.37	VG 132-15*; K 1972-100-03*; K 1984-16-16*
C-1937-2433	KT 0388	Forum NE. e-n: 35-38, sandy fill under Rom paving bedding. NB168 p3 21.5.37	VG 140-21*; K 1984-17-08* *Hesp* Sup 10 p153 s.v. nr 124. *Hesp* 1978 p21 nt29 Par: Pnyx 124*
C-1946-008	KT 0649	SE Bldg. A-D: 18-30 E side main room, from 1.0m NB191 p49 5.xii.46	VG 142-28*; K 1984-18-22A* Smp: IKW 80/192; req for Fitch 3.ix.85 (granted), 6.iv.86*
C-1985-065	KT 0985	E of Theater 94:AX 95:AX. Brown earth w/ rubble in the S baulk — Byz fill. NB778 p25 bsk	K 1985-76-25*(sc ok); K 1985-76-26*(sc ok) Par: *AJA* 7 (1903) p36, 14 103 (CP 1796); cf. *EAD* E27 pp329–30*
C-1968-164	KT 1003	Babbius. Trench 6 NE scarp. 79.758-79.218. NB410 p41 bsk 9 23.v.68	K 1986-41-25*(CGK) *Hesp* 1978 p21 nt.29 Smp: IKW 80/189; req for Fitch 3.ix.85 (granted), 6.iv.86*
C-1980-003	KT 1271	Forum NE 39:AC. Gen fill under Rom forum paving. Lot 1980-25	K 1980-56-28*; K 1986-07-24*(CGK bet?); K 1986-07-25* (CGK)
C-1937-2450	KT 1351	Forum NE. under Forum paving. NB168 p4 21.v.37	VG 141-02* Cxt: found w/ C-1937-2437, C-1937-2446*

5.4. A representative sample of a computer search, using both the General Amphora File and the Knidian Study File. The aim was to find the contexts (together with the photographic and publication information, etc.) of Knidian amphoras found at Corinth that can be dated to the interim period after the Roman destruction of the city in 146 B.C. The two databases were set up in *dBXL* (*dBase III +*) and their "relation" set to a common field—the Study number. Using one *dBase* command, a search was made for all Knidian Types (KTs) in the Knidian file which are dated to Period V (the 30 years after the destruction), and, as each one was found, a further search was triggered through the Corinth amphora file for any records with the same KT number in the Study field. Key fields from each of the databases were then printed in columns, using a primitive *dBase* report form; seven of the nineteen records actually retrieved are shown here.

originally in one place in the card file requires corresponding correction of all the other places where that object is filed.

The computer database not only gathers all the information about each object into one place, but it also allows information to be retrieved by any of the criteria used in the card-file system as well as by many not previously catered for. It is possible, for instance, to ask the computer for all the entries where a certain juxtaposition of letters is present in a name on a stamp; to consult the card file for this very common type of search requires a good deal of very educated guessing, based on a long acquaintance with all possible names and letter combinations.[11] The computer gives a much higher likelihood of producing those, and only those, examples which meet the requirements in any given search than a similar search through the card file can afford.[12] Additions and corrections are made in only one place in the computer database, obviating human error in the cross-referencing needed for card files, and when the information is printed out from the computer database, no additional human errors are introduced in transcription.

The amphora card-file system (not counting the information filed on paper in folders) occupies close to 100 drawers of file cards, mostly with lists of inventory numbers written on the backs of the cards. A copy of these files was urgently needed, and computerization provides very compact, portable storage as well as a means of verifying the data as they are entered. Another obvious benefit from computerizing amphora studies is afforded by the use of simple word processing and list sorting facilities, which save time and can improve accuracy. Finally, disseminating information in database form in addition to more traditional means of publication offers convenience to an increasing number of scholars, and all the more so for those who communicate through electronic networks.

The data in the card files have been collected with meticulous care in recording inventory numbers, measurements, publication references, and context information. Information about each individual amphora fragment is entered first into the "duplicates" (so-called because carbon copies are made as the records are created). These contain the most complete information about each fragment (dimensions, description of fabric, provenance, photographic record, identification of the class of amphora from which the fragment comes, and reading made with the aid of the files of any stamps that may be present on the fragment). The duplicates are arranged by the source of the information (e.g., by excavation and museum collection), and the different classes of amphora are intermingled.

Secondly, one entry for each amphora fragment, often just an inventory number, is made on the back of a "class" file card. These file cards are arranged by class (series or group) of amphora, and contain more up-to-date information about the class and stamp of each fragment; they also include entries that do not appear in the duplicates. The duplicates have also a card copy, and these are kept sorted by class, but it is not possible to update continually all items so filed. These file cards carry an indication of whether the piece cited has actually been seen, or whether the reference is otherwise reliable. For accuracy in making comparisons of stamps (die studies), rubbings made with graphite and very fine paper are glued onto file cards, and photographs reproduced at precisely 1:1 are also attached. Where multiple illustrations of an individual reading exist, selections are made to represent that die as fully as possible, and are added to as better examples are discovered. Photographic reproductions of whole or fragmentary jars are uniformly printed at 1:10 for the best visual comparison of the changes in shape, while profile drawings are made at actual size to include all details.

Computerizing

The adaptation of Dr. Grace's amphora card-file system to a computer database system is being done in three basic phases. These phases are dictated in part by the nature of the original card-filing system, which contains different levels of information about the same object in different card files, and in part by present restrictions, both financial and technical, on computer hardware and software. Structuring the project this way has helped to ensure that the archive can continue to be used during data entry with a minimum of disruption. The bulk of the data entry has been done from photocopies of the original records on IBM portable computers in Athens.[13]

The General Amphora File

In the computer database, all the information about each fragment is entered, one record per fragment, in a General Amphora File (GAF), which can then be sorted automatically by excavation, museum collection, class of amphora, etc., as required. The first phase of data entry consists of entering this material from the duplicates, which contain the bulk of the information about each fragment, and do not, unlike the file cards, have photographs stapled over them which have to be removed for photocopying.[14] This has the additional advantage that all the records from individual sites and museums are entered together, so that requests for identifications, correct readings, and dating information may be issued to those working on the collections.[15] Each data enterer works on a different subset of the data, one on the amphora fragments found at Corinth (see fig. 5.5), for instance, one on those from the British Museum, one on the finds at the German excavations of the Kerameikos in Athens, another on the Athenian Agora, and so on.[16] Database files are kept fairly small, under 64 kb, and can be split or amalgamated for searching as required.[17]

We have composed a 25-page data enterer's manual detailing what type of information should go into each field of the GAF and how it should be formatted,

C-1989-58   Kor   (Co 1366)   Kn   KT 1267
               [Ἐπὶ Ἑρμοφ]αν
               [του Χαρ]
               [μ]οκρατε vase
               υς
               (Σ lunate)
ΧΑΡΜΟΚΡΑΤΗΣ fab ΕΡΜΟΦΑΝΤΟΣ ep %vase
Cxt: Forum SW. 73: A. From well fill from − 4.41 to − 4.94m below E
        rim (upper filling)
        NB823 p25 bsk 16 31.v.89 Lot 1989-78
        Deposit: Manhole 1976-1
        Dated: 5c BC or sl earlier — ERom (44 BC)
Frg: pres hdl w/ upper att and most of vert side
Dim: PH 0.202, W × Th 0.040 × 0.023
Pht: K 1990-05-19*(CGK); K 1990-05-20*(CGK bet);
        K 1990-05-21*(CGK ng)
Par: C-1937-646? C-1977-029 (MSP says same die, CGK poss same
        27.iii)*
Msc: atelier on Datça Peninsula (Empereur et Picon *BCH* Sup 13 1986
        p126 nr6)*

5.5. Representative entry in the General Amphora File for stamped Greek amphoras from the excavations at Corinth. The number at the top left is the Corinth inventory number, at the right the Knidian Type number, for the reading of this particular stamp (see "The Study Files" below and Fig. 5.6). Note that the reading of the stamp includes many letters in square brackets (not legible on this example), and many dotted letters which indicate that only traces of the letter are visible. This badly impressed and badly worn example was identified in the first place by its device ("vase") and its only clear line, showing the US of the end of the name ERMOKRATEUS. When an example of the same type showing all the letters clearly was found, the reading was confirmed by the remaining traces of letters.

together with a few pages of general introduction on the use of the computer and particularly on how to type in Greek.

After information has been entered from the duplicates, there remain amphora fragments on record for which full duplicate entries do not exist. These can best be entered initially through the class files. The second phase of data entry, which is now under way for the Knidian class and will soon begin for the Rhodian, therefore consists of photocopying the backs of the more up-to-date class file cards, and making a computer check of the items listed there. Where an item has already been entered into the GAF, the information from the class file cards serves to verify the class identification and stamp reading in the GAF. Where an item from the back of a class file card has not already been entered in the GAF, a new entry is made for it automatically and the record later supplemented from information elsewhere in Dr. Grace's records. Entering from the duplicates, then doing computer checks with the class files, and vice versa, helps to ensure data accuracy.

Eventually, we envisage a third stage of data entry which will include representation of the photographs, rubbings of stamps, and profile drawings from Dr. Grace's files in the computer database. These will be entered using optical scanning techniques to store images, for the computer screen and also for print-out, in the GAF itself. This will require not only the use of optical scanning equipment, both hardware and software, but also integration of the binary optical scanning data into the database software used for the GAF.

The Study Files

In addition to the GAF, with its one record for each fragment (analogous to the original duplicates), we are also creating a number of Study Files on the analogy of the original class card files. These contain information about the various classes of amphora fragments according to their site of manufacture. As Dr. Grace's extensive work on the dating and connections inside the classes is added to and expanded, these files are being updated continually; new information in the Study File then affects a number of individual items in the GAF files. Each item in the GAF that belongs to a class that has been studied in this way is therefore given a Study number through which the additional information in the Study File can be found. The Study Files thus obviate the need for massive updating of the individual GAF records, and at the same time form the basis for further scholarly work on; for instance, wine manufacturing sites, the dating of their amphora production, and their distribution in commerce. Computer Study Files are being created from Dr. Grace's work on the Knidian amphora stamps, the fabricants and eponyms named in the stamps from Rhodes, stamps on jars from the island of Kos, and the series of amphoras manufactured in Corinth and her colony of Corcyra.[18]

Of these, the most nearly complete at the present time is the Knidian Study File (fig. 5.6). Among the 60,000 amphora stamps of Knidos recorded in Dr. Grace's files, approximately 2,350 different readings have been distinguished, each a composite made from all known impressions.[19] The Knidian Study File contains these readings, together with information relevant to dating all the amphora fragments which bear a stamp with that reading; this additional "study" material may take the form of comparisons of context information, reference to published examples and the discussions of date, references to where illustrations of the type can be found, etc. Each reading has its own KT (Knidian Type) number, and each Knidian stamp of that reading in the GAF is identified by the appropriate KT number. We intend to publish a catalogue of the KT readings in the not-too-distant future.

```
KT-1267
                    Ἐπὶ Ἑρμοφάν
                    του Χαρ
                    μοκράτε vase
                    υς Κνίδιον
                    (Σ lunate)
Per: 4 B                        99 ex.
ΧΑΡΜΟΚΡΑΤΗΣ fab ΕΡΜΟΦΑΝΤΟΣ ep                    eth %vase
Publ:    Dumont 1871 p192 nr 299 (no device mentioned), p192 nr 300,
         p301 nr 196, p350 nr 89, p368 nr 219 (restored), p434 nr 74
         (restored);
         Grace 1934 p257 nr 156 (ill.);
         Canarache 1957 p288 nr 734;
         Tenos 1 1986 p243 nrs 76–77;
         Empereur et Picon BCH Sup 13 1986 p126 nr 6.
```

5.6. An example from the Knidian Study File of the entry for KT 1267. The information applies generally to all stamps with this reading. Dating information is given; the type is dated to Period IVB in Virginia Grace's chronology (see note 3). Roman numerals representing chronological periods have been entered in the computer as arabic numerals to facilitate "greater than" and "less than" search, as are references to publications of examples of this type. Figure 5.5 is an example of a stamp of this type, identified as KT 1267 by careful comparison with photographs and rubbings of the best preserved of all the examples of this type (note "9 ex."!) on file.

The Rhodian Study File, the bulk of which has been entered in raw form, takes a distinctly different form from the others: the Study number represents not the reading of a type of stamp but the name of the fabricant or eponym which appears in the stamps. Each fabricant is given an R number, each eponym an RE number, and a system for recording the combinations of eponyms and fabricants known has been worked out. Where in Knidian stamps both the eponym and the fabricant regularly appear in the same stamp, each Rhodian stamp usually preserves only one name, and we are dependent on finding a whole jar, or the neck of a jar preserving both handles, to establish which fabricant was active in which periods and what types he or she (a number of women are named as fabricants of Rhodian stamps) used at different dates, as well as the sequence, and so the dates, of the eponyms who gave their names to the year and hence provided the dating information for the jars.

Where the Study File has been set up with one reading for each Study number, as in the case of the Knidian, the time-consuming process of entering readings has been much shortened by using the computer to enter the readings from the Study File automatically into each record of the GAF which has a valid KT Study number. The data enterer then updates each Knidian record which has a KT number in the GAF which she or he has completed, and enters only the epigraphical sigla for the individual stamp. This both provides a check on the data entry (does the information from the duplicates match the reading supplied from the Study File?) and ensures that the most up-to-date reading for each stamp appears in the GAF.

Some Mechanics

The number of records in the General Amphora File is now well over 45,000 (of a projected possible 150,000). The bulk of the data entry has been done in Athens, and floppy diskettes are forwarded to North America for proofreading by the authors during the seven to eight months of each year when neither of us is in Athens.[20] Copies of the data are kept in Baltimore and in Toronto as well as in Athens. We designate one person as the owner of the master copy of any given file, usually the data enterer who is creating the file, and no modifications may be made to other copies of the data, except when updates are issued from the master copy, though we still all have access to all the data at any given time. Communication between sites in North America has been immensely facilitated by the use of electronic mail, file transfer, and sharing of computer facilities through a number of networking programs (BITNET, Internet, Telnet, ftp) between Baltimore and Toronto and some other computer sites.

   The choice of IBM PCs was originally made at the project's inception, when classical Greek was not available even for word processing on computers, let alone for databases; the programmability of the IBM PC was then a major requirement, and it has since helped us to keep the amphora project's computer needs as much to standard equipment as possible, despite its special requirements for Greek and epigraphical sigla. While searches of the data can be made on all our machines, the main computer center consists of a Sun386i in Toronto, running both DOS and UNIX, which makes possible much more complex and faster searching, tallying, and consistency checking than is feasible on the PCs. Eventually (properly integrated software, and money, permitting) we hope to include optical imaging equipment for the reproduction of rubbings, drawings, and photographs, for use in conjunction with the character information about each object in the database. For data entry and basic database manipulation, we are still using software written in the C language by Philippa Matheson specially for the needs of a database project requiring Greek and epigraphical symbols. For distribution and multi-relational database functions, data are now also being converted to and from *dBase III+* (*dBXL*), and for the more cpu-intensive types of search we have uploaded certain parts of the database to a Silicon Graphics workstation at the University of Toronto, where the data are converted for use with the *EMPRESS* database management system (made by Rhodnius, Inc.).

The major component is a flat-file database program called *FERRET,* which gives us data files of unlimited size and variable length fields, and also shows epigraphical Greek on the screen, while still using only ASCII low-bit characters (so that data can be manipulated by, and transported to, other programs, including mainframes). It includes the use of a simple full-screen editor with CGA-based graphics for the Greek, sorts up to 3,000 entries, and performs a number of selecting functions, including Boolean AND and NOT, mathematical (greater than, less than, equals), and string comparisons. It also allows output formatting and simple creation of subsidiary databases. For more complicated (and faster!) operations, we use a wide range of UNIX functions on the Sun386i, often in the form of awk and shell scripts, as well as the *EMPRESS* multi-relation system, also running under UNIX on a Silicon Graphics machine.

Printing is done using the graphics capability of a wide range of dot matrix printers to produce the Greek and epigraphical characters. The system of transliteration we use is basically the same as the Beta format used by the Thesaurus Linguae Graecae project, as also by a great many other Greek computer projects which use its data. Our Greek can easily be converted to and from Beta format as required and has been adapted to the Packard Greek font cartridge for use with a LaserJet printer as well as for use with the TeX typesetting program and a Greek PostScript font for the NEC LC-890. This enables us to do the often fiddly and technically demanding typesetting needed to represent the stamp readings accurately for camera-ready copy of amphora publications.

The main advantage of the programs currently in use is their flexibility. Global corrections, importation of data from outside files, and updating while browsing through the data can be done using ordinary commercial word processors, such as *PC-Write, Edix/Wordix,* even *WordStar* (non-document mode) — any word processor that can create and manipulate text in standard ASCII format without the addition of hidden or coded control characters. The Greek and epigraphical passages can be edited in transliteration if needed (and can thus be manipulated also by mainframe editors, such as VI and EMACS in the UNIX system and XEDIT in VMS).

For dissemination and for multi-relational searches, we are also using *dBase III +* (in the form of the *dB III +* clone, *dBXL*) (see fig. 5.4). Conversion of the data from *FERRET* to *dBase* poses few technical problems. A fixed-length database structure like *dBase,* however, requires at least 1.5 kb per record of storage space when loaded into the program for use; for a potential 150,000 records, using the whole database through *dBase* would mean maintaining and manipulating 225 megabytes of data, nearly ten times the size of the database as projected using variable length fields.

While the combination of *FERRET* and *dBase* adequately meets our present needs, and will for the next few years, in the long term we hope to have the use of a more sophisticated database program. The database we choose must eventually allow for the storage, retrieval, and display of images (photographs of stamps and whole jars, rubbings of stamps, and profile drawings, preferably with the added ability to make calculations of capacities from them). Like *FERRET*, the program ideally should enable all our font characters to be displayed as text on the screen. Finally, the size of the database will eventually make it highly desirable to have continuous on-line access to a central copy of the database, which can be used by a computer network. As the database grows, and with the addition of the further enormous storage requirements of imaging data, other media for storage will be needed (such as the erasable compact disk). Developments in the technology and pricing of large data storage equipment, as well as in the software used to read and write the data, and the networking capabilities of that software from mainframe to PC and from country to country, will all affect the decision of what large-scale database management system will be best suited to our needs in three or four years' time. While the technology for all these requirements already exists individually, we have not yet hit upon a combination of software and hardware (preferably within our budget!) which unites them all.

A number of measures have been implemented to protect against error in data entry. Typographical errors in key fields in the GAF are guarded against by computer comparisons of the data entered under Class and Study with a list of permissible entries. Searches are also made using the database program to catch other inconsistencies (if, for instance, "rs" appears in Stpdesc, then "rose" must also be present in Reading; if Date is entered, Context must not be blank, etc.). In the case of data which need to be the same, with only minor variations between individual records, as in the Knidian readings, data entry for that field is done by program (in *dBase*) and each record later updated individually, making a further check on the accuracy of the original entry also for other fields.

The use of two different sources for the information also provides a built-in check of a fairly large proportion of the data: the original archives, filed by collection (duplicates), are cross-referenced to the file cards, filed by class of amphora. Thus each object entered during the second phase, from the class files, is being checked when its inventory number is typed in, and discrepancies either corrected immediately or further investigated. We find that we catch errors frequently by sorting and printing lists of selected fields. Security of data in the usual computer sense (protection against multiple simultaneous updating of a computer file, and protection against unauthorized writing of database files) is not a major concern, since no two people work on the same computer at the same time; we do take care to make sure that only one person is responsible for alterations to any given data file.

A form of security does arise, however, in the nature of the material, which is as yet largely unpublished; the *FERRET* database system had to have built into it a system by which certain fields can be marked as reserved: the contents of the field can be viewed at the computer terminal, but the data in the field are omitted (with the indication "Field reserved" to show that the field was not simply left blank) in printed versions or text files on disk. Unpublished material can, however, always be made available to scholars who have the publication rights to that material (for example, to all who are working with the permission of the excavator on material from an archaeological site).

The Future

At present the advantages of the use of the computer for an academic project are the advantages which any technical improvement in the process of working gives. The introduction of the typewriter produced much the same improvements: greater clarity, accuracy, speed of execution, and multiple copies from a single prototype. The computer, while making further advances in all these directions, adds improved filing and cross-referencing, and the great facility of having all personal data compressed into one machine, with, in theory, access to unlimited amounts of additional information. Some of this additional information is indeed being made available: the TLG is an example in Classics, and the large data archives of published material that are being built up at the Oxford Text Archive and elsewhere are another. Our project will be able to release sections of the database in computer-searchable format as soon as we have published those sections in book form. But what the computer is capable of in terms of data sharing and communications, and what the scholars who control the data are likely to achieve in this field, are very different things. Our own experience of this has been that a form of computer-phobia exists even among those who use them most. Excavators and museums do not want information about unpublished finds disseminated to "unauthorized" scholars; scholars do not want the data on which their publications are based made available in "raw" form; none of us want the state of our bank balances, our income tax returns, and other personal financial details made publicly available. This built-in reluctance to present incompletely studied data will do much to keep the use of computers in archaeology to the level of personal office machines in the immediate future. It seems to us likely that the main influence of our project among classicists will be more in the content of the academic work which the computer enables us to do (dating of archaeological contexts, synthesis of amphora information on trade routes, statistics on import and export for ancient states, etc.) than in the dissemination of computer-searchable raw materials.

With the expanding use of computers, however, a minor communications revolution is taking place which will enable computerized projects such as ours to participate in a wider range of academic research. The use of electronic mail (like the increasing use of FAX machines) for the exchange of information is less disruptive than a telephone call, and less formal and labor-intensive than writing a letter by ordinary post. It is already possible to obtain large amounts of (uncontroversial) raw data "on-line" (and more or less anonymously) by simply sending for the appropriate files from another computer (by Ethernet's ftp or BITNET's LISTSERV, for example). But also for projects such as ours where the information must in most cases be individually tailored to the question, the files of a large computerized database can be searched, and the results edited, to answer a particular query in a much shorter time than is taken to search a file-card system and write the selected information out again to be sent out as an answer in a letter. Since both the original query and the reply are relayed instantly (and any part of your correspondence can be cannibalized for inclusion in another document), the time spent on the consultation is reduced much more nearly to pure thinking time. When you yourself find answering less of a bother, you are also more likely to ask others for information. Projects which have been computerized will thus be available to an increasing pool of scholars, as the physical process of exchanging information becomes less of a barrier to communication in general.[21]

In the next few years we hope to see the development of the perfect database system, customizable for all our font, data, optical imaging, storage, and communications needs. We are not holding our breath until the utopia of total and instantaneous free exchange of information arrives. But despite the occasional frustration and necessary tedium of arriving at our present plateau, and our awareness that there is still the odd technological mountain (such as creating and integrating optical images with the database system) looming in front of us, we have nevertheless already experienced the great satisfaction of being able to ask questions, get immediate answers, and share those answers with others, that working with computerized data gives.

Notes

1. On amphoras in general, see V. R. Grace, *Amphoras and the Ancient Wine Trade*[2], [= *Picture Book 6, Excavations of the Athenian Agora*] (Princeton, 1979).

The authors have given a number of presentations on the AMPHORAS computer project, including twice at the joint meetings of the Archaeological Institute of America and the American Philological Association, in 1984 (a poster session) and 1988 (for the abstract, see "Amphoras on Computers," *AJA* 90 (1986): 224), and at the 9th International Conference on Computers and the Humanities and 16th International Association of Literary and Linguistic Computing Conference in 1989 (Toronto). The computerized data also provided the basis of a paper on the Knidian wine trade given at the AIA/APA meetings in 1990 (see note 7).

We would like to thank a number of people for their support of the project: Virginia R. Grace, for her unstinted academic help and continued patience with our predilection for pushing buttons; Maria Petropoulakou and Andreas Dimoulinis for the welcome they gave the project and all the extra work they have done for it; those who have done the bulk of the (often tedious) work of data entry — Victor Bakich, Sophia Huxley,

Lucy Krystallis, Camilla MacKay, Catherine McCarty, Louise McInerney, Alexandra Zavos, Dinah Zavos (also our project manager in Athens), Peter Zerner, and Carolyn Ferrigno, who has seen to practical details at the University of Maryland, Baltimore County. We are also extremely grateful for the financial support of donors to AMPHORAS through both the University of Maryland, Baltimore County, and the University of Toronto, most especially to the 1984 Foundation.

For permission to publish the photographs in figs. 1 and 2, we thank the Agora Excavations of the American School of Classical Studies at Athens.

2. V. R. Grace, "The Canaanite Jar," in S. S. Weinberg, ed., *The Aegean and the Near East: Studies presented to Hetty Goldman* (Locust Valley, N.Y., 1956), 82–83. P. E. McGovern (Museum Applied Science Center for Archaeology, The University Museum of Archaeology and Anthropology, University of Pennsylvania) has kindly informed me of recent analyses of finds in Egypt that show that the Egyptians copied the Canaanite shape in local fabric as early as the Hyksos period.

3. For information on the Knidian and Rhodian series in general (as well as on other classes), see V. R. Grace and M. Savvatianou-Petropoulakou, *L'Îlot de la Maison des Comédiens*, Explorations archéologiques de Délos, no. 27 (Paris, 1970), in particular the introductions to Knidian (217–314) and to Rhodian (209–302) stamps. Rhodian period dates have been revised since then; see V. R. Grace, "Revisions in Hellenistic Chronology," *Mitteilungen des Deutsches Archäologischer Instituts (Ath. Abt.)* 89 (1974): 193–200, and "The Middle Stoa Dated by Amphora Stamps," *Hesperia* 54 (1985): 7–13 and 42 [hereafter, Grace (1985)]. The Knidian chronology has not been affected by the more recent chronological revisions; see Grace (1985): 13–18 and 31–35, especially for stamps dating before about 183 B.C., and for general sharpening of the chronology, including a working list of Knidian eponym names individually annotated with period dates (31–35).

4. S. I. Rotroff, *Hellenistic Pottery: Athenian and Imported Moldmade Bowls,* The Athenian Agora: Results of Excavations Conducted by the American School of Classical Studies at Athens, no. 22 (Princeton, 1984), 94–106.

5. G. F. Bass, J. R. Steffy, and F. H. van Doorninck, Jr., *National Geographic Society Research Reports, 1976 Projects* (1984), 177.

6. Grace (1985): 25–30.

7. On some amphora evidence for this interim period at Corinth, see C. K. Williams, II, "Corinth 1977, Forum Southwest," *Hesperia* 47 (1978): 21, n. 29. We discussed the statistical evidence for that period, both for the volume of Knidian manufacture, and for the comparative rates of import of Knidian wine into Athens and Corinth, at the annual AIA/APA meetings in 1990 (for the abstract, see *AJA* 95 [1991]: 336).

8. Grace (1985): 7.

9. Dated by Virginia Grace and published by D. T. Ariel, *Excavations at the City of David 1978–1985: Imported Stamped Amphora Handles, Coins, Worked Bone and Ivory, and Glass,* vol. 2, Qedem 30 (The Institute of Archaeology, The Hebrew University of Jerusalem, 1990), 13–98, esp. 18–20.

10. Such a large and expensive undertaking requires, even in view of its usefulness, justification on the grounds of the quality of data. Scholars have demonstrated their appreciation for Dr. Grace's efforts and their absolute reliance upon her rigorous analysis of the data she has collected. When in 1983 we began to explore the possibility of creating a computerized database from Dr. Grace's files, we wrote to 90 scholars in

sixteen countries who had been in some way her "clients," and received letters of support from two-thirds of them (a high rate of return for such an endeavor — and in addition there were a few others who wrote unsolicited letters). All acknowledged their "professional dependence upon [Dr. Grace] and her amphora-stamp studies." One "would characterise the information received as amongst the most important, because so specific (both in date and provenience), which an excavator can receive." Another observed, "Archaeologists usually consult with colleagues at centers specializing in numismatics, glass, weapons, or the like, but in the case of amphoras there really is only one place to turn." It was generally agreed, in the words of a third, that "[the archive] is internationally famous and referring to it has become an almost automatic procedure."

11. Initial identification of the stamps is still done most efficiently by M. Petropoulakou and A. Dimoulinis in Dr. Grace's office in Athens. The stamps are handwritten and very irregular, and a stamp with letters that are not clearly identifiable nevertheless can be read with a high degree of accuracy if another stamp of the same die with clearer letters can be found for comparison. We have all had the experience of showing to Mr. Dimoulinis a blurred, half broken-off impression of a Rhodian stamp, in which we think we can perhaps make out, e.g., a lambda, and being totally convinced a moment later that the stamp actually says [M]IΔAΣ (dots are placed under letters which are not clearly seen, and [ ]s around letters which are missing altogether from the stamp), when he produced from the card file photographs and rubbings of another, sharper example of the same stamp. Human pattern recognition of this sort is still in advance of computers.

12. Recently we used the computer database to help identify a Knidian stamp of which only the right-hand edge, containing two very sharp letters, one at the end of each line, were preserved. At M. Petropoulakou's suggestion we developed a reading-searching database for the Knidian stamps which allows us to specify line ends and beginnings as well as patterns of letters and devices, and so we were able to narrow the search to three possible Knidian types out of the approximately 2,350 known.

13. We have tried as much as possible to make sure that the people who do photocopying also do data entry and vice versa. Photocopying, we discovered, is a trained job, since anything that is not clear on the photocopy must be intelligently annotated by hand, and it is done best by those who understand the problems that arise in data entry. Furthermore, the file cards must be kept in order for refiling. We are particularly grateful to A. Zavos for her meticulous attention to detail in all aspects of data entry and photocopying.

14. Experience with optical character readers (Kurzweil, Hewlett-Packard) made us decide, regretfully, that they could not be used on this material, since much of it is handwritten (in a number of hands, some in pencil of varying shades and degrees of faintness!), and since the data enterers are asked to make some value judgments as to what material to reproduce, as well as to standardize abbreviations and forms of expression for data entry.

15. We have been able to supply printouts to a number of excavations and museums. The excavations at Corinth requested a complete printout, which is being used as part of the inventory system; amphora information from the computer database has recently been supplied to the excavations at Tell el-Fara'in (ancient Buto) in Egypt and at Morgantina in Sicily. Finds from Tel Anafa in Israel, Stobi in Yugoslavia, and the collection of the Royal Ontario Museum in Toronto have all been printed out and contributed to

the preparation of publications of those collections. Excavators at Isthmia have received data on their stamped handles in hard copy as well as in *dBase* delimited text format by electronic mail to Boston University, where computerization of the pottery records from those excavations is in progress.

16. For example, in Athens, D. Zavos has entered the readings in the Knidian Study File and data from Delos and the Kerameikos, A. Zavos is entering material from the Athenian Agora, and C. MacKay has entered the Corinthian Study File; in Toronto, V. Bakich is working on Knidian stamps from Alexandria and the National Museum as well as the Rhodian Study File, while C. McCarty is entering material published in *Inscriptiones Graecae* 12.1, mostly Rhodian stamps in the British Museum, and has embarked on verification and updating of the Knidian records from the cross-references in the card file.

17. The average size of a record in the GAF depends on the amount of the available information for the amphora fragments. The pieces from Corinth average 309 bytes per record; from the Agora in Athens, 188 bytes per record; and from the Kerameikos excavations in Athens, 128 bytes per record. Since the Corinth data are particularly complete, it is probably safest to assume an average record size of 150 bytes or somewhat more for the file in general.

18. A manuscript on the Koan class of amphoras, with photographic plates illustrating the different types of stamps, has been prepared by V. Grace and M. Petropoulakou, with assistance from P. M. W. Matheson. One of the goals of the AMPHORAS project is to establish a series of monographs presenting various amphora classes, in which this volume will appear. The two works which should initiate the series are that presenting all the Knidian Types, by V. R. Grace, M. S. Petropoulakou, P. M. W. Matheson, and C. G. Koehler, and *Corinthian Transport Amphoras,* by C. G. Koehler.

19. New excavation material seldom anymore turns up stamps with unknown Knidian Types, although we await details on the results of recent excavations of kiln sites around Knidos; for a preliminary report, see N. Tuna, J-Y. Empereur, M. Picon and E. Doğer, "Rapport préliminaire de la prospection archéologique Turco-Française des ateliers d'amphores de Reşadiye-Kiliseyani, sur la péninsule de Datça," *Anatolia Antiqua Eski Anadolu* (1987): 47–52.

20. We are more than grateful to D. Zavos for making this schedule possible by coordinating activities in Greece, including maintaining the Project's hard-worked IBM PCs, collecting the data, keeping the accounts, and helping to maintain the consistency of the data entry by drawing attention to the discrepancies between theory and practice which continually crop up.

21. As of June 1993, we have not ourselves so far succeeded in obtaining access to electronic mail from Greece (access to an EARN node is not yet perceived as a necessity by academic institutions, even North American ones, abroad in the same way that it is in the U.S.A. and Canada). But the comparative ease of communication by e-mail within North America has made possible a great many collaborations and consultations which otherwise either would have represented an expensive drain on time or would perhaps not have been undertaken.

6

The Database of Classical Bibliography

Dee Clayman

1. Nature and Significance

The American Philological Association (APA), the Société Internationale de Bibliographie Classique (SIBC), and the City University of New York (CUNY) are working together to create a comprehensive, bibliographical database covering all aspects of Greco-Roman antiquity. When complete, it will contain the entire *L'Année Philologique* (*APh*), the international bibliography of record for classical studies published in Paris by the SIBC, supplemented by specialized bibliographies from related fields. The database will be made available in stages, as it is built, on a compact disk (CD-ROM) that will be updated periodically. The centralization of these scholarly resources and their distribution in machine-readable form is intended to support the study and teaching of Greco-Roman antiquity by increasing access to these materials for everyone, from the most sophisticated scholar to the beginning student, in classical studies and in all humanistic disciplines that trace their origins to ancient Greece and Rome.

1.1. The Source Material

APh is the premier research tool for the study of classical antiquity. It is the first and often the last place scholars look for bibliography on Greek and Latin literature, ancient history, and related subjects, including religion, philosophy, science, economics, art, and archaeology. With almost 15,000 entries each year, it guides researchers through a morass of scattered and varied materials in every modern European language, as well as Latin and Greek. Among publications devoted to the advancement of classical studies around the world, none has done more to facilitate scholarly work at all levels by improving its quality, increasing its efficiency, and teaching by example the virtues of accuracy, consistency, organization, and comprehensiveness. In the field of classical studies there is no bibliographical source material of higher quality or greater value.

The *APh* was founded in 1927 by J. Marouzeau, and it has flourished under the guidance of Juliette Ernst, who became directrice in 1963. Citations are collected at a central office in Paris and by collaborating offices at the University of North Carolina at Chapel Hill, since 1965, and Heidelberg, since 1972. The final editing of the annual volume takes place in Paris now under the direction of Pierre-Paul Corsetti.

Over the years the *APh* has published sixty-one volumes containing more than three-quarters of a million citations. Each includes complete bibliographical information augmented by summaries of articles in journals and Festschriften, and lists of published reviews for each book. Entries are organized under eleven rubrics and hundreds of sub-rubrics including author's names, subject areas (e.g., *Philosophie et histoire des idées*) or types of material (e.g., *Dictionnaires, atlas, recueils*).

1.2. The Value of a Database

Although the printed volumes of the *APh* are a vital research tool as they stand, recasting them in machine-readable form and distributing them on a CD-ROM will make their contents more accessible, increase their utility, and permit wider distribution of scarce resources. There are several reasons why:

1. A bibliographic database can be searched rapidly. Typically, a scholar or student begins a research project by surveying all the relevant bibliography. In classical studies this means consulting each of sixty-one volumes of the *APh* plus a number of earlier and specialized bibliographies. Entries may be scattered throughout each volume, and the indices, such as they are, may be of no use in finding them. For example, a researcher studying "Greek concepts of freedom" would read through the entire divisions of *Auteurs et textes, Histoire, Droit,* and *Philosophie et histoire des idées* at the very least, which total more than 400 pages in vol. 56 alone. Multiply that effort by 61 and the magnitude of the undertaking becomes clear. Without the *APh* the task would be impossible, but even with it, an initial search through the bibliography is a daunting project. In the earliest stages of research, the computer's ability to scan a vast amount of information with great speed is a considerable advantage. High-speed searching is also an advantage at the very last stage of research, when a manuscript is being prepared for publication and all the citations must be verified.

2. A bibliographical database is easily indexed. The *APh* has five printed indices: *Index des rubriques collectives, nominum antiquorum, geographicus, noms d'humanistes, auteurs*. Although accurate and useful, they are limited in scope, to say the least. What is urgently needed and most frequently requested is a subject index to guide a search such as the one just described. The manual preparation of a subject index for the sixty-one retrospective volumes would be a Herculean task, but a computer's searching and sorting capabilities can greatly alleviate the labor.

3. A bibliographical database can be inclusive. With all relevant bibliographic resources in a central place, it is far less likely that researchers will overlook previous scholarship crucial to their work. This is of particular importance to scholars at small colleges and universities without direct access to major research libraries.

4. A bibliographical database on a CD-ROM can produce a fairer distribution of scarce resources. Bibliographies in related, specialized fields like papyrology, numismatics, and archaeology are generally found only in wealthier universities where senior faculty are actively engaged in these areas. Graduate students and faculty at undergraduate institutions who have an interest in these areas often lack the means to pursue them. A comprehensive database of classical studies on an inexpensive CD-ROM that can be read on an ordinary personal computer will dramatically improve the dissemination of these valuable resources.

5. A bibliographical database on a CD-ROM can preserve its source material from decay and potential oblivion. Nine volumes of the *APh* are no longer available, and others will become so as stocks are depleted. There are no plans to reprint them. The earlier bibliographies, which will be added at a later stage, have been out of print for decades. The preservation of these precious resources on optical media is an important priority in a field where standards of documentation are high and good research tools never lose their value.

6. A bibliographic database can be used in conjunction with other databases of classical material. These might be ancient texts like those in the Thesaurus Linguae Graecae, or the Duke Data Bank of Documentary Papyri, collections of information about ancient objects like the *Lexicon Iconographicum Mythologiae Classicae,* which has a database at its American Office, lexicons such as Liddell-Scott-Jones, available through the Perseus Project at Harvard, or the texts of scholarly books and journals, which are often put in machine-readable form for printing. Several of these collections are already available on CD-ROMs and others will be in the future. Scholars equipped with a microcomputer, the requisite software, and a CD reader will have a powerful set of research tools at their command, among which an authorative bibliography is essential.

7. A bibliographical database can be used in conjunction with bibliographical databases in other fields. Related scholarly disciplines, such as modern language studies, philosophy, theology, and history already have large-scale, electronic bibliographies that can be queried on similar issues to produce a wealth of comparative material. A bibliographic database for classical studies would make information about the ancient world more accessible to scholars in these fields, enhancing the contribution of classical studies to interdisciplinary

research. Classical studies lags behind other humanities disciplines in automating its bibliographical resources and will not reach its full potential as a source for interdisciplinary research until it makes available the wealth of its bibliography in a format and medium consistent with that of its sister disciplines.

1.3. A Sample Search

The effectiveness of searching a bibliographical database is best illustrated by example. Suppose a scholar has a special interest in narrative and wishes to explore its form and function in Greek poetry. The *APh* provides no subject indices to assist in finding relevant citations. There is a sub-rubric "narativa," under *Auteurs et Textes,* but this contains listings only for narrative romances that cannot be placed under an author's name. For example, in vol. 56 it offers review notices of a book entitled *Lessico dei romanzieri greci,*[1] and a citation of an article on a verse novel by an eleventh-century Persian poet.[2] A second rubric, "Littérature narrative et historiographie," with 42 entires should be more promising, but it contains nothing at all directly relevant to narrative in Greek verse. Without a database there is no alternative to perusing all the listings under each relevant author. In this case it would be all Greek poets. If one does not know all their names then significant published research may be missed.

When the printed bibliography is converted to machine-readable form and tagged, however, a search on the titles and summaries of all entries for "narra*" (covering narrative, narration, narrate, narrator, narratology, narratio, narrazione, narratif, narrateur etc.), "récit*" (to capture récit, récitateur, réciter etc.) and erzähl* (for Erzählung, erzählen, Erzähler, etc.) produces 153 entries extracted from 44 different rubrics in volume 56 alone. The following entries are a small sample from among those selected automatically that would be relevant to the topic at hand, reproduced here in their original *APh* format:

Rubric: Aeschylus; *APh* vol. 56, p. 4, N° 41.

Goldhill S., *Language, sexuality, narrative, the Oresteia* : Cambridge Univ. Press. 1984 IX & 315 p. | TLS LXXXIV 1985 292 Taplin | CR XXXV 1985 243–246 Heath.

Rubric: Euripides; *APh* vol. 56, p. 102, N° 1621.

González de Tobia A. M., *Doble λόγος en Medea* : Argos VII 1983 [1985] 101–112. | Dans cette pièce, un λόγος extérieur, renforcé par les récits mythiques, et un λόγος intérieur s'entrelacent. Le λόγος intérieur s'exprime le plus clairement dans les vers 85–88 qui annoncent le programme éthique de toute la tragédie.

Rubric: Homerus; *APh* vol. 56, p. 144. N° 2268.

Jong I. J. F. de, *Iliad 1.366–392. A mirror story* : Arethusa XVIII 1985 5–22. | This passage can be classified as a retrospective mirror story dealing with true facts already told in the main story. It shows that a character can assume the same authorial position as the main narrator. It also gives us a clear picture of the mental state of Achilles, one of the principal protagonists.

Rubric: Homerus; *APh* vol. 56, p. 143, N° 2252.

Ferrini M. F., *Espressioni di tempo nell'epica omerica e postomerica* : GIF XVI 1985 15–52. | Ces expressions doivent être analysées en étant reliées à la technique de la communication orale. Elles délimitent et circonscrivent les actions pour mieux les faire entendre. Ainsi l'image de l'aurore et celle du soir ont un caractère naturel d'introduction et de conclusion qui les rend aptes à attirer l'attention sur des moments de passage et de poursuite du récit.

Rubric: Pindarus; *APh* vol. 56, p. 219, N° 3485.

Pinsent J., *Pindar's narrative technique. Pythian 4 and Bacchylides 5* : LCM X 1985 2–8.

Rubric: Mythographie et Folklore; *APh* vol. 56, p. 359, N° 5813.

Prag A. J. N. W., *The Oresteia. Iconographic and narrative tradition* : Warminster Aris & Phillips & Chicago Bolchazy-Carducci 1985 xii & 213 p. 46 pl.

Rubric: Grec et dialectes helléniques; *APh* vol. 56, p. 368, N° 5974.

Calame C., *Noms grecs de jeunes filles. L'anthroponyme comme énoncé narratif* : Cahiers romains d'études littéraires (Bucarest) IV 1984 4–11 56. | La littérature antique use de l'anthroponyme comme d'une véritable figure. Chez Homère, par exemple, des étymologies fantaisistes permettent de fixer dans le nom propre des qualités que le déroulement de l'action attribue à l'acteur concerné. On relève un même jeu, mais à des fins spéculatives chez Hésiode. Chez Alcman, le processus consiste à faire correspondre a posteriori les traits que le nom peut impliquer par l'intermdiaire d'un jeu sur sa morphologie avec les valeurs qui se sont à peu actualisées dans son porteur.

A search such as this on the whole of the available database would be no more difficult than a search on a single volume, though it would, of course, turn up much irrelevant material on narrative in Greek prose, in Latin poetry and prose, and narrative representations on ancient art and artifacts. Specially designed software would permit ways of refining the search so that it could be much more precise. One could search, e.g., for "narrative and Homer," or "narrative and Greek authors," or "narrative and Greek authors and fifth century." It is clear though, that even a broad search of the bibliography based only on the words printed in the *APh* will make the research process far more efficient and accurate.

2. History of the Project

Thanks to the outstanding collections of machine-readable texts assembled by the various projects represented in this volume and in Europe by Antonio Zampolli (Laboratorio di Linguistica Computazionale, Pisa), Wilhelm Ott (Zentrum für Datenverarbeitung, Tübingen), and L. Delatte (Le Laboratoire d'Analyse Statistique des Langues Anciennes, Liège), classicists were acquainted early with the advantages of computer-assisted research. It is not surprising that many began making small bibliographical databases for their own purposes and calling for the computerization of *L'Année Philologique*.

In response to this demand, the Association's Committee on Research created a Subcommittee on Bibliography in spring 1981 to investigate the creation of a bibliographic database. In October of that year the Committee sponsored an international conference on computerized bibliography for classical studies at Columbia University with support from the National Endowment for the Humanities. In attendance were the principals of the APA and the *L'Année Philologique*. A lively discussion of issues took place, but the tangible results were modest: the main office of the *APh* in Paris arranged for its printed volumes to be phototypeset beginning with vol. 53 (1982), and the American office at the University of North Carolina at Chapel Hill became fully automated with support from the David and Lucile Packard Foundation.

Five years elapsed when no progress was made at all, but by 1986 the successful development of the Thesaurus Linguae Graecae and other on-line resources for research in classics made it apparent that the creation of a bibliographic database should have the highest priority. In the spring of that year I was appointed Director of Planning with a mandate to get the project under way again. In the following year three pilot projects were begun at CUNY, UNC Chapel Hill, and Rutgers to test strategies for data entry and searching, a general plan was developed, and a new dialogue was begun with Juliette Ernst. After much correspondence and a diplomatic mission to Paris in January 1987 by the Association's President for 1986–87, Martin Ostwald, and Jay Bolter of the Chapel Hill office, Ms. Ernst agreed that the database project should go forward and that the Paris office would be computerized.

Following these developments, plans were made to bring together representatives of the three *APh* offices and the database project to ensure that all four operations would be sufficiently compatible in hardware and software so that data could easily be shared among them. The meeting took place October 14–16, 1988, in Chapel Hill, with support from the NEH.

In addition to discussing technical issues, agreement was reached on how the retrospective database would be updated and distributed.

Work began on data entry in June 1989 with support from the National Endowment for the Humanities, the Getty Grant Program of the J. Paul Getty Trust, the Florence J. Gould Foundation, the Samuel H. Kress Foundation, the Dorot Foundation, and the Faculty Research Award Program of CUNY. Since that time, 11 volumes of the *APh* (vols. 48–58) have been recast into machine-readable form, proofread, and tagged for searching, creating a database of more than 150,000 records.

3. Technical Goals and Standards

Although the principal language of the *APh* is French, it has always been international in scope, with entries in every western European language including Greek and such minor languages as Danish and Dutch. All of the languages are correctly accented, and all traditional characters such as ɸ and ç are faithfully reproduced. Originally, the accompanying summaries were written only in French, but following the establishment of the overseas offices, English and German abstracts have become increasingly common. A contemporary entry for a Greek text with commentary edited by an American and printed in Germany with a summary in French could therefore contain, within its brief confines, material in four different languages. The complex language mix complicates every stage of production.

3.1. Procedures and Standards for Input

A pilot study, supported by the David and Lucile Packard Foundation, to test the feasibility of using optical scanning techniques for data entry was conducted on samples from all the volumes of the *APh,* and the results were so poor, it was determined that input would have to proceed by keyboarding. Accordingly, printed volumes provided by the Paris office are sent to a commercial input center where the bibliography is typed at a computer console using standard double-entry procedures. Data is coded in ASCII (ANSI X3.4) with the extended Latin character set designed for MARC (ANSEL = ANSI Z39.47). Greek characters are entered in the TLG Beta Code which has become a de facto standard in the field, and non-Roman characters represented in neither of these sets are rendered in SGML (ISO 8879) with our own extensions. For example, entry 4113 on page 259 of vol. 56 is entitled, "Sappho fr. 32,14 L-P, χλωροτέρα ποίας." In the database it appears as "Sappho fr. 32,14 L-P, <G>XLWROTE/RA POI/AS<G>," and E. Lipinski, the author of entry number 11161 on p. 650, appears as E. Lipi<C>nacute<C>ski. Software will be provided with the disk to translate these codes back into their original appearance.

Following entry, the data is forwarded on disks to CUNY where it is proofread twice by a team of graduate students trained as editors and formatted in a 71-field database template designed for the special requirements of the *APh*. The field definitions with examples from various volumes follow:

1. **AnAuth1** (Analytic Author) — Person responsible for artistic content of a work, including ancient authors.

Example of a single analytic author, modern:

Tomasco D., *Su Apuleio, De deo Socr.* I 116,9-II 119,10 *Th.* : Vichiana IX 1980 166-172.

    AnAuth1   Tomasco D.

Example of a single analytic author, ancient:

Accius Tragicus — *I frammenti delle tragedie,* a cura di Antò V. d' ; cf. APh LI N° 1.

    AnAuth1   Accius Tragicus
    Subauth1   Antò V. d'
    APhRub   Accius Tragicus

2. **AuthCom1** (Author Comments) — Comments in square brackets added by the *APh* within or after author's name.

Example of author with author comment:

Thomae B. [= Thomasson B. E.], *Laterculi praesidum,* II ; cf. APh XLIX N° 10635.

    AnAuth1   Thomae B.
    AuthCom1   Thomasson B. E.

3. **Anauth2** (Second Analytic Author).

Example of two or more analytic authors individually named:

El-Sawy A., Bouzek J. & Vidman L., *New stelae from the Terenouthis cemetery* [inscriptions] ; cf. N° 6500.

    AnAuth1   El-Sawy A.
    AnAuth2   Bouzek J.
    AnAuth3   Vidman L.

4. **Authcom2** (Second Author Comment).

5. **Anauth3** (Third Analytic Author).

6. **Authcom3** (Third Author Comment).

7. **Anauth4** (Fourth Analytic Author).

8. **Authcom4** (Fourth Author Comment).

9. **ManyAuth** (Additional Analytic Authors).

Example of two or more analytic authors, some unnamed:

Olivier J. P. [et al.], *Une épingle minoenne en or avec inscription en linéaire A* ; cf. N° 6286.

> AnAuth1   Olivier J. P.
> ManyAuth   et al.

10. **SubAuth1** (Subsidiary Author) — Name of translator, editor, etc.

11. **AuthRol1** (Subsidiary Author's Role) — "ed.," "trans."

Example of a single subsidiary author:

Die griechische Anthologie, übertr. von Ebener D., I : *Buch* I-VI ; II : *Buch* VII-X ; III : *Buch* X-XVI : Bibl. der Antike Griech. R. Berlin Aufbau-Verl. 1981 LXXVIII & 282 ; 547 ; 580 p.

> SubAuth1   Ebener D.
> AuthRol1   übertr. von

12. **SubAuth2** (Second Subsidiary Author).

Example of two or more subsidiary authors, one role:

Cento anni bibliografia ambrosiana (1874-1974), a cura di Beatrice P. F., Cantalamessa R., Persic A., Pizzolato L. F., Scaglioni C., Tibiletti G. & Visonà G. : Studia Patristica Mediolanensia XI Milano Vita e Pensiero 1981 XXVI & 529 p.

> SubAuth1   Beatrice P. F.
> AuthRol1   a cura di
> SubAuth2   Cantalamessa R.
> SubAuth3   Persic A.
> SubAuth4   Pizzolato L. F.
> SubAuth5   Scaglioni C.
> Subauth6   Tibiletti G.
> ManySubs   Visonà G.

13. **AuthRol2** (Second Author's Role).

Example of two or more subsidiary authors, two or more roles:

Giuliano l'Apostata nelle Storie di Ammiano [extraits des 1. XV, XVI, XVII, XVIII, XX, XXI, XXII, XXIV, XXV], introd., testo & comm. a cura di Selem A., trad. di Chiabò M. : Nuovi Saggi LXXIII Roma Ed. dell'Ateneo e Bizzarri 1979 606 p.

SubAuth1	Selem A.
AuthRol1	introd., testo & comm. a cura di
SubAuth2	Chiabò M.
AuthRol2	trad. di

14. **SubAuth3** (Third Subsidiary Author).

15. **AuthRol3** (Third Author's Role).

16. **SubAuth4** (Fourth Subsidiary Author).

17. **AuthRol4** (Fourth Author's Role).

18. **SubAuth5** (Fifth Subsidiary Author).

19. **AuthRol5** (Fifth Author's Role).

20. **SubAuth6** (Sixth Subsidiary Author).

21. **AuthRol6** (Sixth Author's Role).

22. **ManySubs** (Additional Subsidiary Authors).

23. **SerEd1** (Series Editor).

24. **SerEdRo1** (Series Editor's Role).

Example of series editor and role:

Handbuch der Dogmengeschichte, hrsg. von Schmaus M. [et al.] : Freiburg Herder : — II,3a,1 : Scheffczyk L., *Urstand, Fall und Erbsünde von der Schrift bis Augustinus* : 1981 VI & 239 p.

AnAuth1	Scheffczyk L.
SerEd1	Schmaus M. [et al.]
SerEdRo1	hrsg. von

25. **SerEd2** (Second Series Editor).

26. **SerEdRol2** (Second Series Editor's Role).

27. **SerEd3** (Third Series Editor).

28. **SerEdRol3** (Third Series Editor's Role).

29. **AnalTitl1** (Analytic Title) — Title of article, chapter.

30. **Antitl2** (Second Analytic Title) — Title of an individual part when an article is published in parts.

Example of analytic title and second analytic title:

Moraux P., *Anecdota Graeca minora, IV : Aratea* [en all.] : ZPE XLII 1981 47-51.

Analtitl1	Anecdota Graeca minora, IV
Analtitl2	Aratea

31. **MonTitle** (Monographic title) — Title of single volume.

Example of analytic title and monographic title:

Walsh P. G., *Apuleius and Plutarch* : Essays in honour of A. H. Armstrong (cf. N° 11788) 20-32.

AnalTitl1	Apuleius and Plutarch
MonTitle	Essays in honour of A. H. Armstrong

32. **SubTitle** (Title of individual volume in a set of volumes of the same name).

Example of monographic title and subtitle:

The complete works, II : Orations XVII-LIII, transl. by Behr Ch. A. : Leiden Brill 1981 VII & 502 p. [286

MonTitle	The complete works
Subtitle	Orations XVII-LIII
BookVol	II

33. **TitleCom** (Title Comments) — Comments in square brackets added by the *APh* within or following title.

Example of title comment:

Sergent B., *Le royaume d'Arcadie* [dans les tablettes mycéniennes] ; cf. N° 9495.

TitleCom	dans les tablettes mycéniennes

34. **Lang** (Language) — Comment added by the *APh* and DCB to denote language of work or abstract. Appears in *APh* after title or after extent.

Example of language comment:

Sergejev V. M., *L'analyse structurale du texte du disque de Phaistos et l'identification de sa langue* [en russe] : Structure du texte-81 (cf. N° 11762) 165-167.

Lang	russe

35. **SerTitl1** (Series Title) — Numbered series of volumes.

36. **SerVol1** (Series Volume) — Number.

Example of a simple series:

Salzmann D., *Untersuchungen zu den antiken Kieselmosaiken. Von den Anfängen bis zum Beginn der Tesseratechnik*: Archäol. Forsch. X Berlin Mann 1982 139 p. 102 pl. ill. 2 cartes.

MonTitle	Untersuchungen zu den antiken Kieselmosaiken. Von den Anfängen bis zum Beginn der Tesseratechnik
SerTitle1	Archäol. Forsch.
SerVol1	X

37. **SerIss1** (Series Issue).

38. **SerTitl2** (Second Series Title).

39. **SerVol2** (Second Series Volume).

Example of two nested or parallel series:

Gero S., *Byzantine iconoclasm during the reign of Constantine V with particular attention to the Oriental sources* : Corp. script. Christ. Orient. CCCLXXXIV Subsid. LII Louvain SCO 1977 xiv & 191 p.

SerTitle1	Corp. script. Christ. Orient.
SerVol1	CCCLXXXIV
SerTitle2	Subsid.
SerVol2	LII

40. **SerIss2** (Second Series Issue).

41. **SerTitl3** (Third Series Title).

42. **SerVol3** (Third Series Volume).

43. **SerIss3** (Third Series Issue).

44. **BookVol** (Volume Identification) — Volume number for book or journal.

Example of one volume from a set:

Aristides Rhetor — *Opera quae extant omnia*, I ; cf. APh XLIX N° 351.

MonTitle	Opera quae extant omnia
BookVol	I

45. **JourSerI** (Journal Series Indicator).

Example of an article in a journal with journal series indicator:

Smolak K., *Sol calet igne meo (Anthologia Latina 221 im Mittelalter)* : WS N.F. XV 1981 233-248.

AnalTitle1	Sol calet igne meo (Anthologia Latina 221 im Mittelalter)
MonTitle	WS
BookVol	XV
JourSerI	N.F.

46. JourIsID (Issue Identification) — Issue number or issue name of journal.

Example of an article in a journal with journal issue identification:

Bossi F., *Appunti per un profilo di Archiloco* : QS VII 1981 N° 13 117-142.

AnalTitle1	Appunti per un profilo di Archiloco
MonTitle	QS
BookVol	VII
JourIsID	13

47. Jourseq (Sequels to Journal Article).

48. Ed&Rep (Edition and Reprint Information).

Example of a previously published work:

Woodhead A. G., *The study of Greek inscriptions*, 2nd ed. : Cambridge Univ. Pr. 1981 XIV & 150 p. 4 pl. 3 ill. (pour la 1<C>rsup esup<C> éd., cf. APh XLI p.564).

Ed&Rep	2nd ed.

49. PubImp (Publisher's Imprint) — Unnumbered series.

Example of a publisher's imprint:

Alchimica — **Les alchimistes grecs,** *I : Papyrus de Leyde, Papyrus de Stockholm, Fragments de recettes,* texte établi & trad. par Halleux R. : Coll. G. Bud Paris Les Belles Lettres 1981 237 p. en partie doubles lexique.

PubImp	Coll. G. Bud

50. PlofPub1 (Place of Publication).

51. Publish1 (Publisher) — Includes university for dissertations.

52. PlofPub2 (Second Place of Publication).

53. Publish2 (Second Publisher).

Two publishers in separate cities:

Science and speculation. Studies in Hellenistic theory and practice, ed. by Brunschwig J., Burnyeat M. F. & Schofield M. : Cambridge Univ. Pr. &

Paris Maison des Sciences de l'Homme 1982 XXVII & 351 p. (dépouillé dans le présent vol.).

Publish1	Cambridge Univ. Pr.
PlofPub1	Cambridge
Publish2	Maison des Sciences de l'Homme
Plof Pub2	Paris

54. **DatofPub** (Date of Publication).

55. **DateCom** (Date Comments) — Comments in square brackets added by the *APh* within or after date.

Example of date and date comment:

Meritt B. D., *The Choiseul marble again* : AE 1978 [1980] 95-108.

| DatofPub | 1978 |
| DateCom | 1980 |

56. **Location** (Location) — Range of pages in a book or journal.

Example of location of an article:

Gerber D. E., *Archilochus fr. IV West. A commentary* : ICS VI 1981 1-11.

| Location | 1-11 |

57. **Extent** (Extent of Work) — Total and types of pages in a book.

Example of extent:

Kopecek T. A., *A history of neoarianism* : Cambridge, Mass. Philadelphia Patristic Found. 1979 V & 553 p. en 2 vol.

| Extent | V & 553 p. en 2 vol. |

58. **ExtCom** (Extent Comments) — Comments in square brackets added by the *APh* within or after extent.

59. **Medium** (Medium) — If other than ordinary print.

Example of medium:

Palaima T. G., *The scribes of Pylos* : Diss. Univ. of Wisconsin Madison 1980 270 p. [microfilm]. | Cf. summary in DA XLI 1981 4383A.

| Medium | microfilm |

60. **Type** — Type of publication: aj = article in journal; ac = article in collection; m = monograph; c = collection; e = edition; d = dissertation; r = review; s = summary.

Examples of types:

Tomasco D., *Su Apuleio, De deo Socr.* I 116,9-II 119,10 *Th.* : Vichiana IX 1980 166-172.

Type   aj

Bili<C>nacute<C>ski B., *Appio Claudio Cieco el' aspetto sociale della sua sentenza Fabrum esse suae quemque fortunae* : Lett. compar. (cf. N° 11834) 283-291.

Type   ac

Bynum W. F. & Nutton V., *Theories of fever from antiquity to the Enlightenment* : Med. Hist. Suppl. I London Wellcome Inst. Hist. of Medicine 1981 IX & 154 p.

Type   m

Médecins et médecine dans l'antiquité, art. réunis & éd. par Sabbah G., avec en complément les Actes des Journées d'étude sur la médecine antique d'époque romaine (Saint-Étienne 14-15 mai 1982) : Mém. du Centre Jean Palerne III Saint-Étienne Publ. de l'Univ. 1982 191 p.

Type   c

Apollonius Rhodius — *Argonautiques,* III : Chant IV, texte établi & comm. par Vian F., trad. par Delage E. & Vian F. : Coll. G. Budé Paris Les Belles Lettres 1981 273 p. en partie doubles 3 indices 4 cartes en dépliants.

Type   e

Blank D. L., *Studies in the syntactic theory of Apollonius Dyscolus* : Diss. Princeton Univ. Princeton, N.J. 1980 143 p. [microfilm]. | Cf. summary in DA XLI 1981 3094A.

Type   d

Shackleton Bailey D. R., *Towards a text of the Anthologia Latina* ; cf. APh L N° 215. | RPh LV 1981 185 André | CR XXXI 1981 39-42 Courtney.

Type   r

Mandouze A., *Prosopographie et histoire de l'Église.* Le dossier Petrus abbas (523-525) : Résumé dans BSAF 1977 141-142.

Type   s

61. **Reviews** (Book reviews).

Example of multiple reviews:

Heisserer A. J., *Alexander the Great and the Greeks* ; cf. APh LI Nᵘ 8595.
| Platon XXXII-XXXIII 1980-1981 400-402 Mitsos | G & R XXVIII 1981
101 Mosley.

Reviews   Platon XXXII-XXXIII 1980-1981 400-402 Mitsos
                           | G & R XXVIII 1981 101 Mosley

62. **Summary** — Location of summary in DA or elsewhere.

Example of summary of American dissertation:

Palaima T. G., *The scribes of Pylos* : Diss. Univ. of Wisconsin Madison
1980 270 p. [microfilm]. | Cf. summary in DA XLI 1981 4383A.

Summary   DA XLI 1981 4383A

Example of summary of book:

Novara A., *Les idées romaines sur le progrès d'après les écrivains de la
république. Essai sur le sens latin du mot progrès*, I : Coll. d'ét. anc. Paris
Les Belles Lettres 1982 560 p. [rés. dans IL XXXIII 1981 111-119].

Summary   IL XXXIII 1981 111-119

63. **APhVol** (*APh* Volume).

64. **APhPage** (*APh* Page).

65. **APhID** (*APh* ID Number).

66. **APhRub** (*APh* Rubric).

67. **APhCRef** (Cross Reference Information).

Example of a cross-reference within volume:

Shelmerdine C. W., *Nichoria in context* [dans les tablettes en linéaire B] ;
cf. N° 9394.

APhCRef   9394

68. **CrRefCom** (Cross Reference Comment) — e.g. "suite" or "depouille."

Example of cross-reference to another volume with a comment:

Guarducci M., *Epigrafia greca, IV : Epigrafi sacre pagane e cristiane* :
Roma Istituto Poligraf. dello Stato 1978 X & 601 p. ill. (pour le tome III,
cf. APh XLIX N° 8804).

AphCRef   XLIX 8804
CrRefCom   pour le tome III

69. **Notes** — Miscellaneous information printed with entry.

70. **LastDate** — Last date record was modified by DCB. Used for editorial housekeeping. Will not print out.

71. **Abstract** — *APh* summary.

Example of *APh* abstract:

Matthews V. J., *Who were the kings of the Aigialans?* <G>BASILEUE/
TORES *AI)GIALH/WN<G> <MD49>in *Antimachos 10 Wyss* : AncW
III 1980 113-114. | Antimachos does not use the word <G>*AI)GIALH/
WN<G> for the Greeks in general.

Abstract	Antimachos does not use the word <G>*AI) GIALH/WN<G> for the Greeks in general.

An uncomplicated journal article would look like this in the printed volume:

Schwartz J., *L'empereur Alexandre Sévère, le SB X 10295 et le P. Fay. 20* :
ZPE LXI 1985 122-124. | Revidierter Text, Übersetzung, Kommentar zu SB
X 10295. Der Brief ist Alexander Severus zuzuschreiben und gewinnt an
Aussagekraft, wenn man ihn mit P. Fay. 20 vergleicht, der denselben Kaiser
betrifft.

And like this after formatting:

AnAuth1	Schwartz, J.
AnalTitl	L'empereur Alexandre Sévère, le SB X 10295 et le P. Fay. 20
MonTitl	ZPE
BookVol	LXI
DatofPub	1985
Location	122-124
Type	aj
APhVol	56
APhPage	97
APhID	1533
APhRub	Epistulae
Abstract	Revidierter Text, Übersetzung, Kommentar zu SB X 10295. Der Brief ist Alexander Severus zuzuschreiben und gewinnt an Aussagekraft, wenn man ihn mit P. Fay. 20 vergleicht, der denselben Kaiser betrifft.

An edition of an ancient text would be changed from this form:

Euripides' Kresphontes and Archelaos, introd., text & comm. by Harder A.
: Mnemosyne Suppl. LXXXVII Leiden Brill 1985 xi & 302 p.

To this:

AnAuth1	Euripides
SubAuth1	Harder A.
AuthRol1	introd., text & comm. by
MonTitle	Euripides' Kresphontes and Archelaos
SerTitl1	Mnemosyne Suppl.
SerVol1	LXXXVII
PlofPub	Leiden
Publish1	Brill
DatofPub	1985
Extent	xi & 302 p.
Type	e
APhVol	56
APhPage	100
APhID	1591
APhRub	Euripides

Initial reformatting is partially automated so that articles in journals and collections, book reviews, dissertations, and simple cross-references are tagged automatically. Monographs and editions will soon be treated in the same way, but the intricacy of the printed entries, their multilingual nature and the variety of European citation formats will prevent us from automating the process completely. Although the bibliography could be produced and searched without any formatting, as if it were a text, defining the logical parts of each entry offers great advantages for the most essential database functions: indexing, searching, and formatting output.

3.2. Indexing and Searching

Searching a full text is quickly done, but searching an index is faster still and much more efficient. This advantage is especially important for those searching CD-ROM, which are comparatively slow, using microcomputers without large amounts of memory; it will be most apparent when the database begins to approach its full size. The DCB will provide indices of all fields which can be searched individually or in groups. This feature not only increases searching speeds, but also allows maximum control for the user in the searching process. For example, one could search for "West M." in the author fields and produce a list of everything Martin West has written relating to classical studies (handy for preparing an edition of his *Kleine Schriften*), but if one only wants to verify a citation of his edition of the *Theogony,* a search for "West M." in the author fields AND "Theogony" in the title fields would lead straight to the desired entry, which would be printed with all its reviews as a bonus. If the reviews were not wanted, the search would be for "West M." AND "Theogony" AND NOT "r" in the type (of entry) field.

With all fields in the database indexed, it will be a simple matter, for example, to produce a list of all publishers of classical texts, all American dissertations, or all of the abbreviations used in classical bibliography. It is hardly possible to guess all of the purposes this information could serve.

Subject searching, an area where the database has the most dramatic advantage over the printed volumes, will be based on a master index of words that appear in the titles and abstracts. This will be, in effect, a constantly growing, multilingual thesaurus of subjects and technical terms relevant to the study of classical antiquity. Users will be able to access the word list directly as an aid in searching or use it in tandem with other databases.

When the word list is used directly, one can find all instances of any word or set of words. A search on "Antigone," for example, will turn up all the entries for books and articles that have her name in the title and/or abstract fields. Thus, it would find M. Davies, "Sophocles' Antigone 823ff. as a Specimen of Mythological Hyperbole," *Hermes* 113 (1985): 247–49, and also H. Patzer, "Methodische Grundsätze der Sophoklesinterpretation," Poetica 15 (1983): 1–33, which is accompanied by the following abstract in *APh* vol. 56, p. 275: "Les tragédies de Sophocle doivent être interprétées en fonction du système signes poétiques propre à cet auteur (système qui reste à définir) et en tenant compte de la «théologie tragique» qui est à la base de l'imaginaire athénien du ve s. Interprétation de l'Antigone à titre d'exemple."

A search on "Antigone," however, will not find a book like Cedric Whitman's *Sophocles* (Cambridge, Mass., 1951), which has a chapter on the *Antigone* that is not described in the standard bibliographical reference. The best guarantee to finding all the relevant references would be to request all the entries for "Antigone" and "Sophocles" and "Poésie dramatique" and then be prepared to spend some time in the library. Although this leaves the researcher with a good deal of sifting and reading to do, it is far more efficient than looking through each of the printed volumes.

In the case of Antigone it is clear what broader categories one should search in order to find the narrower subject, but suppose one were interested in third-century epigrammatists. A search on the word list for "third century" or even "epigrammatists" is likely to turn up only a fraction of the desired references. It would, of course, be possible to assemble a list of relevant authors' names, but suppose the searcher is a student who does not know the names or where to find them. In this case the search can succeed by using two related databases: the bibliography and a machine-readable version of Luci Berkowitz and Karl A. Squitier, *Thesaurus Linguae Graecae Canon of Greek Authors and Works,* 2d ed., 1986, 3d ed., 1990, which could be incorporated into the searching software (for discussion of the *TLG Canon,* see chapter 2 above). The *Canon* contains entries for 2,884 ancient Greek authors with essential information about their life and work including each author's date by century, place of origin, works, genre of works, and recommended editions. From an initial scan of the *Canon* the program could create a list of all epigrammatists, then all third-century epigrammatists, and finally, it would match these names against authors' names in the bibliography using a list of alternative spellings. In this way, the student searching for third-century epigrammatists, who had never heard the name of Asclepiades of Samos, could assemble a set of articles on his work and the work of his contemporaries from bibliographical citations that mention neither the date nor the genre.

This approach to searching, by using multiple, related databases, enhances the value of the *APh* summaries, eliminates the tedious and expensive task of adding keywords to the bibliography, and offers the possibility of incorporating additional thesauri of terms for special subjects, like mythology and ancient history. Indices designed orginally to enhance searching the database of classical iconography maintained by the U.S. office of the *LIMC,* for example, could also be used with the DCB to facilitate a search for bibliography on all "Iliadic heroes" or all "Olympians," because the *LIMC* indices define each mythological figure in a range of different categories.[3] In theory, there is no limit to the number of databases that can be related, and we can look forward to the day when all of the databases described in this volume can be searched with and through each other.

3.3. Output

The division of each entry into logical fields also provides maximum flexibility in formatting output because the parts can be reassembled in any desired order. Software will allow entries to be output to a disk or a printer in a variety of standard formats including the original *APh* format, *TAPA, MLA, Chicago Manual A & B,* and *TEI-2* (SGML). It will also be possible to output the data in tagged or delimited form so that it can be imported into any standard database management system. This will be particularly useful to those pursuing large-scale research projects who will want to create their own more focused bibliographical databases. If none of the options provided suffice, users will be able to produce output according to their own design.

3.4. Distribution

The project will begin distributing its database with attendant indices and software on a CD-ROM as soon as sufficient funding is available. The directory and file structure of the data on the disk will follow ISO 9660, the so-called "High Sierra" format. Software, provided by the project, will permit the disk to be searched on a variety of standard machines including both DOS (IBM) and Macintosh equipment. Search screens will be available in English, French, and German, and all non-Roman characters including the entire Greek alphabet will be correctly printed. The software will be developed by a commercial vendor from an existing product.

4. Future Development

Following the production of the first CD-ROM, the database will be expanded backward, to include all previous volumes of the *APh* and earlier bibliographies; forward, to include future volumes of the *APh;* and sideways, to include bibliographies in related areas. Following the agreement with the Paris office reached at the meeting in Chapel Hill, movement forward in time will be restricted in order to protect the sales of the most recently printed volumes. The overall rate of development, approximately ten volumes added in each two-year cycle, will also be limited both by the labor-intensive nature of proofreading and editorial work and by the level of financial support the project can reasonably expect.

The addition of earlier bibliographies and those in related fields will follow the completion of the *APh* unless they can be supplied in machine-readable form and do not require extensive proofreading. An international board of consultants, appointed by the American Philological Association in cooperation with the SIBC, will be charged with determining priorities for entry of material after the completion of the *APh*.

A sizable expenditure of human and financial resources will be necessary to bring the project to completion, but it will be more than worth the effort. When it is complete, classical studies will have a bibliographical database of incomparable value.

5. Additional Samples

Article in a journal:

Pannoux S., *La représentation du travail ; récit et image sur les monuments funéraires des Médiomatriques* : DHA XI 1985 293-328. | Une approche sémiologique de la structure, du fonctionnement et des éléments constitutifs des représentations du travail sur les monuments funéraires gallo-romains des Médiomatriques, de la documentation témoignant de modes de figuration, de valeurs, de normes sociales, fait apparaître le fonctionnement du rapport des hommes au travail, les formes de dépendance, leur rôle dans le système de production. [8286

AP vol. 56, p. 490, N° 8286, rubric: Gaule et Germanie.

AnAuth1	Pannoux S.
AnalTitl	La représentation du travail ; récit et image sur les monuments funéraires des Médiomatriques
MonTitle	DHA
BookVol	XI
DatofPub	1985

Location	293-328
Type	aj
APhVol	56
APhPage	490
APhID	8286
APhRub	Gaule et Germanie
Abstract	Une approche sémiologique de la structure, du fonctionnement et des éléments constitutifs des représentations du travail sur les monuments funéraires gallo-romains des Médiomatriques, de la documentation témoignant de modes de figuration, de valeurs, de normes sociales, fait apparaître le fonctionnement du rapport des hommes au travail, les formes de dépendance, leur rôle dans le système de production.

Article in a collection:

Knabe G. S. *L'espace historique et le temps historique dans la civilisation de la Rome antique* [en russe] : Civilization de la Rome antique (cf. N° 12208) II: 109-166. [5707

APh vol. 56, p. 353, N° 5707, rubric: Littérature narrative et Historiographie.

AnAuth1	Knabe G.S.
AnalTitl	L'espace historique et le temps historique dans la civilisation de la Rome antique
MonTitle	Civilization de la Rome antique
Lang	en russe
BookVol	II
Location	109-166
APhvol	56
APhPage	353
APhID	5707
APhRub	Littérature narrative et Historiographie
APhCRef	12208

N.B. Software will be designed to fetch the cross-referenced volume automatically:

Collection:

SubAuth1	Kolosovskaja Ju. K.
ManySubs	et al.
AuthRol1	éd. par
MonTitle	Civilization de la Rome antique
Lang	en russe

```
BookVoI      I & II
PlofPub1     Moskva
Publish1     Nauka
DatofPub     1985
Extent       2 vol. de 432 & 398 p.
Type         c
APhVol       56
APhPage      705
APhID        12208
APhRub       Civilisation romaine
CrRefCom     dépouillé
```

Monograph:

Deiss J.J., *Herculaneum. Italy's buried treasure* : London Thames & Hudson 1985 xviii & 222 p. 118 ill. [11498

APh vol 56, p. 667, N° 11498, rubric: Monde romain et byzantin

```
AnAuth1      Deiss J.J.
MonTitle     Herculaneum. Italy's buried treasure
PlofPub      London
Publish1     Thames & Hudson
DatofPub     1985
Extent       xviii & 222 p. 118 ill.
Type         m
APhVol       56
APhPage      667
APhID        11498
APhRub       Monde romain et byzantin
```

Reviews:

Brilliant R., *Visual narratives. Storytelling in Etruscan and Roman art* ; cf. LV N° 8516. | CR XXXV 1985 169-171 Colledge | AJPh CVI 1985 523-527 Pollini.

APh vol. 56, p. 52, N° 8932, rubric: Archéologie romaine.

```
AnAuth1      Brilliant R.
MonTitle     Visual narratives. Storytelling in Etruscan and Roman art
Type         r
Rev          CR XXXV 1985 169-171 Colledge | AJPh CVI 1985 523-
             527 Pollini
APhVol       56
APhPage      52
APhID        8516
```

APhRub   Archéologie romaine
APhCRef   LV 8516

N.B. Searches will generally produce all of the published reviews of a book as well as the original publication information unless specifically limited.

Edition of an ancient author:

I cosmetici delle donne, introd., testo, trad. e comm. a cura di Rosati G. : Il convivio Coll. di class. greci e lat. Venezia Marsilio ed. 1985 96 p. [3096

APh vol. 56, p. 197, N° 3096, rubric: Ovidius.

AnAuth1	Ovidius
SubAuth1	Rosati G.
AuthRol1	introd., testo, trad. e comm. a cura di
MonTitle	I cosmetici delle donne
PubImp	Il convivio Coll. de class. greci e lat.
PlofPub	Venezia
Publish1	Marsilio ed.
DatofPub	1985
Extent	96 p.
APhVol	56
APhPage	197
APhID	3096
APhRub	Ovidius

Dissertation:

Arnold B.M., *Neoteric Vergil. Alexandrian themes in the Eclogues* : Diss. The Univ. of Washington Seattle 1984 408 p. [microfilm]. | Cf. summary in DA XLV 1985 3342A. [5100

APh vol 56, p. 317, N° 5100, rubric: Vergilius.

AnAuth1	Arnold B.M.
MonTitle	Neoteric Vergil. Alexandrian themes in the Eclogues
PlofPub	Seattle
Publish1	The Univ. of Washington
DatofPub	1984
Extent	408 p.
Medium	microfilm
Type	d
Summary	DA XLV 1985 3342A
APhVol	56
APhPage	317
APhID	5100
AphRub	Vergilius

Notes

1. Conca, et al., *Lessico dei romanzieri greci, I* (Cisalpino-La Goliardica, Milano 1983).

2. Hägg, "Metiochus at Polycrates' Court," *Eranos* 83 (1985): 92–102.

3. The concept of relating various databases of classical material was first described in a paper entitled "Databases for Research in Classics," delivered by J. Penny Small at the annual meeting of the American Philological Association on Dec. 30, 1986, in San Antonio.

7

The Perseus Project
Data in the Electronic Age

Elli Mylonas, Gregory Crane, Kenneth Morrell, and D. Neel Smith

We conceive the humanities as a pickle factory preserving human "values" too tender and inert for the outside world. The world goes its way but supports us, museumlike, to show what, had it been composed of people like us, it might have become. This cozy conspiracy is sustained by both sides. The harsh world wants to imagine a finer world and we pretend to dwell in it. But our students and the society from which they come will not permit this illusion to continue unchanged; nor will a technology which has volatilized print; nor will our own thinking, our "theory," about what we are and do.

RICHARD LANHAM, "The Electronic Word"[1]

Introduction

As cultures transform their primary forms of discourse from oral to written, different ways of thinking and communicating emerge, engendered by the new technology of writing. The use of computers, in the scholarly domain and outside it, is bringing about a similar paradigm shift.[2] The Perseus Project, which has as its goal to transfer information traditionally used in the study of Classics and archaeology into electronic form, must also learn how to transform that information so that it is functional in its new form. By taking into account the new ways of using information, we are concentrating not only on collecting the information and presenting it to our audience but also on structuring it and recreating it in an electronically viable form. The results of this effort may not be immediately apparent to readers of the Perseus CD-ROM, but they will nevertheless ensure the survival of the material in Perseus beyond any one machine or any single use. It is important that this work be done by classicists and archaeologists in a research project like Perseus: if we, who know the material best, do not do it first, it will be done by publishers and others whose goals are very different and whose end results may not be the best for our work.

The goal of the Perseus Project is to put the information traditionally used in the study of Classics and archaeology into electronic form and to disseminate it in a system that not only facilitates familiar ways of using these materials but also makes possible new types of research that may not have been feasible previously. In order to do this a number of problems must be solved: we must find ways to translate print texts, drawings, and photographic images into useful computerized formats, discover clear ways in which to present this information to the student and scholar, and create tools that will enable several different uses of the same materials. In addition, we must ensure that the basic, archival form in which we store Perseus data is general and system-independent enough that it will outlast any one software or hardware system. In order to determine the success of all such aspects of the project, we have made an effort to evaluate the project as it comes into being and is put to use in different types of classes all over the United States.

The Perseus Project grew out of a fascination with words. The Thesaurus Linguae Graecae (TLG), publicly released in 1982, spawned at Harvard a software project which developed a powerful full-text retrieval system. The more we worked with the data at our disposal, the more we thought about how computers could help us explore and study the ancient world. The Perseus Project, with its broad range of materials, was designed to complement the textual focus of the TLG. Perseus will contain information from a variety of sources and in a variety of media — texts in the original and in translation, plans of sites and buildings, color photographs of archaeological objects and places, and such secondary materials as a Greek-English Lexicon, a classical encyclopedia, and an overview of Greek history. These will be linked together so that a user of the system can move easily from one source to another. As a result, students will be able to explore the ancient world more easily and to discover and even synthesize information faster than they might have in the traditional library, and scholars will be able to incorporate materials into their research that they might not otherwise have broached.

The purpose of this article is to describe the Perseus Project, the different types of information being included in it, and the methods and reasons for their preparation. It will also discuss the ongoing evaluation process, as that will influence how the project will develop in the future. Some aspects of the Perseus system, such as the software tools that allow users to annotate and link its different parts, are beyond the scope of this article. (See the bibliography for more on these aspects.)

Origins of Perseus and Modus Operandi

Work on Perseus began in 1990, and was planned to take five years. The first year was spent in doing preliminary research and preparing a "proof of concept" so that funding for the full project would be granted.[3] The project applied for its full funding during that year and received a grant to carry it through four years, until winter 1993. The plan was, during this time, to collect about 100 mb of textual data and over 10,000 images, release four versions of the Perseus database on compact disk and videodisc, and evaluate how these materials are used in various academic situations.

Perseus is a large undertaking, and it can only be accomplished through the collaboration of many people. It is already a collective effort by classicists and archaeologists from several institutions in the United States. In addition to the authors of this article, significant contributions have been made by T. R. Martin of Pomona College and by several other scholars who have contributed translations of Greek texts and descriptions of archaeological objects. The Perseus classical encyclopedia already includes articles on geography and prosopography by graduate students from Brown University and the University of Wisconsin at Madison. As work on the basic formats of the Perseus system progresses, we plan to solicit more such contributions and, ultimately, to accept submissions as a refereed journal.

Perseus, because it explores the transferal of a variety of data onto the media of computers, is by nature a research effort. However, we are also committed to producing working versions of the system during the course of its development, so as to gather information about its use and to modify it accordingly. To this end, there will be four yearly versions of Perseus, beginning in the winter of 1990. The first versions of Perseus run under HyperCard on the Macintosh computer and are distributed on a combination of compact disk and videodisc.[4] When work on the basic database has progressed further, we plan to explore other hardware and software platforms as well as taking into account developments in distribution media.

Textual Material

Texts comprise a significant part of the Perseus Project. In this we are not attempting to emulate the exhaustive coverage provided by the TLG. We are, instead, intent on collecting a smaller number of classical texts, providing them with such ancillary material as translations and lexicographical tools, and incorporating them into the contextualized whole that is Perseus. The texts we have chosen to include are primarily those of the fifth century B.C. complemented by some later material that serves as an important reference for the classical period. A decision was made early in the development of Perseus to focus on one period and to create a rich collection of materials for the study of this period. We also want to provide the texts that are used most often in teaching classical Greek. We decided to begin by concentrating on the fifth century and to slowly extend coverage in either chronological direction as the project progressed. In addition to Aeschylus, Sophocles, Herodotus, and Pindar, our early versions also include Pausanias, Pseudo-Apollodorus, and the Greek lives of Plutarch. We are in the process of adding Homer, Aristophanes, the Attic orators, Thucydides, lyric and elegiac poetry, Plato, and some Aristotle. We will later add relevant parts of Diodorus Siculus and Strabo.

Sources and Basis of Selection

For Perseus to be a viable system, the textual material it contains has to be at least as useful and useable, if not more so, than printed texts. Our goal therefore is to discover how to transport and display information that was created for the scroll, and has been adapted to the codex, onto the computer screen. On the one hand, we need to discover and use features inherent in the electronic form of a text; on the other, we must not lose the time-tested features of the book. For example, although a text's electronic incarnation may not impose page breaks — an artificial division — these may act as important reference markers that enable a reader find a particular place. So, although the text ought not to be broken up into page sized chunks, it may be necessary to record where the page breaks of a definitive edition occurred. Such holdovers already appear in print editions of classical texts, where the canonical referencing for an edition derives from the pagination of an earlier edition (e.g., Stephanus pages in Plato).

One important advantage of electronic texts is that they may be displayed in different ways, depending on the purpose for which they will be used, and in different combinations. Perseus can use the same set of textual components to create different "editions." A text may be viewed in Greek only, or in Greek and English, with accompanying notes or with a metrical analysis, for example. It may also form a part of a different logical "document," as in the case of a section of text included in a multimedia essay.

Works in Perseus consist of original Greek text and an accompanying translation. The choice to include translations is to allow students and other scholars who are not fluent readers of Greek to work with the texts and to broaden the circumstances in which Perseus will be consulted. In addition to the original text and the translation, we also plan to accumulate other data that pertain to these texts, such as notes, metrical analyses for choral odes, and some critical apparatus. (Some of these materials will derive from contributions submitted to the project by scholars who have developed them in the course of their teaching and research; others will be entered by the project from extant sources.) Our goal is not only to provide as much information as there is in a critical edition but to present the same information in such a versatile manner that it can be used by people at different levels of proficiency and for different purposes. Traditionally, each of these levels or purposes requires its own printed edition, which provides different types of information, or sometimes the same information but with a different emphasis. In its electronic incarnation, the same basic form may be used for different purposes with only a few changes or additions.

Most of the textual material currently in Perseus comes from books that already exist in print. Since the Perseus database will be widely distributed, it is necessary to make sure that any information within it, textual or otherwise, either is clearly owned by Harvard,[5] is within the public domain, or that permissions have been obtained for its use within Perseus. With these constraints in mind, we decided to rely on the Loeb Classical Library for a large portion of our Greek and English texts. Although the texts are usually quite accurate, the English translations of the Loeb texts are often archaic and difficult to read. These are being revised to eliminate archaisms and to make them more accessible.[6] Other sources for Perseus texts are out-of-copyright editions that are still considered authoritative and original translations not under copyright. We are including significant notes such as Frazer's from the Loeb Pseudo-Apollodorus, and, initially, the notes from Jebb's *editio maior of Oedipus Tyrannus*.

Production

Although simple data entry was the first hurdle we encountered in transferring texts onto the computer, it is by no means the most difficult problem to solve. Texts are scanned in by an optical character reader, or, when there is more complex typesetting or Greek, keyboarded. They are then proofread so that the errors introduced in the data-entry process are removed. Keyboarding, which is more expensive up front, is often more cost effective, because the results tend to be more accurate and require less correction later. Scanning is initially cheaper but requires substantial correcting and proofreading.[7]

For these texts to be useful in their new, electronic form, they must undergo substantial work that will make explicit their inherent structure and other important features. Classical texts have a variety of implicit structures and features, most of which will be necessary for different applications. Most important is the canonical reference structure which is used to refer unambiguously to any part of a text, regardless (usually) of the contemporary edition. This must be preserved; in addition, many of the indications of lineation and alternate numbering that are left up to the reader to intuit must be written out. Further, there are metrical structures in verse, different types of discourse in historical and rhetorical prose, and the additions of ancient editors, such as speaker names in drama, that are essentially part of the received text. Most of these structures are indicated in one way or another by the typesetting of the text on the page. However, the typesetting is less an end in itself than a means for conveying this information.

Structuring Text

One of the important goals of Perseus is for the data it creates to remain useful beyond the lifetime of any one piece of hardware or software. This means that it must be easily portable to different systems. To make it so, we have to seek

```
<CHAPTER NUM ="88" >
<SECTION NUM ="1" >*darei = os de \ meta \ tau = ta h(sqei\s th =
sxedi/hl to \n a)rxite / ktona au)th = s *mandrokle / a to \n *sa/mion
e)dwrh / sato pa = si de/ka: a)p' w( = n dh \ *mandrokle/hs a)parxh
\n zw = l a graya / menos pa = san th \n zeu = cin tou = *bospo / rou kai\
basile / a te *darei = on e)n proedri/hl kath/menon kai\ to \n strato \n
au)tou = diabai / nonta tau = ta graya / menos a)ne / qhke e)/s to \
*(/hraion,e)pigra / yas ta / de.</SECTION>
<SECTION NUM ="2" >
<ORACLE METER ="&dact;" >
<LINE>*bo / sporon i)xquo / enta gefurw / sas a)ne / qhke</LINE>
<LINE>*mandrokle / hs *(/hrhl mnhmo / sunon sxedi / hs,</LINE>
<LINE>au(tw = l me\n ste / fanon periqei / s, *sami / oisi de \ ku = dos,
   </LINE>
<LINE>*darei / ou basile / os e)ktele / sas kata \ nou = n.</LINE>
</ORACLE></SECTION></CHAPTER>
```

7.1. Part of Book 4 of Herodotus, tagged in SGML.

out generic and supportable archival formats for all our data. In the case of
text, we have decided to use SGML[8] to encode all the texts in Perseus. SGML
provides a means for marking the structure of a text using elements that are
significant because of their content and not their appearance; it also codifies
that structure so that anyone who is given the text can interpret it. Instead of
indicating page breaks and indents, we mark off reference chunks and changes
of meter or speeches. Instead of entering long and short lines of verse, we
mark them as hexameter or pentameter. This is done using human-readable
tags with intuitive names. SGML is also an ASCII encoding scheme which
restricts the character set used for both text and tags to a subset that can be
transmitted across networks and read on different types of computer.[9] Greek
characters and accents are encoded in a subset of Beta code, an ASCII scheme
developed by David Packard and used in the TLG. Beta code is designed for
encoding not only Greek characters but page formats as well. We use only the
parts that encode letters, accents, and special characters (see figure 7.1).

   Once a text has been tagged using SGML and verified so that its structure
is correct, we can start to use that structure to get more information about the
text. Using the reference structure, the texts are indexed, and all forms of all
words, together with their references, are merged into a morphological database of all the texts in Perseus. We also use the SGML structure to create the
version that readers of Perseus currently see, which is distributed in Hyper-
Card. Although a text in HyperCard does not contain all the information that

was preserved using SGML, we can draw on that information, in the form of the morphological databases, and use it to determine the visual presentation of the text itself. Furthermore, since the principal, archival form of the text is the SGML version, we can always return to it as we move to more powerful and capable distribution systems.

The most difficult and labor-intensive part of text preparation is not, as might be thought, the data entry but the verification and structuring of a text. Although these are the most costly parts of the process, they are also the most worth investing in. The structured texts will not only outlast our current delivery system — HyperCard and the Mac — but they will also outlive our current purpose. By putting them into this new form we are able to put them to new uses. As they are used by more and more people, their structures can be expanded and made more detailed so they may lead to forms of study that we cannot yet predict.

Morpheus

The text-analysis systems developed in the early 1980s did not exhaust the possibilities inherent in an electronic medium. Scholars could not, for example, search directly for φέρω but needed instead to ask for strings that more or less defined the stems of this word (e.g., φερ-, οἰσ-, ἐνεγκ- and ἠνεγκ-, etc.). For words with short stems (e.g. ἄγω) or very irregular forms (e.g. εἰμί), electronic searches were not very effective. Perseus set out to develop a system that understood Greek morphology which, if it were asked to locate φέρω, would also be able to locate ἔφερον, οἴσετε, ἠνέγκατε and other forms.

Morphological Information in Perseus

At present, the Perseus Project has a working morphological-analysis system. Every text that is included in the Perseus database is put through the analyzer and the results of the analysis are stored in a morphological database. Thus, when the parser sees ἠνέγκατε, it records not only the fact that it saw a second-person plural aorist form of φέρω, but that the stem is ἐνεγκ-, that it has an augment in this form, and that the ending is -ατε. Furthermore, the parser understands that there are different dialects: if it sees the form χώρης, it records not just the analysis but the fact that this form is Ionic; if it sees πέμψατε, it realizes that this could also be an unaugmented aorist indicative in Epic or Ionic. Whatever the parser can determine about each word is recorded, and this information can subsequently be recalled from the database.

Greek morphology is not entirely unambiguous (the average form can have 1.7 analyses), and this method thus has its limits. Nevertheless, it tends to include rather than to exclude possibilities: thus, it makes no attempt to determine whether αἰσχύνη is from αἰσχύνω or αἰσχύνη or whether πέμπω is indicative or subjunctive. Its users do, therefore, get some irrelevant information. Nevertheless, the parser rarely fails to locate a word of text that it has analyzed, and when it does, its dictionary is updated so that it will identify this form in the future.

A morphological database of this complexity is large and cannot fully be included in the general Perseus database. We do, however, include enough basic information so that anyone using Perseus can locate virtually all possible forms of a given word that appears in the database. Since most major works of Greek literature through the fourth century will ultimately be included in the database, the database itself is a powerful tool that will augment the capabilities offered by the TLG.

Ultimately, however, it would be desirable to distribute the full morphological database on a CD-ROM by itself as a resource aimed primarily at classical philologists. A scholar could then query the database to compare, for example, the frequency of abstract nouns ending in -σις in Herodotus and Thucydides, trace the relative frequency of optative forms over a period of time in early Greek prose, or search the texts themselves for all examples of ἵνα followed within ten words by a verb in the subjunctive. Generally speaking, Perseus as a whole contains far more information than we can for the foreseeable future distribute, and a complex morphological database is only one possible derivative work.

Developing the Parser

Our work on Greek morphology began at Harvard in 1984, was continued at Berkeley in 1985–86, and returned again to Harvard in 1987, where it was essentially completed by the end of 1989. A considerable amount of work had already been done in this direction before we began. In the early 1970s, David Packard had developed a system (*MORPH*) that could analyze Greek morphology, and this system was, and is still, widely used.[10] We adopted the basic algorithm of this system: our parser separates off possible preverbs and then divides stem from ending.

We set out to extend Packard's model. For the sake of simplicity, *MORPH* ignored accents and thus did not distinguish between τιμῇ and τίμη. At the time, such ambiguity was of marginal importance, and an editor could subsequently choose the correct interpretation. Likewise, *MORPH* did not address Greek dialects: χώρην and χώραν were both simply accusative singular nouns. Since the system was designed to work with one dialect at a time, there was no reason to instill in it a complex model of Greek dialects.

We decided to build a parser that would extract as much information as possible from a given Greek word. We did this both to have the most accurate database possible and also so that we could see whether designing such a system was in fact feasible — the history of computational linguistics is strewn with projects that looked simple but proved to be impractical. An automatic parser of Greek morphology is, in fact, an electronic model of the language, and we were seeing how much knowledge we could in fact represent in this new form. Human beings constantly apply their own intellectual skills to fill in the gaps of a written description.

A normal grammar will, for example, record first-declension endings in one place and simply assume that the reader can apply these endings to the one hundred odd nouns, adjectives, and participles that follow this pattern. A dialectical grammar will content itself with observing that -εω- appears as -ιω- in Laconian and will leave the reader to recognize ἀνιοχίων as a particular instance of this general rule. An electronic parser cannot, however, perform such substitutions unless it is specifically taught to do so.

Ultimately, the parsing process itself was only one of several rule-based systems. We developed entire generative models for inflections and various verb stems so that, if we dealt with a new dialect in which inflections or vowel contractions differed, we could change one entry in the database and the change would propagate itself throughout the system. Thus, if we added -αισι as a dative plural to the main list of first-declension nouns, then this ending would appear throughout. If we added the new rule "-εω- appears as -ιω- in Laconian" to our list of contraction rules, then the system would recognize this as a general phenomenon.

The most onerous task was not the programming but the development of a database of stems and endings that could support the parser, for no parser will get far with ἔπεμπε unless it knows that πεμπ is an Ω-class stem that can take the augment and an ending -ε. We used the morphological entries in the *Intermediate Liddell-Scott Lexicon* as the starting point for our database of stems and endings. The entire text was entered, and then, over the space of almost two years, the morphological information embedded within it was slowly converted into a format that the parser could use. This in turn forced us to develop a formalism to describe Greek morphology (e.g., "ἔχω takes a syllabic augment"; "φιλέω is a regular epsilon contract verb but καλέω is not"). The more words we added, the more we learned, and we often had to redo substantial amounts of work. In the end, however, the system worked fairly well. In analyzing Pausanias, a standard prose author not covered by the *Intermediate Liddell-Scott,* the parser was able to analyze roughly 97 percent of the unique strings within the text. When we include a new Greek text in Perseus, we simply add to the database whatever stems the parser needs.

Greek Morphology and Semantic Browsing in Perseus

Using of the database of morphologically parsed texts, not only classicists but other scholars and students who want to read Greek but are not expert in the language — sophomores toiling through Homer or philosophy professors with only a few years of Greek — can point to any word in a Perseus text, call up the possible morphological analyses, and then view the definition. This is possible because along with the digested morphological data from the *Interme-diate Liddell-Scott* we included the definitions.

Once we entered the definitions, however, it was a simple matter to create a rough English-Greek lexicon. It is therefore possible to discover which words contain a particular English word in their definitions, examine the definitions to identify synonyms and related terms, and thus expand the range of the search. Once a list of words is assembled, the system can use its morphological database to determine which of these words actually appears in Aeschylus as opposed to Pindar. That done, the investigator can proceed to call up each passage and examine the text itself. We discovered that this function was extremely powerful, for it allowed us to explore general semantic categories (e.g., "wealth", "honor", "anger") much more broadly and rapidly than would otherwise have been the case.

By placing the pedagogically oriented lexicon into the larger database — with its morphological information, Greek texts, and ability to index English — we allow individuals to approach this lexicon from a different direction (i.e., English to Greek) and thus transform it into a qualitatively different tool that serves a very different function. This example illustrates two general phenomena that can be expected during the transfer from a print to an electronic environment. First, simply moving the information into an electronic environment changes its value. Second, it is impossible to anticipate accurately the value of this transformation until it takes place — we had, of course, always known that we could use the new electronic lexicon as an English-Greek lexicon, but we had not fully appreciated how versatile this could be.

Archaeological Material

Archaeological publication in Perseus, as in print, involves a wide range of visual as well as textual information. Given the storage capacity of optical discs and the navigational flexibility of inexpensive hypermedia systems, it is technologically feasible to present multimedia information in a single environment. The challenge for Perseus is, instead, intellectual: how should that variety of material be integrated into a whole?

Applications of computing technologies in archaeology today are both widespread and wide ranging, but at the beginning of the Perseus Project this diversity was as much an obstacle as a help. It is interesting to note that every project member had extensive experience with the TLG prior to beginning work on Perseus; that experience helped shape ideas about working with texts in an electronic environment and provided a common point of reference for all project members. No archaeological research provided a comparable common experience; the archaeological issues raised by Perseus were consequently less well defined at the inception of the project. We began by intensively exploring very specific problems and only much later began to synthesize a system to coordinate the disparate pieces.

An Initial Example

Consider the apparently straightforward problem of describing an artifact. Several existing models suggest what descriptive drawings, photography, and text might look like in Perseus.

1. *It could be modeled after an image archive.* Perseus contains thousands of photographs, motion video, drawings, and computer-generated graphics: users should be able to browse through these as easily as browsing through a well-organized photo archive. But photo archives typically subordinate documentation of objects to the photograph: to find out about an object (e.g., its date) it is first necessary to find a photograph of the object. A more serious drawback is that, when there are many photographs, the photographs can be clustered into groups based on the things they depict; within such groups, information about the objects pictured is often duplicated, and such duplication discourages thorough and consistent documentation of objects.

2. *It could be modeled after an excavation or museum database of artifacts.* Typically a database of artifacts provides much fuller descriptions of objects than a photo archive; because it is oriented toward the objects, it permits queries based on our knowledge of the objects rather than on our photographic documentation of them. But just as an image archive tends to subordinate documentation of objects to images, the artifact database tends to subordinate the documentation of images to the objects and might hinder casual browsing of our image collection.

3. *It could be modeled after a publication with, like many archaeological catalogues, a text volume and a volume of plates with cross references to each other.* At their best, descriptive multi-volume catalogues can unite textual and visual documentation in ways approximating the benefits of both photo archives and object databases, but they share the limitations of any paper publication. Their size is restricted. (How often can museums afford to include exhaustive lists of unpublished photographs in a catalogue of objects? How often can an excavation afford to reproduce more than a small selection of data recorded in the field?) Scholars rarely refer in print to unpublished sources, and they often do not provide a very precise idea of what unpublished data lies behind the catalogue's selection. All of this isolates and devalues unpublished archives of information.

In rethinking archaeological description for the new environment of Perseus, we gradually realized that Perseus must simultaneously provide the functionality of all of these models to describe artifacts. It must offer the completeness of a catalogue/database and the image-browsing capability of an image archive, and at the same time rival published catalogues in quality of both visual and textual information, while uniting visual and textual material in new ways.

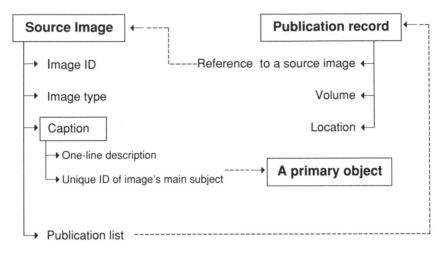

7.2. Relation of image archive and publication records in Perseus. A primary object can be an artifact or a context and will have a fuller structure of its own.

Thus we eventually created three interrelated kinds of "Perseus objects" that together describe an artifact: textual documentation, images in the Perseus archive (these might be drawings, slides, or motion video), and publications of images.

A textual description of an artifact is tied to a list of all images of it in the Perseus archive. In looking, for example, at the description of a red-figure amphora by the Berlin Painter in the Yale University Art Gallery, it is possible to discover that the Perseus archive includes ten original color slides of the amphora, but no drawings. The records of the images are tied to records of their publications, so that a reader can also learn that these color photographs have, for example, been published on the first Perseus videodisc. (See fig. 7.2.)

Structure of Archaeological Data

A major task for the archaeologists working on Perseus has been to define primary structures for archaeological data. The network of information in Perseus is intended to enable Perseus authors and users to present and formulate interpretations; it is not intended to impose a single point of view on users. Given the multiplicity of theoretical approaches to archaeology today,[11] how can a system like Perseus define an underlying archaeological model that would be acceptable to all?

Two observations about archaeology are pertinent.[12] First, while there is an extraordinary range of thought about archaeological interpretation, there is surprising consensus about archaeological description. Archaeologists, in general, agree on how to describe a pot, even if they disagree about what it means.[13]

Second, archaeological fieldwork imposes a special burden, since excavation means the permanent loss of unrecorded information. Consequently, archaeologists may criticize the omission of some category of information; they will rarely object to including information. No matter what their theoretical orientation, there are certain kinds of data that archaeologists in the field will inevitably record. Perseus attempts to supply structures for working with these essentials, without imposing assumptions about how these components must be described in detail, and without limiting the kinds of questions that can be posed of the data. Artifacts must be documented; their find spots are located in a geographic hierarchy (of which the depositional context is the lowest unit); standard interpretive components include dating and optional comparanda. Beyond this very basic level, Perseus contributors are free to define more detailed schemata for particular corpora. (See fig. 7.3.)

Range of Material and Basis of Selection

After the structure of the data, perhaps the most important archaeological questions concern the range of material to be included and the criteria of selection. Perseus is by no means a comprehensive database of classical Greek archaeology. Other large projects focused on a limited range of material, such as the Beazley Archive's database on Attic painted pottery, attempt to cover particular corpora exhaustively; Perseus complements these efforts by placing a significant selection of material in the much wider context of the total Perseus environment. Other projects may see themselves as the reference tool expanded beyond its paper limits: the Beazley Archive represents an extension of ARV and ABV. Perseus is more like a library shrunk to personal size. It includes reference works analogous to atlases, Travlos' *Pictorial Dictionary of Athens,* and the *Princeton Encyclopedia of Classical Sites;* it includes textbook-like introductory essays on various subjects (e.g., classical sculpture); it offers documentation of artifacts comparable to museum catalogues and secondary literature. Like a small library, its coverage is not uniform. This is not ideal, but it is no more of a problem than it is in a library — some excavations or museum collections will be covered in much greater depth than others, just as they are in any library; the user must take account of what material is included and what is not.

The method of selection might be described as "guided opportunism." Where a corpus of material is small enough for us to cover exhaustively, as is the case with original classical sculpture, we attempt to do so, at least at a minimal level of coverage. Where we necessarily have to be selective, as in our coverage of Attic painted pottery, we attempt to put together a core selection that would offer a representative survey of the corpus from any of a number of points of view (e.g., for painted pottery, a stylistic history, an iconographic survey, or a study of techniques). Beyond that, we cover particular collections in more depth as feasible; where we could afford to acquire or

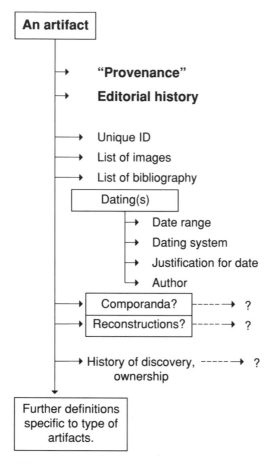

7.3. Schematic representation of the structure of an archaeological artifact in Perseus.

commission photography of particular collections, our visual documentation is richer; where we could acquire rights to printed catalogues, our textual documentation is richer. Thinking again of the library shelf, we could imagine our guided selection of core material as similar to the pieces chosen for an introductory textbook.[14] On the shelf near it, Perseus offers examples of more detailed catalogues.

Sources

Archaeological material in Perseus derives from a variety of sources. In some instances where we received permission to republish, we have reproduced the text of printed works. Other textual material was commissioned from "Perseus authors," specialists in a particular content area who are not part of the project staff, while further material was assembled directly by project staff.

Photography also includes a mix of donated, purchased, and commissioned work. For topography and architecture, personal slide collections are a rich resource. For artifacts, however, more specialized photography is necessary. There are of course numerous photographic archives for classical archaeology, some independent, some based at publishing houses or museums, and where possible we have purchased rights to publish existing photographs. In theory, we could obtain the coverage we need for Perseus entirely from existing photography, but in fact many photo archives are either unwilling to disseminate their collections in electronic forms, or set their price structure so high that it has, to our surprise, proven to be more cost effective for Perseus to hire a full-time staff photographer. This gives us closer control over the quality of photography and over the rights to the photographs.

To convert existing drawings to an electronic environment, scanning is inadequate, so all drawings in Perseus are done by drafters working for the project. In almost all cases, these drawings are based on composites of published drawings, redrafted according to Perseus conventions.[15] Redrawing both regularizes the drawings and creates a new copyright.

Production

Throughout the Perseus project, formats for data have to meet two potentially conflicting requirements. Because we do not want to limit Perseus to any particular software or hardware platform, portability is essential. Because data collection is the most expensive part of the project, the data format must retain the maximum amount of information possible.

Image Technologies. The archival principle (capture the maximum amount of information, even if it cannot all initially be published) is crucial for photography. While videodiscs with 54,000 frames per side make it possible to publish all the still photography we can acquire on a single platter, the NTSC standard, an artifact of television's early days, is seriously limited. Its color fidelity is poor, its maximum resolution low, and most users view video on monitors with only 250 lines of resolution. The technologies for transferring slides to video are limited by the inherent drawbacks of the NTSC standard, but the slides, properly cared for, will be good for several years before they begin to fade; in the meantime, we have begun digitizing slides directly; the digital data can be copied and manipulated without loss of information. We plan to distribute large numbers of digitized photographs at various resolutions on CD-ROM.[16]

For computer graphics, bit maps do not satisfy either criterion: they are difficult to port across systems and can capture only as much information as their maximum resolution. Vector graphics can represent data of arbitrary resolution and are essentially limited only by the resolution of the source data. (A very high-resolution source drawing may have to be scaled up many times for a drafter to work at an effective virtual resolution on screen or printout, but that is an inconvenience, not an absolute limit.)

Because of its easy portability, we initially selected Postscript as the standard format for our graphics.[17] It is entirely appropriate for such drawings as rollouts of vases or perspective reconstruction drawings, and Postscript drawings from our library today can be easily sent by electronic mail (Postscript files are pure text files), viewed, and printed on a number of hardware and software platforms.

For measured drawings, such as site and building plans and elevations, we would ideally prefer to use a CAD system linked to a database of quantitative information about the objects depicted. Our experiments with CAD to date have been limited by the fact that there is simply not enough published data to generate good CAD drawings for most of the buildings and sites we are documenting. In the real world, CAD is primarily used for design, not recording. It is a good choice for new drawing on sites where a sufficient number of measurements can be taken, but in the published record, if the only published dimensions are implicit in the scale of a published plan, then we are better off redrawing with Postscript's bezier curves.[18]

Text Technologies. Perhaps the most daunting problem posed by Perseus's archaeological component is not a question of design: it is the simple problem of amassing the necessary quantities of documentary and interpretive texts to make the archaeological material meaningful and useful to the diverse users of Perseus. In fact, this problem has clear implications for the system's design: Perseus cannot possibly foot the costs of assembling the quantities of archaeological information we would ideally want; therefore, we must design a system that will not merely permit but encourage collaboration.

As we settled on the contents of such disparate elements as descriptions of vases and histories of archaeological sites, we began to draw up guidelines, or style sheets, for contributors. In one of the most fruitful cross-fertilizations within the project, we eventually recognized that Elli Mylonas's structuring of the primary texts with SGML, as described above, simultaneously held the key to formalizing our archaeological guidelines and could permit us to establish a text-only interchange format.

Whatever the origin of the textual data, it is archived as ASCII files marked up in SGML. From this point on, the data may in fact be processed by a number of applications: database programs, text-indexing programs, spelling checkers, or other programs attempting to verify the data by machine where possible.

General Conclusions

Even at this early stage, Perseus presents a realistic model for archaeological work. It encompasses a wide range of archaeological material, much of it published in exhaustive depth. It is a working system that has proven capable of coping with the irregularities of real data in significant quantities. The implications of the Perseus Project as a whole force us to rethink our ideas about the role of collaboration, the functions of publications, and the relation between published and unpublished information (see concluding section); the archaeological material specifically challenges us to reconsider our basic view of archaeology's relation to other disciplines. Here, too, Perseus presents an opportunity to move beyond theorizing in the abstract, as it places a significant corpus of archaeological material in juxtaposition with significant collections of other material.

Evaluation

Purposes and Methodology

Evaluation plays a significant role in the creation of the Perseus Project. For the project to succeed in the long term, all types of users must feel, first, that the information in the Perseus system is accurate and useful, and second, that Perseus is efficient, reliable, and generally easy to use. Thus, the first goal of evaluation concerns the development of the project: it is to ensure the quality of the materials and the viability of the delivery system. By collecting and responding to feedback from beta testers, the project developers aim to guarantee that Perseus creates enough learning opportunities to offset the barriers inherent in electronically based information systems, such as machine and network access and compatibility.

The second, summative goal of the evaluation is to determine how Perseus affects the learning process. The scope of this second effort will extend from the influence of Perseus on the way instructors prepare and deliver their lectures, conduct discussion sessions, and create assignments to the ways in which learners, whether advanced scholars or beginning students, use Perseus in their study and research.[19]

In order to make sure that the evaluation process is not influenced in any way by the actual builders of the database, evaluation is in the hands of an independent group. The principal members of the evaluation team are Gary Marchionini, Delia Neuman, Peter Evans, all from the University of Maryland, and Kenneth Morrell from St. Olaf College. The evaluation plan calls for at least three distinct instances of data collection at each site to be evaluated.[20] The first visit is designed to give the evaluators an opportunity to familiarize themselves with the students and the variables of the educational setting, which include class size, structure, physical setting, and computing environments. At the time of the second visit, roughly half-way through the semester, instructors and students are in the ideal position to provide a critical estimation of the strengths and weaknesses of the Perseus materials and system. Finally, the third visit at the end of the semester has three objectives: to get a third set of responses from the instructor and students to the same interview schedules that were used in the first two visits; to permit the participants in the course to reflect on the overall success of the course in terms of the instructor, the role of the Perseus materials, and their own involvement; and, finally, to collect data on the performance of the students.

In April 1989, Gary Marchionini and Delia Neuman made their first site visit to Harvard University to begin the development of an evaluative approach in connection with the use of Perseus materials in Gregory Crane's course, Literature and Arts 52: Classical Greek Literature and Fifth Century Athens. During the fall semester of the 1989–90 school year, Marchionini and Neuman visited Bowdoin college, where Neel Smith was integrating Perseus materials into his Archaeology 101 course. The evaluation team followed essentially the same approach at Bowdoin as they had at Harvard. Beginning with site visits to Maryland and St. Olaf in April and May 1990, the evaluation team made at least two visits to each site, one either before or during the initial introduction of the system and another approximately one month later. The paired visits to Maryland and St. Olaf represent a closer approximation of the approach outlined above.

Observations and Interviews. As it has evolved through the initial site visits, the general approach for on-site evaluation now includes the collection of data through observation and interviews. As the project progresses, the evaluators will also conduct document and learning analyses. Observations fall into three types. The first are structured, nonintrusive observations that are designed to identify the characteristics of the general group as a whole, including both the instructor and students. These observations take place in classes, discussion groups, and individual study sessions and use a protocol that focuses on "such general issues as instructor's approaches and students' apparent levels of comfort and skill with the Perseus materials."[21] The structured observations serve as a means of identifying a sampling of students who then become the subjects of participant observations in which they interact with the evaluator.[22] Finally, the evaluation team is currently reviewing options for observing the actions of the user through software and hardware that will create a journal of events that occur on the screen. At this point the evaluators hope to make this screen journal available to the students as well for purposes of self-assessment.

At present the team uses one interview schedule for the instructor, including instructional assistants, and another for the students. To aid in achieving the first, formative goal of the evaluation, the interview schedules during the initial series of site visits contained questions primarily about the system design and interface. Because the initial implementations used limited subsets of materials, the interviews did not ask questions about the scope or accuracy of the contents. To gauge the impact Perseus had on the learning process, instructors responded to questions that were grouped in three general areas: how Perseus affects methods of instruction, how Perseus affects the students' learning, and whether Perseus plays any role in the instructor's research. The students answered questions about how they used Perseus, how easy it was to navigate in and learn with Perseus, and whether the instructor made effective use of Perseus.

With the distribution of Perseus 1.0b1, the first beta release, in July 1990, the evaluation team will have the first opportunity to see how users respond to a more complete system. The fifty-one primary beta testers at thirty-nine sites belong to one or more of three categories: instructors who will use the material in classroom settings as an aid to lecture presentations, as a source of readings, or an environment for assignments; scholars who will use Perseus as a source of information during their research; and system specialists whose primary interest lies not in the content as much as in the design of the system, including the adaptation of HyperCard, the underlying data structures, and graphic interface. The evaluation team has implemented an off-site evaluation program that uses questionnaires designed for the three categories of users as the initial source of data. Instructors will respond to questions grouped under four headings: physical environment, system use, instructional potential, and general information (which included questions about how much the tester used Perseus, former computing experience, and general overall impressions). The questionnaire for system specialists contains sections on the physical environment, the performance of the system, the interface, documentation and support, and general information, which in this case focused on the testers' familiarity. Once the team collects and analyzes the responses to the written survey, they will conduct a series of telephone interviews with a subset of the total pool of beta testers. In the interviews over the phone, evaluators will follow up on issues that arise in the initial survey, as well as lay the groundwork for subsequent site visits that the team will undertake at two to four beta sites over the 1990–91 academic year. The observation protocols and interview schedules for the on-site evaluation will undergo revision to reflect the more complete system and variables in the implementation of Perseus at a wider variety of sites. Visits to Harvard, Bowdoin, Maryland, and St. Olaf, which are now formally designated as development sites, will also continue both in conjunction with the beta materials and the testing of elements scheduled for inclusion in subsequent releases of Perseus.

Initial Results

At Harvard, Crane projected images from the Perseus videodisc on one screen and notes from the display of a Macintosh on another to supplement his lectures.

Students had access to a set of texts in a computer laboratory. Students used the texts and a path-building function in assignments that called for them to connect a series of passages from the database with their own commentary. The responses from students and teaching assistants indicated that the use of Perseus in lectures and as an environment for student work faces two primary challenges, both related to the adaptation of the new technology to a conventional educational atmosphere. The expanded role of visual images in the lectures was generally perceived as a positive enhancement, but assimilating the amount of added information in different media posed a problem for some. It raised the possibility that in some contexts more information and the ideas and responses that they generate may increase the degree of confusion and dissatisfaction among students — at least until they develop a greater facility for integrating the sources. When asked to abandon a familiar type of written assignment for an electronically annotated pathway through the database, most students expressed doubts as to whether the pedagogical gains outweighed the anxiety, frustration, and inconvenience posed by first having to overcome the problems of limited access to the materials, which were only available in the computer laboratory, and then having to deal with an unfamiliar system to complete the assignments.[23]

The impact of Perseus in Archaeology 101 at Bowdoin was limited to the lecture component of the course. As Crane had done in Literature and Arts 52, Neel Smith projected video images alongside other archaeological material and notes during his lecture. The role, however, that visual images played in the lectures of Archaeology 101 seemed more integral to the students than the images in Literature and Arts 52 because the subject matter was inherently visually oriented. The goal of the professor was to increase the interactivity and spontaneity of the learning process. Professor Smith felt that having rapid access to the videodisc and the information on the Macintosh during the lecture allowed for a type of interactivity not usually possible in more familiar lecture formats relying on a selection of slides in a predetermined sequence. The experiences from both Literature and Arts 52 and Archaeology 101 suggest some of the problems that arise when a new technology disrupts traditional instructional methods. Instructors who integrate Perseus into their lectures will also have to demonstrate to their students the advantages of a richer learning environment. As more and more instructors include information from a variety of multimedia sources in their lectures, students will develop a greater familiarity to them as well as strategies for assimilating the added information.

In contrast to the early implementation of visual images and texts in translation at Harvard and visual images with archaeological information at Bowdoin, at both Maryland and St. Olaf students used Greek texts with the morphological analyzer and Greek-English lexicon in tightly focused language-learning environments. At Maryland, Eva Stehle used the text of Sophocles' *Antigone* in her upper-division Greek 688 course. The most noticeable impact that Perseus had on the learning process was in shortening the time required to analyze a word and identify a suitable meaning in the lexicon. Without Perseus the two undergraduates in the course normally took as much as 3.5 hours to work through 100 lines of text, sometimes spending between five and ten minutes to identify and look up a single verb. In spite of the fact that the students did not give a comparable estimate of the time the assignment took without Perseus, the general impression of the students that Perseus dramatically shortened the time normally spent paging through a grammar and lexicon is significant, especially because the students developed a more favorable attitude toward the learning process. The one graduate student in the course, whose language skills were more developed, remained unconvinced that use of Perseus offers any clear learning advantage over the traditional use of printed materials, but she did feel that the system saved her time and simplified her research when tracing the use of certain cognate words to determine their relative meanings for the characters in the play.

At St. Olaf, after reading selections from Herodotus' *Histories* from a printed edition, students in Greek 73 switched to using Perseus for their reading assignments from Thucydides and Xenophon in the second half of the semester. Unlike the situation at Maryland, where Perseus was available on a single dedicated machine in the library, students in Greek 73 had access to the Perseus materials from over 100 machines in fifteen locations through the campus-wide network. Perseus appeared to increase the speed with which students could complete their reading assignments. Students spent from one-third to four-fifths of their study time in analyzing and looking up words, so even modest gains in efficiency made a noticeable impact on them. This impression of increased efficiency may be related to how the students made use of the time while they waited for the system to complete the analysis and lookup. Rather than simply waiting for the results, students generally put this time to good use either by working further on the text or by looking up a second word in a printed lexicon.

A number of issues arose that will receive further attention in the evaluation process. One was the effect that Perseus has on collaborative learning. Translating a text may be a highly individualized process or it may be a collaborative effort, depending on the structure of the course and direction of the instructor. The evaluators observed students using Perseus independently at the same time in a computer laboratory but frequently consulting with each other on the possible interpretation of a word. Students reported that without Perseus they would often study together to improve the efficiency of coming up with a suitable translation for a word. Perseus appears to fit into this type of learning as if it were another type of student. If the goal of the course or instructor is to foster individualized study, Perseus may not necessarily contribute to that goal.

Conclusion

The Perseus Project has thus set itself a large task: to move primary and secondary materials used in Classics and archaeology into a new medium, and to explore and evaluate how they are used. In order to do so, we have to spend most of our time and manpower on the structure and organization of our data, but the results of this effort will be the true lasting effect of the Perseus Project's research. Over the last two years, as we have been developing Perseus, we have observed some of the innovations that putting archaeological and classical materials in electronic form brings out.

The electronic environment is already forcing us to rethink our notions of collaboration. With the use of an agreed-upon interchange format, scholars and students working with a variety of hardware and software can contribute directly to joint projects like Perseus. We have successfully integrated material deriving from optical scanning of printed publications, from staff members working directly with databases, hypermedia systems, and other software, and from content experts who simply used a word processor with a set of "style sheets" we supplied. There is no technological reason that even larger projects cannot exchange information with equal facility. If new or existing projects to assemble and manage databases in archaeology and Classics do not support this kind of collaboration, we must ask, why not?

In the past, publishing a book (or a monograph series, depending on the scale of the project) was considered an adequate means of disseminating information. Paper publication might still be necessary, but we believe that in at least three ways it is not sufficient. First, paper publications must be extremely selective; research projects in the electronic environment should consider exhaustive publication. Why publish only a selection of a slide archive if it is smaller than the 54,000 frames that can fit on a videodisc, or the myriads of compressed color images that can be squeezed onto a CD-ROM? Second, printed publications have been the standard for so long that we sometimes tend to aim not only our publication but also our data collection at the printed target. A prime example of this is the bias for black-and-white transparencies over color slides in most photographic archives; the color information has been ignored because it is more difficult and more expensive to reproduce in print. However, as the technology becomes cheaper and more effective, the barrier to high quality data collection will increasingly shift away from the cost of reproduction towards the expense of the raw materials. Because gathering good information is so expensive, it is imperative that we follow the archival principle mentioned above: at the same time that we plan for immediate publication, we need to collect the maximum amount of information possible, and to store it in a well-planned, generalized form, so that we will be prepared to take advantage of predictable new technologies as they reach the consumer marketplace.

Finally, the large amount of diverse material in Perseus invites the reader to synthesize information that is often treated separately in traditional publications. Primary textual and visual data, accompanying databases of identifying information, and secondary sources are all intermingled and easily cross-referenced. As a matter of fact, although they may have been originally created as separate entities, the information they represent may be displayed as completely integrated. This is possible due to the attention that has been paid to their structuring when they were converted from paper to electronic form. If other such scholarly databases also follow these principles, it will be possible for a reader to move through them seamlessly as well.

Notes

1. Richard W. Lanham, "The Electronic Word: Literary Study and the Digital Revolution," *New Literary History* 20 (1989): 287.

2. Walter J. Ong, *Orality and Literacy* (London, 1989), 80 and 135–38; and J. David Bolter, *Turing's Man: Western Culture in the Computer Age* (Chapel Hill, 1984), passim, esp. 10.

3. Perseus is funded primarily by the Annenberg/CPB Project. Additional funding is provided by Apple Computer, Inc., the Packard Humanities Institute, Harvard University, Bowdoin College, and St. Olaf College.

4. Gregory Crane and Elli Mylonas, "The Perseus Project: An Interactive Curriculum on Classical Greek Civilization," *Educational Technology* 28 (1988): 11; and idem, "Perseus Project-Work Plan," *Perseus Working Papers* 6 (February 1990).

5. Harvard is a legal entity, whereas Perseus is not. Therefore only Harvard can hold rights or copyrights.

6. Revisions are made by advanced graduate students and are then reviewed by an older scholar who is a specialist in that author.

7. Scanning can be very cost-effective when the text is destined for editing or revision. In that case, the student or scholar does the proofreading as they revise. The Dante Project at Dartmouth opted for this method.

8. Standard Generalized Markup Language, an encoding standard for text adopted by the International Standards Organization in 1986 and currently required by the U.S. Department of Defense for all equipment documentation.

9. This necessarily brief description of SGML is rough and oversimplified. For more information see: introduction to C. M. Sperberg-McQueen and Lou Burnard, eds., *Text Encoding Initiative: Guidelines for the Encoding and Interchange of Machine-Readable Texts* (Chicago and Oxford, 1990), and Martin Bryan, *The Author's Guide to SGML* (New York, 1988).

10. David W. Packard, "Computer-Assisted Morphological Analysis of Ancient Greek" in A. Zampolli and N. Calzolari, eds., *Computational and Mathematical Linguistics: Proceedings of the International Conference on Computational Linguistics, Pisa 1973*, vol. 2 (= *Linguistica* 37): 343–56. For a discussion of how the CCAT Project at the University of Pennsylvania has used this system extensively, see John J. Hughes, *Bits, Bytes and Biblical Studies* (Zondervan, 1987), 550–56.

11. See, for example, the range of theoretical approaches described in Bruce G. Trigger, *A History of Archaeological Thought* (Cambridge, 1989); or the chapter titles in Ian Hodder, *Reading the Past: Current Approaches to Interpretation in Archaeology* (Cambridge, 1986).

12. The description in this section is necessarily extremely brief for this publication; the archaeological model of Perseus is more fully described in D. Neel Smith, "An Interchange Format for Archaeological Information," *Perseus Working Papers* 12, forthcoming.

13. This is not "blind empiricism"; see, for example, the comments in chapter 1 of Anthony M. Snodgrass, *An Archaeology of Greece: The Present State and Future Scope of a Discipline* (Berkeley, 1987) esp. 14–16 and 32–34, including the observation by Stanley South, "The fact that Noël Hume uses the particularistic approach does not mean that the descriptive classifications and data emerging from his work cannot be used for other approaches."

14. It is interesting to note how limited and repetitive the selection of material is in typical textbooks. Gregory Crane surveyed both standard handbooks on Greek vase painting, including John Boardman, *Athenian Black-Figure Vases: A Handbook* (London, 1974), idem, *Athenian Red-Figure Vases: The Archaic Period, A Handbook* (London, 1975), idem, *Athenian Red-Figure Vases: The Classical Period* (London, 1989), A. D. Trendall, *Red Figure Vases of South Italy and Sicily* (London, 1989), and less traditional art historical publications such as Eva C. Keuls, *The Reign of the Phallus: Sexual Politics in Ancient Athens* (New York, 1985), and Claud Bérard, ed., *A City of Images* (Princeton, 1989). Of 1,762 objects cited, ten museum collections accounted for 62 percent of the references, and twenty collections accounted for 79 percent.

15. These conventions are described in Candace Smith, "Drawing Guidelines for Perseus," *Perseus Working Papers* 11, forthcoming.

16. In order to include motion photography of some Greek sites, we have also shot a limited amount of the best quality video we could in Greece, but most of our image archive consists of 35mm slides.

17. Postscript is a page description language developed by Adobe Systems, Inc., and widely used for output and display.

18. At the time this was written, the Perseus project was undertaking cooperative work with the Center for the Study of Architecture at Bryn Mawr; as part of our exchange of data, we hope to include in future versions of Perseus three-dimensional CAD work done at CSA.

19. See the section on general goals in Gary Marchionini, Delia Neuman, and Kenneth Morrell, "Perseus Evaluation Plan," *Perseus Working Papers* 5 (March 1990): 9.

20. Ibid., 30–31.

21. Ibid., 28.

22. We should note that in conducting interviews and making observations, the evaluators obtain permission from the subjects in compliance with the regulations that govern the use of human subjects at the various institutions.

23. See Gary Marchionini, Delia Neuman, and Peter Evans, "Perseus Evaluation Report: Harvard University–Spring 1989," *Perseus Working Papers* 6a (March, 1990), esp. 12–14 ('Perseus and learning from lecture' and 'Perseus and learning from assignment').

8

Hypertext and the Classical Commentary

Jay David Bolter

For the past several years I have been collaborating in the development of a computer program called Storyspace, a program for creating and presenting hypertexts. It is my experience with this system that has prompted me to offer the following discussion of hypertext and its relevance for classical scholarship. My collaborators (Professors Michael Joyce of Jackson Community College and John B. Smith of the Computer Science Department at the University of North Carolina) and I first envisioned using our hypertext program to create interactive fiction — hence the name Storyspace.[1] However, we have come to regard Storyspace and other hypertext systems as general writing tools, applicable to technical writing, essays, and pedagogy as well as fiction.

Hypertext systems are certainly appropriate to the reading and writing practiced by scholars in the humanities. Scholarly writing is highly relational: it explains texts in terms of other texts, both primary and secondary. In particular, classical philology is the art of explicating an ancient text by exploring its relationships to other specific texts and to the corpus of ancient literature as a whole. Electronic hypertext is the very embodiment of the technique of relating one text to others, and it therefore provides a new writing space for traditional classical studies. At the same time the computer as hypertext calls traditional scholarly assumptions into question, assumptions about the relationship of the scholar to the text and indeed about the nature and permanence of classical texts themselves. The computer as hypertext manages at the same time to reinforce and to undermine the kind of scholarship that has defined Classics for the past 200 years (since the invention of *Altertumswissenschaft*) or indeed for the past 500 (since the invention of printing).

Consider the following example, a hypertextual commentary of *Oedipus Tyrannus*. The reader of the commentary sees three windows on the computer screen. Text in Greek appears in two facing windows; a window below is reserved for the editor's comments. The reader controls the appearance of text in the windows by clicking with the mouse.[2] The underlining in the Greek text is "hot": the reader activates a note by clicking on an underlined word or phrase. The editor's comment then fills the smaller window at the bottom, while a passage for comparison may appear in the other facing window. (See figure 8.1)

What is hypertextual about this program? The underlining marks out electronic links that have been associated with words and phrases in the text. I call these marked passages "topics." To divide a text into topical units and make these units available to the reader in a variety of orders is to write "topographically."[3] A hypertext system in the computer allows us to write in this fashion, defining topics and establishing links between them. A traditional commentary is also an example of topographic writing in print. It uses the conventions of the printed page to link various notes to the original text. We have only to look at Jebb's masterful commentary on *Oedipus Tyrannus* to see how thoroughly linked the text is.[4] There are notes to passages elsewhere in the play, to other notes on other passages, to Jebb's own appendices or introduction, to other plays by Sophocles, to other Greek and Latin authors, and to modern scholarly articles and books. While making his or her way through the text, the reader has the option of following these links or ignoring them. In a printed book like Jebb's, however, readers must themselves do the work of following out the link: they must search for the appropriate line number at the bottom of the page or thumb through the text to find the endnotes. In the computer this task is automated. As we shall see, this automated and fluid movement changes the relationship between the text and the notes.

Jebb's commentary is no school edition but a work of serious scholarship. By the same token a hypertextual system can serve for scholarship as well as teaching. Except for word processing, classicists tend to regard computers as pedagogical tools, useful chiefly for the simplest aspects of language learning, ultimately for drilling students in Greek and Latin grammar. In fact, memorization and drills are necessary for language learning, and many students find the computer a valuable aid for such work. On the other hand, the computer as hypertext is nothing less than a new kind of book; it can serve all the various functions that printed books have served in the past. To regard the computer only as a machine for grammatical exercises makes no more sense than regarding the printing press solely as a technology for producing grammar workbooks. Indeed, once we understand the computer as hypertext, the distinction between pedagogy and research tends to dissolve for the computer as it has for the printed book. The Perseus Project, described just previously in this volume, illustrates how the boundaries blur. Although the primary aim of Perseus is to create a suite of tools by which students can approach ancient texts and archaeological materials, it is clear that these same tools (texts, translations,

ΟΙ. ἦν δ' εὖ σκοπῶν εὕρισκον ἴασιν μόνην,	ΚΡ. Καὶ νῦν ἔθ' αὐτός εἰμι τῷ βουλεύματι.
ταύτην ἔπραξα· παῖδα γὰρ Μενοικέως	ΟΙ. Πόσον τιν' ἤδη δῆθ' ὁ Λάιος χρόνον
Κρέοντ', ἐμαυτοῦ γαμβρόν, ἐς τὰ Πυθικὰ	ΚΡ. Δέδρακε ποῖον ἔργον: οὐ γὰρ ἐννοῶ.
ἔπεμψα Φοίβου δώμαθ', ὡς πύθοιθ' ὅ τι	ΟΙ. ἄφαντος ἔρρει θανασίμῳ χειρώματι: 560
δρῶν ἢ τί φωνῶν τήνδε ῥυσαίμην πόλιν.	ΚΡ. Μακροὶ παλαιοί τ' ἂν *μετρηθεῖεν χρόνοι.*
Καί μ' ἦμαρ ἤδη *ξυμμετρούμενον χρόνῳ*	ΟΙ. Τότ' οὖν ὁ μάντις οὗτος ἦν ἐν τῇ τέχνῃ:
λυπεῖ τί πτάσσει· τοῦ γὰρ εἰκότος πέρα	ΚΡ. Σοφός γ' ὁμοίως κἀξ ἴσου τιμώμενος.
ἄπεστι πλείω τοῦ καθήκοντος χρόνου. 75	ΟΙ. Ἐμνήσατ' οὖν ἐμοῦ τι τῷ τότ' ἐν χρόνῳ:
Ὅταν δ' ἵκηται, τηνικαῦτ' ἐγὼ κακὸς	ΚΡ. Οὔκουν ἐμοῦ γ' ἑστῶτος οὐδαμοῦ πέλας.
μὴ δρῶν ἂν εἴην πάνθ ὅσ' ἂν δηλοῖ θεός.	

Oedipus's problem is with time. The past will not stay past, but threatens to overwhelm Oedipus's present. The killing that happened long ago (and the details of Oedipus's birth and adoption) are catching up with him. The play exhibits a curious vacillation between the desire to incorporate the past in the present and the desire to suppress the past.

8.1. Two passages from *Oedipus Tyrannus* with an editor's comment.

digitized photographs) can aid research and writing for classical scholars and those in related disciplines.[5]

Technologies of Writing

As the ubiquitous word processor has already shown and hypertext is now showing, the computer constitutes a new medium for writing. The special qualties of this new medium need to be explored and exploited. The computer permits us to place our text in a new writing space, but in so doing we must adapt texts to the limitations and possibilities of this space. The changes will apply to old texts (such as classical authors) that we transfer to the computer and a fortiori to new texts (such as commentaries on those authors) that we write at the computer keyboard.

As classicists we should certainly be prepared to appreciate the relationship between the medium of writing and the written text. Milman Parry and the oral theorists have brought to our attention the significance of writing itself for the art of epic poetry — by arguing not only that the Homeric poems were composed without the aid of writing but even that writing destroyed the oral epic technique.[6] In the same spirit Eric Havelock traced the development of literate culture in Greece into the fifth and fourth centuries B.C. and claimed that full literacy, achieved at that late date, left its mark on the writings of Plato and Aristotle.[7] Havelock and to a lesser extent the oral theorists are controversial. But whatever we may think of their conclusions, they compel us to reconsider the meaning of alphabetic literacy for Greek culture.

It is not only literacy itself but the degree and kind of literacy that matter, and these depend in turn upon the technology of writing available to a culture — the alphabet or syllabary, the materials, and the techniques applied to these materials. Several different technologies enter into our study of ancient culture. Texts have come down to us on stone, on fragments of papyrus rolls, and in medieval codices, and there were appropriate texts for each medium: laws and decrees for stone, literary and administrative texts for papyrus rolls, and later literary and scientific texts for the codex. As the German scholars who defined *Altertumswissenschaft* in the early nineteenth century realized, texts in all these media must be studied in order to achieve a comprehensive picture of antiquity. Classical scholarship became the first multimedia study. As a result even contemporary students of Greek or Latin literature cannot wholly ignore the manuscript tradition when they read Sophocles, Plato, or Vergil. The contemporary classical scholar feels the constraint of the received text much more strongly than does a student of modern literature, who may do important work on Dickens or Virginia Woolf with hardly a glance at a variorum edition. Classical studies still regard the textual tradition as the foundation of any further work, and textual criticism remains for many the most reputable, least speculative form of scholarly contribution.

The printed book was a writing space that ancient writers and medieval scribes never knew, but the press is perhaps the most important technology in defining the activity of modern classical scholarship. The scholars of the nineteenth and twentieth centuries who turned textual criticism into a high art knew that their results would be recorded in print, and that knowledge helped to define their work. Elizabeth Eisenstein has argued that the printing press changed Renaissance humanism by introducing a new appreciation of fixity and permanence. The press made it possible for the quality of ancient texts to improve with each edition, whereas in the Middle Ages texts tended to degenerate with each recopying.[8] The desire to fix the text reached its zenith in the nineteenth and twentieth centuries.

The implicit goal of textual criticism is to establish the Urtext, the original and perfect version of the play, poem, or treatise, which printing can then preserve for all time. It was the high standards of transmission of printed editions that gave scholars this goal. The irony is that for classical authors the Urtexts are irretrievable, and the texts now established through textual criticism will always be unstable, vacillating among various readings offered by manuscripts and editors. Yet the drive to fix these texts has been stronger for classical scholarship than for scholarship in modern texts, where the task is less desperate. Textual criticism does not occupy as high a status in English or French literary studies as it does in Classics, and yet the textual critic of recent authors has so much more material to work with. The textual critic of a twentieth-century author is often faced with an overabundance of evidence — handwritten materials, typescripts, proofs, editions, letters, and other instructions by the author. Such a scholar then has to admit that the Urtext is a matter of definition. Is it the best manuscript or typescript? The first edition? Does it include corrections that the author made to later editions? Corrections he or she failed to make but claimed to want to make? Certainly the recent controversy over Gabler's edition of *Ulysses* shows how hard it is to maintain any simple view of the Urtext and poetic intentionality.[9]

An accomplished classical editor such as R. D. Dawe knows that there is a problem. In the introduction to his edition of *Oedipus*, Dawe cites the playwright Tom Stoppard on the question of the authentic text: When Mr. Stoppard lectured in Cambridge in 1980 on the relationship between the dramatist and the text, he drew attention to the great number of alterations which may take place between the time of composition of a play and its first performance on stage. He described how the reception accorded to the play by the public might lead to further, and in some cases drastic, revision of the original words; and he mentioned that the text printed in book form after the stage production was over might again be at variance with the words actually spoken by the actors on stage. Most dispiriting of all, to the practicing textual critic, he made it clear that the question "Which of all these various evolving versions do you regard as your own *authentic* text?" is one that had no meaning for him.[10]

Stoppard's answer is dispiriting to Dawe, because Dawe believed and continues to believe that the Urtext must represent the intentions of the playwright. He readily admits how far he is from the Urtext of Sophocles, but that ideal still informs his work. Dawe still commends the goal of "striving to get as close as possible to the poetic mind of Sophocles."[11] This simple view of poetic intentionality becomes harder to maintain in the electronic medium, which in fact suggests a new relationship between the reader, the editor's text, and the whole textual tradition.

Rereading and Rewriting the Oedipus

I have suggested that a traditional commentary is a hypertext in print, because it defines a network of notes on the primary text and offers the reader a variety of paths through that network. But there remain important differences. In a printed commentary the text is static, and one reading order is preferred to all others, the order defined by the pages of the book. The reader can never break entirely free of that order. There is usually no point in trying to break free, because the commentary is arranged to make the best sense if the reader begins at the beginning. Usually there is an introduction, followed by the primary text itself. The notes then proceed serially either at the bottom of the page or at the end of the volume. In either case the reader works through the text and the notes by moving from the front of the book toward the back. There is a sense of progress, as more and more lines of the primary text are worked through. The primary text defines the natural reading order, while the notes are digressions from that order.

Consider the careful typography of Jebb's commentary on *Oedipus Tyrannus*. In its third edition published in 1893, it is a good example of typography in the heyday of print. The Greek and its translation face each other across the opening; the apparatus runs in a thin band underneath both text and translation; the notes occupy the bottom half of both pages. This arrangement brings all the book's textual strands into a visual whole. It is, I think, much more effective than the modern practice, represented by Dawe's commentary, of putting the text and apparatus first, followed by the notes. We could say that Jebb's commentary follows the Victorian practice of filling up space (think of the books of William Morris), while Dawe reflects the modern preference for simple lines and an uncluttered page. But perhaps the explanation lies in the diminishing craftsmanship of modern publishing: today's publishers are unwilling to go to the trouble and expense of matching notes and text on the same page. Both in Jebb and Dawe, the reader makes progress by moving page by page through the primary text.

The computer can not yet, and perhaps never will, compete with the visual precision of a commentary like Jebb's. But printed typography can afford to be precise, because each page is fixed at the time of publication and copied hundreds or thousands of times. The computer substitutes motion for precision. It can draw and replace words or graphics in seconds: no one text remains on the screen for long. If the reader does not like the current presentation of text, he or she can change it by pressing a few buttons. Movement under programmed control is the computer's defining quality as a technology of writing. Hypertextual links are instructions to the computer to move among places in a text at the reader's tacit or explicit request.

In a computer commentary, then, the deployment of materials, the "typography," is different, and our concept of the commentary changes accordingly.

The reader cannot see and feel the electronic pages. Readers will not know that they are approaching the end of the text, unless the author chooses to give them some indication. The typography is defined by the unit of text (the topic) on the screen and by the reader's movement from one screenful to another. If we are looking at lines 20–40 of *Oedipus Tyrannus* on the screen, it should be almost as easy to flip to line 800 as it is to move on to line 41. If we do choose to branch to line 800, we may have no sense of skipping over the intervening material, because there are no pages to flip. Humanists sometimes criticize the computer for not having pages, arguing that we cannot browse through a text in the machine as we do through a printed book. But in fact, a programmer could construct an interface that closely resembled the "look and feel" of a printed book. The program could frame the text with a drawing of the covers of a book, and the reader could be required to reach up with the mouse and turn down the pages. Such a system, however attractive, would be an example of what I would call technological nostalgia, a desire to recreate a familiar technology in the new one. The computer's typography does not make browsing impossible: new arrangements of the text and new representations of structure simply call for new methods of browsing. These arrangements need not, and probably will not, make the screen look like a printed page or a bound volume.

In an electronic commentary the reader need not measure his or her progress in a strictly linear fashion. The notes need not function as mere interruptions in a relentless march to the end of the primary text. Instead, electronic typography encourages us to read the text as the center of a field of interrelated words and ideas. Notes lead us away from that center, and they may later return us to the same passage in the primary text or to another passage. The notes may take us to another primary text altogether. We may start reading *Oedipus Tyrannus* and soon find ourselves reading *Antigone,* if both are available in the same electronic network. The typography in which notes radiate out from the primary text was perhaps already present in the medieval commentaries, where the text was surrounded by one or more layers of glosses and comments. In this way, as in others, electronic writing has more in common with the medieval codex than with the printed book. But more than the codex and much more than the printed book, the electronic commentary encourages a multidimensional view of text: it offers layer upon layer of references without a strong sense of hierarchy that dictates which layer is more important than the others.

It is certainly possible to include in an electronic commentary all the various information that one now finds in an elaborate printed commentary, such as Jebb's. Such programs are already envisioned — in particular, the Perseus Project with its encyclopedic resources for studying Greek literary texts. The question I wish to pose here is whether and how the electronic medium might change the emphasis and critical character of a commentary. I suggest that this new medium can make both commentator and reader more sensitive to the text as a network of verbal references, a network that works against or around the linear sequence of lines. This network can be explored even with the simple electronic typography shown in figure 8.1 above. The two large windows work contrapuntally in displaying the text of the *Oedipus*. The reader begins by calling up text in the left window. To follow a link, the reader clicks with the mouse, and the computer locates the linked passage and displays it in the facing window on the right. The window at the bottom contains a comment (in English) on the connection between the two passages. This arrangement of windows is well suited for examining the way in which similar words and expressions reach out to one another across tens or hundreds of lines of intervening text.

I have in mind such instances as the remarkable figures of litotes and negation in the play. In our hypertext, the figures can be explored in the following manner. The reader encounters Teiresias's threat at 372–73: there is no one who will fail to hurl insults at Oedipus, once his true condition is revealed. The underlining in figure 8.2 indicates that this passage is linked to another. If the reader clicks on an underlined word, Teiresias's next threatening negation appears in the right window (see fig. 8.2). Putting these passages side by side on the screen allows them to resonate. Oedipus's condition is so horrendous that it can only be expressed by negation, by saying what it is not: it is not like the condition of anyone else. Later in the play (862), Jocasta utters an apparently innocuous litotes: she says she would do nothing that is not φίλον to Oedipus. But the line could be read with dark irony, because of Oedipus's too-dear relationship with Jocasta. Elsewhere (1058 and 1065), Oedipus invokes figures of negation to emphasize that he cannot fail to discover the truth of his birth. We could move out from these passages to a host of other negative expressions. And reading all these passages in succession creates the impression that all the characters are endeavoring to avoid speaking the truth straight out. The truth cannot be said but only alluded to. Indeed even allusion becomes too much for Jocasta, and she refuses to speak further. She announces that she will speak ἄλλο δ' οὔποθ' ὕστερον (1072), and with this negation she leaves the stage to commit suicide.

Figures of negation form a path or thread that weaves its way through the play. One could choose dozens or hundreds of other candidates for this kind of threading, including the complex of words for knowing (φρονέω, οἶδα), words for covering and for revealing (στέγω, etc.), words for nourishing or feeding (such as τρέφω), phrases for measuring time (Oedipus's problem is that the past will not stay past but threatens now to overwhelm him), and so on. The play is dense with such threads. My point is simply that computer-ontrolled juxtaposition (the following of links) is a remarkably suggestive way to read the *Oedipus*. Reading the play always evokes associations in the reader's mind, but the computer is the first technology that can activate these associations easily and consistently. In the computer each line of association constitutes a particular order in which the play may be read. The order defined

OI. Ἀλλ' ἔστι, πλὴν σοί· σοὶ δὲ
τοῦτ' οὐκ

ἔστ', ἐπεὶ
τυφλὸς τά τ' ὦτα τόν τε νοῦν
τά τ' ὄμματ' εἶ.

TE. Σὺ δ' ἄθλιός γε ταῦτ'
ὀνειδίζων ἃ σοὶ
οὐδεὶς ὃς οὐχὶ τῶνδ'
ὀνειδιεῖ τάχα.

OI. Μιᾶς τρέφῃ πρὸς νυκτός,
ὥστε μήτ' ἐμὲ

μήτ ἄλλον ὅστις φῶς ὁρᾷ
βλάψαι ποτ' ἄν.   375

TE. Οὐ γάρ με μοῖρα πρός γε σοῦ
πεσεῖν. ἐπεὶ

ἱκανὸς Ἀπόλλων ᾧ τάδ'
ἐκπρᾶξαι μέλει.

OI. Κρέοντος ἢ σοῦ ταῦτα
τάξευρήματα:

TE. ἅ σ' ἐξισώσει σοί τε καὶ τοῖς
σοῖς τέκνοις.

Πρὸς ταῦτα καὶ Κρέοντα καὶ
τοὐμὸν στόμα

προπηλάκιζε· σοῦ γὰρ οὐκ
ἔστιν βροτῶν

κάκιον ὅστις ἐκτριβήσεταί
ποτε.

OI. Ἦ ταῦτα δῆτ' ἀνεκτὰ πρὸς
τούτου κλύειν:

Οὐκ εἰς ὄλεθρον: οὐχὶ
θᾶσσον: οὐ πάλιν   430

ἄψορρος οἴκων τῶνδ'
ἀποστραφεὶς ἄπει:

TE. Οὐδ' ἱκόμην ἔγωγ' ἄν, εἰ σὺ
μὴ 'κάλεις.

There is no one who will not reproach Oedipus, when the king's true condition is revealed. Likewise there is no mortal who will ever be as miserably crushed as Oedipus. Oedipus's condition is so horrendous that Teiresias can only say what it is not.

8.2. The reader clicks on the underlined passage in the left-hand window, and the associated text appears in the right.

by the figure of negation (or the image of concealment or phrases for the measuring of time) is an interpretive reading of relevant passages in the play. This reading takes these passages out of their original narrative context and inclines us to read them with a peculiar emphasis. That is precisely the effect of any interpretation in a commentary or an essay.

Some classicists may still contend that a philological commentary is not an interpretation but is instead prior to interpretation. On this view the philologist attempts to establish the facts about the words in the text from which the literary critic can proceed.[12] But a look at almost any page of Jebb's printed commentary on *Oedipus* will show how distinterested philology shades into interpretation. How can Jebb tell us what a passage "means" in a grammatical sense without at the same time telling us what it "means" as a literary expression? Even the simple act of reference is interpretive: when Jebb refers us from one passage in the play to another, he is challenging us to compare the two passages. If we follow the reference, then we are following Jebb's recommended interruption in our reading of the text. A hypertextual commentary is in this sense no different. The difference lies instead in the typography. The electronic commentary shows us the reference explicitly on the screen and compels us to confront the fact that this rereading is an act of interpretation.

Whether in print or as a hypertext, a commentary is an interpretation, as is an interpretive essay. Both the commentary and the essay tell the reader how to read the primary text. The difference is that the commentary maintains the organization of the primary text, while the essay offers its own organization. The essay insists on its own order in which to present interpretive ideas; passages from the text are rearranged to suit this new order. An essay can be thought of as a commentary in which the comments have rebelled, joined themselves together into a linear narrative, and reduced the primary text to fragments. The essay is both visually and figuratively the inverse of the commentary, where the editor's words are squeezed around or set behind the primary text. In defining the relationship between primary text and interpretive comments, our hypertextual commentary falls between the traditional commentary and traditional essay. In the hypertext the reader may start reading *Oedipus* in the order of the primary text and may continue to read in this fashion using the links to point out parallels. But it is as easy and as legitimate to follow the parallels one after another. Here the reader is following the interpretive line rather than the narrative line: he or she is reading the editor's rewriting of *Oedipus*. In the electronic medium, it becomes clear that a commentary is not only a reading but also a rewriting of the text.

In the hypertext system I have outlined, we could say that the interpretation belongs to the editor who establishes links for the reader to follow. The obvious next step is to allow the reader to become an editor—to add his or her own links in the passages. The reader would simply call up two passages, select a word or phrase from each, and then draw the link (see fig. 8.3). This technique would enable the reader to pursue further the strands established by the original editor or to add new strands. This is reading at its most active, in which the reader inscribes his own words into the hypertext, an activity that is impossible for printed books.

I should add, if there is any question, that the reading and writing of the associative links in the text is *not* a first reading of *Oedipus Tyrannus*. The play has a strong narrative line, perhaps one of the strongest in extant Greek tragedy, and demands to be read straight through.[13] Associative reading is appropriate for the second, third, or tenth reading of the play. This electronic commentary is envisioned for scholarly reading, which presupposes that the reader

ΤΕ. ἃ σ' ἐξισώσει σοί τε καὶ τοῖς σοῖς τέκνοις.	ΟΙ. Πῶς εἶπας: οὐ γὰρ Πόλυβος ἐξέφυσέ με:
Πρὸς ταῦτα καὶ Κρέοντα καὶ τοὐμὸν στόμα	ΑΓ. Οὐ μᾶλλον οὐδὲν τοῦδε τἀνδρός, ἀλλ' ἴσον.
προπηλάκιζε· σοῦ γὰρ οὐκ ἔστιν βροτῶν	ΟΙ. Καὶ πῶς ὁ φύσας ἐξ ἴσου τῷ μηδενί: 1019
κάκιον ὅστις ἐκτριβήσεταί ποτε.	ΑΓ. 'Αλλ' οὔ σ' ἐγείνατ' οὔτ' ἐκεῖνος οὔτ' ἐγώ.
ΟΙ. 'Η ταῦτα δῆτ' ἀνεκτὰ πρὸς τούτου κλύειν:	ΟΙ. 'Αλλ' ἀντὶ τοῦ δὴ παῖδά μ' ὠνομάζετο:
Οὐκ εἰς ὄλεθρον: οὐχὶ θᾶσσον: οὐ πάλιν 430	ΑΓ. Δῶρόν ποτ', ἴσθι, τῶν ἐμῶν χειρῶν λαβών.
ἄψορρος οἴκων τῶνδ' ἀποστραφεὶς ἄπει:	ΟΙ. Κᾇθ' ὧδ' ἀπ' ἄλλης χειρὸς ἔστερξεν μέγο:
ΤΕ. Οὐδ' ἱκόμην ἔγωγ' ἄν, εἰ σὺ μὴ 'κάλεις.	ΑΓ. 'Η γὰρ πρὶν αὐτὸν ἐξέπεισ' ἀπαιδία.

Oedipus is made equal to his children through incest with Jocasta. On the other hand the messenger stands in the same relationship with Oedipus as does Polybus; neither is really related to him. Oedipus's relationships are either too close or too distant. Note also |

8.3. In hypertext the reader can add new links and comments. To do so, the reader might underline two passages on the screen and draw a line between them. The computer would then register the link.

is familiar with the text and so already possesses it as a structure of words and episodes in his or her memory. The purpose of scholarly reading is to explore and elaborate the structure, to find new paths and therefore new readings of the familiar text.

The Challenge of Hypertext

Hypertextual reading can be done for modern literature as well as for ancient. In fact, hypertext poses a challenge to all disciplines in the humanities, which are all defined by the study of a particular body of texts and whose methods all presuppose the technology of print. The responses from these challenged disciplines may vary. Classics is a special case, both because of its long history and because of its current isolation. As has often been remarked, classical studies in the twentieth century have responded quite slowly to changing literary-critical trends. Trends in English and the modern foreign languages often barely reach into classical scholarship. Classical studies today are still dominated by methods that were popular in the nineteenth and the first half of the twentieth century: by biographical and historical criticism and by the New Criticism. A few classicists have imported notions from structuralism and more recently from deconstruction and other postmodern theories. But postmodernism, which has been so hotly debated in other fields, has hardly disturbed classical studies.

Deconstruction in its most radical form may now be passing from favor. Indeed, the computer as hypertext calls for a revision of deconstruction and other postmodern methods. Hypertext allows us to get beyond the postmodern impasse, because it shows how the notions of the instability and contingency of the text can be turned against themselves, that is, exploited by writers to forge new and interesting texts. Classicists, who were never worried by deconstruction, will not be much concerned by its eclipse. But hypertext will have implications for classicists, too. As we said, classicists still follow methods appropriate to ("old") historicism and New Criticism. And in one sense our hypertextual *Oedipus* commentary can be seen as a vehicle for a New Critical reading: the links can be used to point up correspondences, symmetries, and ironies in the play. The comments in English can be used to elucidate the unifying effects of these correspondences. In another sense any hypertextual commentary is necessarily postmodern. The temporary quality of text on the computer screen means that the hypertext can make no lasting assertions because a hypertext is different for each reader and for each act of reading. And if the reader can add new links, then the text is never complete: its meaning is always open to modification and contradiction. A hypertext is always equivocal, and the equivocality of a hypertextual commentary must always infect the primary text as well. Equivocality cannot easily be maintained in print. The certainty of the printed page works against an equivocal reading of the text. It makes the reader strive for the right reading. Univocality cannot possibly be maintained in a hypertext read at the computer. The changing character of the text cannot be captured in any static statement of meaning.

The aim of much classical scholarship is to establish a univocal meaning. Philological and literary commentary seeks to tie the text down, to fix it in all its possible literary and social relations. Classical scholarship aims at completeness, what contemporary literary theory calls "closure." What classicist even today is not excited by the prospect of taking an enormous commentary off the shelf, say Eduard Fraenkel's commentary of *Agamemnon?* Even though we know better, we cannot help feeling that such a commentary (in three volumes and over 1,000 pages) confronts or at least touches upon all the problems inherent in Aeschylus' 1,673-line text. Such an encyclopedic commentary presumes to exhaust the primary text, although this is a goal that can never be achieved. It is the same goal that led German scholars to attempt to create in *Pauly-Wissowa* a comprehensive encyclopedia of classical studies, or an encyclopedic lexicon of the Latin language in the *Thesaurus Linguae Latinae*. Print technology leads the scholar to hope that a subject can be covered once and for all, fixed between the two covers of a printed book or in a series of such books. The *Thesaurus Linguae Latinae,* begun early in this century and currently on P (having skipped N to avoid the word *non*), is projected to continue into the twenty-first century. Of course, as the editors know, when the last letters are published (and even N is completed) it will be time to begin revising the first volumes, which will then be a hundred years old. The *Thesaurus* is an open-ended project, one that can continue as long as there is funding and scholarly interest. The project seems to have an end only because of the technology of the printed book.

An electronic book—commentary, lexicon, or encyclopedia—makes no pretense to closure. It opens up to other texts, primary and secondary, and invites the reader to participate in the writing. Perhaps an early sign that classics is accepting the new medium will be a proposal to create an ongoing commentary on some major author, such as Aeschylus or Plato. The difference would be that editors of this commentary would admit from the outset that the project has no planned end. The project would in this sense resemble a journal rather than a single publication. Contributors would continue to add their own notes to Plato's text and to the notes of other contributors. But the point would be not to have the last word, but rather to watch each layer of reference expand and interlace itself with other layers.

What will happen in particular to traditional textual criticism in the age of the electronic commentary? It may be that interest in textual criticism will diminish, for the reasons I have already suggested. Textual criticism aims at fixing the text once and for all—putting the "right" readings in the body of the page and the interesting but "wrong" readings and conjectures in small print at the bottom. Nothing distresses the textual critic more than having to put a crux in the text, for the crux is really an admission that the text at that point is not fixed. In the worst case, the editor can offer no good suggestion, so that the text is radically open: it may need the change of a few letters or it may be lacking whole words or lines. In the best case, the editor may be convinced that the choice is between two or three readings listed in the apparatus, but he or she cannot decide which. Here the text oscillates among the possible readings, and even this oscillation is unwelcome: it cannot be represented in the typography of the printed page.

Most classicists already prefer a kind of reading that makes only limited use of textual criticism and the apparatus. If scholars begin to create hypertextual commentaries and essays, they may find even less need to focus on textual problems. The instability of the text will be less bothersome to them, and they will adopt critical methods that do not depend on textual certainties that cannot be established. They will eschew interpretations that depend on a single word or short phrase in the text because the word or phrase may vacillate in the tradition. We could go further and imagine a kind of literary criticism that not only accepts but even emphasizes the instability of the received text, a method that takes into account the vacillating history of the text. Such criticism would need to look at the apparatus again, but with a different perspective.

We could argue that textual criticism as it has been practiced in the late age of print is already a kind of hypertextual reading. The editor is a reader who is re-writing the text to suit his or her own conception. This is particularly true for Greek tragedy, say for a chorus of Aeschylus and to a lesser extent for Sophocles and Euripides. The whole manuscript tradition of the author, together with the apparatus of previous editions, constitutes a hypertext, offering various paths to follow in form of readings to choose. The editor who chooses among those readings is in fact fashioning his or her own text of *Agamemnon* or *Oedipus Tyrannus* out of all the possible permutations that the tradition offers. Such an editor is no passive reader. Finding no manuscript or previous edition to his or her liking, the editor may choose to devise a new reading, which then becomes part of the hypertext that is passed on to future editors. The editor is literally rewriting the text as he or she goes. The resulting edition is a reading, which is to say an interpretation. Clearly, there is no way to disentangle a troubled chorus in *Agamemnon* without at the same time deciding what the text "could" or "could not" mean (and editors often talk this way), and such decisions are inevitably bound up with one's interpretive strategy for the play. Once again, editors seldom admit that textual criticism is a form of interpretation.

The computer encourages scholars to be more honest about the relationship between the textual tradition and the adding of a new commentary to that tradition. As the computer always undermines the distinction between the author and the reader, so for classical scholars it will undermine the distinction between the original author (as received in the complex manuscript tradition) and the scholarly reader. A good electronic commentary will invite the reader into the whole complex tradition by which an author such as Aeschylus or Sophocles has come down to us — invite the reader to participate in constituting the text. This is an attitude that a few energetic readers have already adopted in the age of print. The computer will perhaps increase the number of such active readers even for classical texts. But there will be a cost. These new readers will not be inclined to revisit the problems or adopt the strategies favored by classical scholars in the age of print.

Notes

1. Using Storyspace, Michael Joyce has produced an interactive fiction called *Afternoon*, published by Eastgate Press (Cambridge, Mass., 1990).

2. The structure of this example (the connections among texts) can be built in the current version of Storyspace. However, the particular configuration of windows I describe is not yet supported. In the coming months I hope to modify Storyspace to provide the kind of relationship among windows envisioned in this example. In general, Storyspace serves as both an authoring and a presentation system. In this case, Storyspace can be used both by the editor who constructs the commentary and the reader who examines the result.

3. I discuss the notion of topographic writing in more detail in my (printed) book, *Writing Space: The Computer, Hypertext, and the History of Writing* (Hillsdale, N.J., 1991).

4. See Richard C. Jebb, *Sophocles: The Plays and Fragments. Part I: The Oedipus Tyrannus* (Cambridge, 1914). The first edition was in 1883, the second edition in 1887. Passages from *Oedipus* cited in this article are taken from Jebb's edition.

5. See the article in this volume. See also Gregory Crane, "Redefining the Book: Some Preliminary Problems," *Academic Computing* 2.5 (February 1988): 6–11 and 36–41.

6. This is A. B. Lord's well-known argument in *The Singer of Tales* (New York, 1968); see especially 124–38.

7. See Eric Havelock, *The Literate Revolution in Greece and its Cultural Consequences* (Princeton, 1982).

8. See Elizabeth Eisenstein, *The Printing Press as an Agent of Change* (Cambridge, 1979), in particular 175ff.

9. The controversy over the Gabler edition and reprints of earlier editions of *Ulysses* has become so heated that even the *New York Times* noticed it: E. McDowell "After 2 Steps Forward, One Back for 'Ulysses,' " *New York Times,* June 28, 1990.

10. R. D. Dawe, *Sophocles: Oedipus Rex* (Cambridge, 1982), 23.

11. Ibid., 26.

12. For example, the statement of the editorial board of *AJP* 108.3 (1987): vii–ix seems to suggest that a philological reading of an ancient text can be prior to any theory. This statement was part of the impetus for the volume *Classics: A Discipline and Profession in Crisis?* edited by Phyllis Culham and Lowell Edmunds (New York, 1989). See Edmunds's introduction, p. ix. See also Martin Bernal, "Classics in Crisis: An Outsider's View In," 67–74, and John Peradotto, "Texts and Unrefracted Facts: Philology, Hermeneutics and Semiotics," 179–98.

13. It is a commonplace to note that *Oedipus* as a play was never meant to be read and studied but performed. In fact, we have only the verbal text; we can never hope to recapture the conventions (music, staging, rhetorical practice) of the Greek dramatic festivals. It is as a text to be read that the play has come down to us in the manuscript and printed traditions — with accompanying scholarly commentary. And it is as a hypertext that the play will be translated into the electronic medium.

Selected Bibliography

Because the purpose of this volume is to record the development of new means and tools for classical scholarship, the following bibliography is limited to those works which were cited in the preceding essays and which concern this development. Omitted are citations of traditional databases and collections of corpora and secondary classical sources unrelated to computers and computerization. Also omitted are citations of the APA and TLG *Newsletters,* all of which are to be found in Brunner's essay on the TLG.

Bagnall, Roger. "The Camel, the Wagon and the Donkey." *Bulletin of the American Society of Papyrologists* 22 (1985): 1–6.

———. "Papyrology and Ptolemaic History, 1956–1980." *Classical World* 76 (1982): 13–21.

———, ed. *Research Tools for the Classics: The Report of the American Philological Association's Ad Hoc Committee on Basic Research Tools.* APA Pamphlets 6 (1980).

Bateman, John. "Report of Action by the Directors." *Transactions and Proceedings of the American Philological Association* 99 (1968): xliii.

———. "Report of Action by the Directors." *Transactions and Proceedings of the American Philological Association* 100 (1969): lv–lvii.

———. "Report of Action by the Directors." *Transactions and Proceedings of the American Philological Association* 102 (1971): lxii–lxv.

Berkowitz, Luci. *Thesaurus Linguae Graecae Canon of Greek Authors and Works from Homer to A.D. 200.* Costa Mesa, Calif.: TLG Publications, Inc., 1977.

Berkowitz, Luci, and K. A. Squitier. *Thesaurus Linguae Graecae Canon of Greek Authors and Works.* 2d ed. New York and Oxford: Oxford University Press, 1986. 3d ed., 1990.

Bolter, J. David. *Turing's Man: Western Culture in the Computer Age.* Chapel Hill: University of North Carolina Press, 1984.

———. *Writing Space: The Computer, Hypertext, and the History of Writing*. Hillsdale, New Jersey: Lawrence Erlbaum, 1991.

Brunner, T. F. "Data Banks for the Humanities: Learning from the Thesaurus Linguae Graecae." *Scholarly Communication* 7 (1987): 1 and 6–9.

———. "Overcoming Verzettelung." *Humanities* 9 (May/June, 1988): 4–7.

Bryan, Martin. *The Author's Guide to SGML*. New York: Addison Wesley, 1988.

Comfort, Howard. "Report of the Delegates to the Féderation Internationale des Associations d'Études Classique." *Transactions and Proceedings of the American Philological Association* 97 (1966): xlvi–xlvii.

Crane, Gregory. "Redefining the Book: Some Preliminary Problems." *Academic Computing* 2.5 (February 1988): 6–11 and 36–41.

Crane, Gregory, and Elli Mylonas. "Perseus Project: Work Plan." *Perseus Working Papers* 6 (February 1990).

———. "The Perseus Project: An Interactive Curriculum on Classical Greek Civilization." *Educational Technology* 28, no. 11 (1988): 25–32.

Culham, Phyllis, and Lowell Edmunds, eds. *Classics: A Discipline and Profession in Crisis?* New York: University Press of America, 1989.

Eisenstein, Elizabeth. *The Printing Press as an Agent of Change*. Cambridge: Cambridge University Press, 1979.

Greenberg, Nathan A., et al. "Report of the Advisory Committee for Computer Activities." *Transactions and Proceedings of the American Philological Association* 102 (1971): xlv–l.

Havelock, Eric. *The Literate Revolution in Greece and its Cultural Consequences*. Princeton: Princeton University Press, 1982.

Hodder, Ian. *Reading the Past: Current Approaches to Interpretation in Archaeology*. Cambridge: Cambridge University Press, 1986.

Hughes, John J. *Bits, Bytes, and Biblical Studies: A Resource Guide for the Use of Computers in Biblical and Classical Studies*. Grand Rapids: Zondervan, 1987.

———. "From Homer to Hesychius: The Thesaurus Linguae Graecae Project." *Bits and Bytes Review* 1.7 (1987): 1–6.

———. "Studying Ancient Greek Civilization Interactively: The Perseus Project." *Bits and Bytes Review* 2 (1988): 1–12.

Keenan, James G. "Papyrology and Roman History, 1956–1980." *Classical World* 76 (1982): 23–31.

Koehler, Carolyn, and Philippa Matheson. "Amphoras on Computers." *American Journal of Archaeology* 90 (1986): 224.

Lanham, Richard W. "The Electronic Word: Literary Study and the Digital Revolution." *New Literary History* 20 (1989): 265–90.

Levy, Harry L. "President's Corner." *Proceedings of the American Philological Association* 104.2 (1974): 71–72.

Marchionini, Gary, Delia Neuman, and Kenneth Morrell. "Perseus Evaluation Plan." *Perseus Working Papers* 5 (March 1990).

Marchionini, Gary, Delia Neuman, and Peter Evans. "Perseus Evaluation Report: Harvard University — Spring 1989." *Perseus Working Papers* 6a (March 1990).

Minton, William M. "Report of Action by the Directors." *Transactions and Proceedings of the American Philological Association* 98 (1967): xxxviii.

Oates, John. "The Duke Data Bank of Documentary Papyri." In S. Cacaly and G. Losfeld, eds., *Sciences historiques, sciences du passe et nouvelles technologies d'information,* 253–60. Lille, 1990.

———. "Sale of a Donkey." *Bulletin of the American Society of Papyrologists* 25 (1988): 129–35.

Ong, Walter J. *Orality and Literacy.* London: Routledge & Kegan Paul, 1989.

Packard, David W. *Concordance to Livy.* 4 vols. Cambridge, Mass.: Harvard University Press, 1968.

———, et al. "Report of the Advisory Committee on Computer Activites." *Transactions and Proceedings of the American Philological Association* 101 (1970): xliii–xlv.

Raben, Joseph. *Computer-Assisted Research in the Humanities: A Directory of Scholars Active.* 3d ed. New York: Pergamon Press, 1977.

"Report of the Advisory Committee on Computer Activities." *Transactions and Proceedings of the American Philological Association* 100 (1969): liv.

"Report of the Special Committee for Computer Problems." *Transactions and Proceedings of the American Philological Association* 99 (1968): xli.

Small, Jocelyn Penny. "Advanced Revelation: A Review." *Archival Informatics Newsletter* 2.1 (Spring 1988): 2–5.

———. "Computer Index of Classical Iconography." *ACH Newsletter* 9.1 (1987): 12–14.

———. "Computer Index of Classical Iconography." *Humanities Communication Newsletter* [University of Leicester] 8 (1987): 4–8.

———. "A Database for Classical Iconography." *Art Documentation* 7 (1988): 3–5.

———. "Designing a Computer-Index of Classical Iconography." *Journal of the Rutgers University Libraries* 50 (1988): 104–14.

———. *How to Choose a Database.* American Philological Association, 1986.

———. "The NEH and Research Data Bases: A Classical Experiment." In T. F. Moberg, ed., *Databases in the Humanities and Social Sciences 1985* 3 (Osprey, 1987): 467–69.

———. "Retrieving Images Verbally: No More Keywords and Other Heresies." *Humanities in the 90s. Library Hi Tech Journal,* forthcoming.

Smith, Candace. "Drawing Guidelines for Perseus." *Perseus Working Papers* 11, forthcoming.

Smith, D. Neel. "An Interchange Format for Archaeological Information." *Perseus Working Papers* 12, forthcoming.

Sowa, Cora. "Report of the Advisory Committee on Computer Activities." *Transactions and Proceedings of the American Philological Association* 103 (1972): xlviii.

Sperberg-McQueen, C. M., and Lou Burnard, eds. *Text Encoding Initiative: Guidelines for the Encoding and Interchange of Machine-Readable Texts.* Chicago and Oxford (privately published by the editors): 1990.

Squitier, Karl A. "The *TLG Canon:* Genesis of an Electronic Data Base." *Favonius* 1 (1987): 15–20 (suppl.).

Trigger, G. *A History of Archaeological Thought*. Cambridge: Cambridge University Press, 1989.

Waite, Stephen V. F. "Report of the Supervisor of the American Philological Association Repository of Classical Texts in Machine-Readable Form." *Transactions and Proceedings of the American Philological Association* 101 (1970): xlvi.

———. "Report of the Supervisor of the Repository of Greek and Latin Texts in Machine-Readable Form." *Transactions and Proceedings of the American Philological Association* 103 (1972): xlviii–lii.

Index

About the Editor

Jon Solomon is Associate Professor of Classics at the University of Arizona with special interests in ancient Greek, music and poetry, and the classical tradition. He has received six awards for teaching from three universities. He and his brother, Robert Solomon, coauthored *Up the University,* a book on how to restructure the American university.